ACHIEVEMENT ADDICTION DETOX

7 Steps
To Creating The Life You Deserve
Without Killing Yourself

Elena F. Rand
JD, MSW

Achievement Addiction DETOX
7 Steps To Creating The Life You Deserve Without Killing Yourself

Copyright © 2023 by Elena F. Rand JD, MSW

Published in NY, NY, by Monaco Legacy Press

ISBN: 9781736628201

Cover Photo: Rob Goldman, Inc.
Cover Design: Rob Goldman, Inc./Fleury Design
Interior Design and Production: Jera Publishing, LLC

In memory of my mother
Maria Concetta Catalano Rand
(March 9, 1947-May 31, 2020)

A lady among women.
A queen among ladies.
An empress among queens.
An icon among mortals.
An eternal light among God's angels.
An endless heartbreak until I see you again.
Forever loved.
Forever missed.
Forever mine.

CONTENTS

INTRODUCTION

How Achievement Addiction Almost Killed Me

Like many of the high-achieving professionals who have sat across from me for executive career coaching over the past twenty years, my résumé reads like a perfect dream come true. By the time I was thirty-six, I had, by all appearances, done it all, balanced it all, and become the Madison Avenue definition of a successful you-can-have-it-all woman.

Take a deep breath because what I am about to share with you nearly killed me.

I was top in my class from elementary school onward, am fluent in four languages, am well-traveled, was raised in two countries, went to Princeton University on scholarship, where I graduated magna cum laude, attended Georgetown Law School, graduated with honors, was a litigator at two national law firms in New York, was happily married to a successful international real estate developer and architect, had two healthy and beautiful children by the age of thirty-one, and was raising them while embarking on a new entrepreneurial career in executive coaching. At the same time, I was completing my master's in clinical social work from NYU and finishing a one-year fellowship at NYU in psychoanalytic studies, while launching LawScope (my executive coaching company) and practicing as both a therapist and an executive coach working with Am Law 100 law firms. I owned and cared for two large homes—one in Scarsdale, New York, and the other on the New Jersey shore. I was running regularly, practicing yoga, cooking, entertaining, serving on the boards of several nonprofits, and being interviewed by NPR and quoted in the *Wall Street Journal* as a career expert. I had a weekly early morning standing appointment to have my ethnic curly hair straightened and my nails manicured, wore only breakneck high heels and couture dresses to work, starved myself to maintain my weight at a size six, owned several European cars, traveled regularly with my family to Europe and the Middle East, and possessed a cadre of great, fascinating girlfriends who showed me how to spend money in the most ridiculous ways, all while drinking several gin martinis in one sitting.

Are you gasping for air yet? Looking back, I know I was. Gasping for air but unwittingly inhaling more and more toxic fumes. This kind of behavior characterized by an unchecked and autonomic compulsion to achieve, achieve, achieve at all costs will kill you. Or at least try to. This highly applauded variant of ambition gone wild is an affliction. I have named it Achievement Addiction™.

And as you will read in client story after story in this book, it nearly killed many of my clients. And it almost did me in.

By the time I turned forty, Achievement Addiction was the proverbial monkey on my back. Achievement had become my single obsession. I was trying to rise to the unattainable standard of someone else's definition of success and killing myself in the process. But the truth is that not unlike many of the client stories I share here, underneath all that achievement, I was dying. I was living in some fog-drenched, sleepwalking trance, slowly killing myself to reach the next achievement, only to devalue it the moment I attained it. And even before the ink dried on one accomplishment, I found myself sprinting toward another achievement mirage. One that I just knew for sure this time would be the key to my enduring happiness.

The achievement race never ended. No matter how desirable, no achievement could fill me up, quell my worries, and make me feel lasting joy. No matter the cost to me or others, the next milestone was always the one that held the magical promise of a happy life. I was in a masochistic marathon without a finish line where the road behind me and the miles already logged quickly vanished with my every step.

I can honestly admit that at that point in my life, none of my achievements—other than my children—really ever brought me lasting joy, peace, or an improved sense of self-worth. Sure, I enjoyed the first fleeting moments of euphoria that high achievement offered me. And I won't deny that I hungrily lapped up every last drop of the societal praise that came along with my achievements as if my very life force depended on it. And to top it all off, when I wasn't busy chasing the next crazy achievement, I spent whatever energy I had left trying to give the breezy appearance that all my success was effortless and that I was brilliantly A-OK.

But even before the dizzying champagne bubbles could reach the top of my flute glass in celebration of my most recent accomplishment, I was already off and running, obsessing over the next achievement that would *really* make me happy.

For as long as I can remember, it was always the next achievement that held the supernatural power to unlock the key to success, happiness, and absolute joy. And I can see now that achievement has had me by the throat since the age of twelve. So much so that by the age of forty, my Achievement Addiction was a runaway train ready to jump the tracks.

Because if you had only looked a little more closely at my forty-year-old life, you would have discovered that beneath my perfectly successful, achievement-addled façade,

- I had been diagnosed with depression, PTSD, and anxiety.
- I was living beyond my means and flirting with financial disaster.
- My marriage of nearly fifteen years was falling apart.
- I was often miserable, exhausted, and unpredictable.
- I felt like a failure, a charlatan, and a chronic disappointment to my immediate family.
- I felt hopeless, worthless, unlovable, broken, and thoroughly unfixable.

But damn, I looked great! And damned if I didn't spend every ounce of energy making sure no one knew the multiple fault lines underlying my seemingly successful but Achievement-Addicted world.

But by my late thirties, the rapid-cycling nature of my Achievement-Addicted life was starting to catch up with me. I was fully resigned to the belief that chronic dysfunction, ill health, and misery were the price I had to pay for high achievement and success.

Until one day . . .

I was driving my two little children, ages six and nine, to school, then running to the Metro-North train to get to an 8:30 networking breakfast for women entrepreneurs before starting my day. My schedule that day involved a three-hour workshop at a major law firm in NYC, followed by four individual coaching clients, followed by a nonprofit board meeting, followed by cocktails and dinner (and then more drinks) with board members. My schedule was fully packed, and I remember thinking that my heart was beating unusually fast that morning. But I was used to that. I chalked it up to lousy sleep, my three-mile run at 6 a.m., and the three espressos I had downed on an empty stomach.

That's when I noticed that my left arm had started tingling. I was driving, so I shook it out a couple of times, thinking it had fallen asleep. But the tingling was growing in intensity, as was the beating of my heart. I could hear my heartbeat in my ears, I felt a sharp pain radiate down my arm, and then I couldn't feel my arm anymore.

I quickly pulled over. I leaned over the steering wheel as I felt the pressure in my chest escalating. I couldn't breathe. I heard my son's voice yelling, "Mommy!" and the little one's crying. But every voice around me seemed muffled underneath the sound of my heartbeat growing louder and louder in my ears. I couldn't respond. My God! I was having a full-on heart attack in front of my children. I managed to press speed dial #1 and called my husband. He called 911, then told the nanny to meet me with her car and take the kids to school. He stayed on speakerphone calming the kids. I remember fading in and out of awareness as I slumped over the steering wheel, eyes closed, gripping my left arm, and sweating profusely. I was convinced I was dying, and that I was going to die right there in front of my kids. My last sad, conscious thought was *But, God, there's so much more I want to do with my life.* Then I passed out.

I awoke to find myself on a gurney in White Plains Hospital and attached to lots of wires and tubes. I took a quick inventory. I was breathing. My vision was clear. I wiggled my fingers and toes. Good. My body was still intact. Then I remembered what had happened. But I was bewildered. Had I really just had a heart attack at forty?

After hours of testing, the ER doctor ruled out my nightmare. It wasn't a heart attack. Instead, he prescribed Xanax and ordered cardiovascular testing to be done over the next couple of weeks.

I spent the next few weeks bopping around from one cardio test to the next. The Park Avenue cardiologist who finally sat down with me to review all the test results was a balding, avuncular older man with a slight Jewish, Eastern European lilt to his speech. He reminded me of all the rabbinical-looking men I used to see in Brooklyn when I was a kid.

He looked me over, gestured for me to have a seat in the chair across from his desk, flipped through a couple of pages in the open file on his lap, and said nothing. Finally, he spoke while shaking his clean-shaven head: "Nothing. Nothing. Nothing."

I was silent.

"My dear, I am sorry to inform you that there is absolutely nothing wrong with your heart."

Whew. That was a close one, I thought to myself. *Wait—"sorry" to inform me?* He must have seen the confusion on my face.

"Why am I sorry, you might ask?" he continued. I smiled inside. He had mastered the slightly annoying Talmudic art of rhetorical discourse, and I was now his reluctant student. His question/answer routine continued. "Why? Because if you had heart disease, or high blood pressure, or a murmur or, God forbid, something like an occlusion, well, then I could prescribe you something, and you would take it and *poof!*" he snapped his fingers. "Just like that, you would feel better. But not with you. Not you. Why not with you, you might ask? Well, I'm glad you asked. This, my dear," he said, picking up the reports and raising them in his hand, "this here, my dear, is what they call 'complicated.' *You*, my dear, are complicated," he said triumphantly.

I winced. I could feel my face flush, and I bit the inside of my lower lip to the point of tasting blood so I wouldn't blurt out the torrent of expletives that were lining up like antiaircraft missiles on the tip of my tongue. Instantaneously, my mind became a Category 5 hurricane of thoughts:

Are you fucking kidding me?! Exactly where did you get your medical degree? I could have saved us both a lot of time and money, Doc. . . "Complicated" is in my fucking DNA! And do you seriously expect me to believe this load of bull that I nearly died behind the wheel of my car because I am COMPLICATED?!

But, trying hard not to adopt an Achievement Addict a--hole posture, I kept my battalion of questions to myself and sat stewing quietly in a stinking puddle of my arrogance. That's when I noticed that my heart was pounding fast and hard again . . . just like that life-threatening morning only weeks before.

What is happening to me? This can't be happening again, can it? Get a grip. . . Breathe.

It turned out the good doctor's harmless reference to my being "complicated" had just triggered some less-than-pleasant personal flashbacks that I was not in the mood to entertain that morning.

You see, I have been a card-carrying member of the "Complicated Club" since kindergarten, when, for starters, my newly divorced, Roman Catholic, Sicilian immigrant mother converted us both to the Jewish faith to marry the man who would go on to become my legally adopted dad (and only father I would ever know). At the age of four, I found myself converted to Orthodox Judaism, stripped of my baptismal gold cross around my neck, and deposited into an Orthodox Jewish yeshiva day school swarming with fundamentalist rabbis. So, before most "uncomplicated" children had even learned their ABCs, I had netted a newly devoted Father, the loss of God's Only Son, and a more-than-slightly traumatized Holy Spirit.

But I don't want to get ahead of myself...

Restless under the doctor's gaze, and itching to get out of his office, I started to rummage through my designer bag for my phone. I put my over-size, Jackie-O sunglasses back on my face and started for the door, saying, "Look, Doc, I have a meeting to get to and . . ."

He was unfazed.

"Sit down," he ordered. "I mean it. Sit."

I whipped around and glared at him. I DID NOT WANT TO HAVE THIS TALK.

With my coat and sunglasses still on, I lowered myself into the chair and teetered on its edge. Everything inside me was on high alert. I was a lightweight boxing champion, readying myself in my corner, waiting for the bell and my next knockout round with my opponent. Because this is how an Achievement Addict views someone who is about to serve her some unvarnished truth.

"Lemme give you a valuable piece of advice," he continued very slowly. "Can you listen to an old man?" His voice was gentler now.

And despite my almost uncontrollable urge to bolt, I nodded that, yes, I was listening.

So he continued.

"So here it is: There is nothing wrong with you, pretty lady. Nothing at all." He peered at me over his rimless round glasses, paused, and added the warning shot with a solitary finger poked in the air for effect: "For *now*. Nothing wrong with you. FOR NOW. You understand me?" He had leaned way over his side of his desk, and the finger was now pointing directly at me.

Trust me when I tell you that no Achievement Addict likes a finger pointing close to their face. Much less an Achievement Addict who grew up in Brooklyn, New York, in the '80s. It's an invitation to trouble. I was so distracted by this doctor's fearless flirtation with violence, I genuinely didn't understand what he was saying. I collected my thoughts and responded with all the maturity of a sulking twelve-year-old. "No," I said flatly. "I have no idea what you're talking about."

He took a deep breath, closed my file, tilted his head to the side, and took a long, sad look at me like I was a five-year-old kid lost at the county fair.

Then he sighed.

"Something is very, very wrong in your life, my dear. Something big. And it is your very, very difficult job to figure out what it is. I am not in the business of guaranteeing anything when it comes to the heart or heart disease, but if you don't do anything about whatever is going on in your life, and if you don't make some big, and I mean *big*, changes in your life, I can guarantee you 100 percent that you will be back here in five years, and then, well, then I can guarantee there *will* be something very wrong with your heart. Do you understand me now?"

I looked up at his eyes for the first time and saw the genuine concern of a wise elder.

I suddenly felt the stony grip around my heart release a little.

He nailed me. There was no escaping what he had to say about my life. "Yes. I understand," I said softly. I could feel hot tears stinging my eyes.

He stood up, slowly came to my side of the desk, and perched himself on its edge. He was now looking down at me with sincere but stern kindness in his voice.

"Whatever the price, do it fast before it is too late. Because if you don't, it will cost you your health. Be the really smart girl you are and make the changes now."

With that, he nodded with satisfaction, took my file off his desk, and handed it to me as if to say, "Okay, it's in your hands now, not mine."

After almost forty years, this kind doctor woke me from my trance. His words ring in my ears to this day. I can still see him standing, leaning toward me to hand me the file of my cardiology tests.

He broke my hard shell and shook me wide awake. I credit him with saving my life.

Shortly after that meeting, I did make some drastic changes in my life. I resigned from my nonprofit board and started spending more time working from home. My husband and I reduced our expenditures, sold our homes, and decided to separate. It was a long process, but I started to take stock of my life seriously.

And then I did the unthinkable: I asked for help. Lots of it. From all sorts of people. Over those years and onward, I enlisted the help of therapists, coaches, wise elders, Al-Anon, religious leaders, spiritualists—you name it. I was lucky to find a good therapist who helped me understand that my bottomless materialism and relentless drive for achievement were sorely misaligned with my deepest values and beliefs.

All I knew at that time was that I needed to examine those choices and values that were now wreaking havoc in my life. I needed to go back. I needed to retrace how, when, and why my once-healthy ambition had mutated into the dysfunction that was now costing me my health, my sanity, and possibly even my life itself.

Eventually, I would come to understand that Achievement Addiction had hijacked my life.

WHAT IS ACHIEVEMENT ADDICTION?

The truth is that I stumbled upon the syndrome of Achievement Addiction as a byproduct of my own life crisis and need for transformation. Executive career coaching was my niche, but clients were now also asking for more life coaching. As my life started to change so did my coaching style and the clients who were finding their way to me.

Clients were opening up about their deeper frustrations with their careers. They were coming to coaching wanting to find a solution to their misery. Many wanted help managing feelings of worthlessness that no level of outward success could assuage.

Eventually, I began to see a unifying pattern emerging with all my clients. There was something similar to all their stories. In working with thousands of high-performing, accomplished professionals, I realized that while the details of their frustrations were different, nearly all of my coaching clients shared one common compulsion that seemed to be at the heart of their unhappiness. This compulsion was elusive and insidious. It was the same one that had dominated my own life and psyche for decades and had caused me endless suffering.

Suddenly, this consistent pattern came into sharper focus. The closer I looked, the more I realized that much of my clients' pain seemed to orbit around a common nucleus: **The Chase For More Achievement** ("**The Chase**").

The Chase fuel injected many of my clients' other destructive compulsions, addictions, bad choices, and general life chaos. **The Chase** controlled their mood, their sense of self-worth, and overall quality of life. **The Chase** had them on a non-stop, G-force roller-coaster ride that was making them all physically and emotionally sick. And they all believed that the only way to manage their suffering was to increase **The Chase! The Chase** had them in the grips of an addictive loop that only worsened with time.

But no one was talking about hyper-achievement as the possible source of the problem. It didn't exist in any academic, psychological, or self-help literature. If anything, it seemed to me that there was an over-proliferation of books promoting success at all costs and the virtues of endless achievement! I was determined to understand more—for myself and my clients.

With the help of my clients, I unearthed something new. I call it *Achievement Addiction*™.

One by one, as I reviewed my client files, Achievement Addiction revealed itself at the root of many of the personal and professional miseries that later surfaced. It was becoming apparent to me that many of my wildly successful clients shared a fundamental core delusion—*a singular delusion that chasing achievement was worth complete and utter self-annihilation.*

Why? Because these same paragons of success truly believed that *without their achievements they and their lives were utterly worthless.*

I came to discover that without their achievements my clients felt hollow and lost. Without their achievements they had no idea who they were or what their value was or whether they even had a right to live! Achievement was the real drug of choice among my clients. No price was too high for the next achievement-fix, because without their achievements, many believed their lives were meaningless. And I came to observe that there was a rapid-cycling quality to my clients' addiction to achievement. As long as they were seeking the next-higher rung of achievement, they were fine. Some even felt euphoric, super-human. But the minute they reached their achievement goal, they tanked again. Some fell into a deep depression. Some suffered suicidal thoughts. Achievement Addiction was in control and hijacking their lives just as it had once hijacked mine. One client summed it up to me this way, "I am my achievements. Without my achievements I am nothing. I am no one."

I turned the mirror around, and there it was. For me and others, Achievement Addiction was driving many of the decisions and behaviors that caused or exacerbated much of our unexplainable misery. In fact, when I looked at myself and my clients, it felt as if we were all in the grip of some alien *trance* (more on this later) that had us robotically moving from achievement to achievement. Never stopping to question what it was doing to our health, our mental state, or our families. Slowly and steadily our drive for achievement had become autonomic and self-destructive.

The ugly truth was that the very same relentless ambition and drive for achievement that had once served me and others so well had now betrayed us.

This realization cut deep and forced me to change many things in both my life and work.

My coaching method changed as I started to understand and address my clients' struggles through the lens of Achievement Addiction. This new approach became known as the IMAGO Coaching Method. Using this new approach, clients started to DETOX from Achievement Addiction. And throughout this book, you will be guided to coach yourself using the IMAGO Coaching Method that helped so many others.

Over time, I was able to see that there were 7 Steps at the heart of my clients' Achievement Addiction DETOX. Clients working these 7 Steps using the IMAGO Coaching Method manifested their career goals while simultaneously embarking on lasting, meaningful personal changes that improved the overall quality of their lives.

And now it's YOUR turn to experience Achievement Addiction DETOX!

In *Achievement Addiction DETOX*, I will be

> ➤ Introducing you to some new Achievement Addiction terminology like the *Achievement Trance*, the *Achievement Avatar*, and *Achievement Amnesia*. By the end of the first section of this book, you will better understand the full nature of Achievement Addiction, its characteristics, its origins, and how it manifests itself in high-performing, success-driven individuals.
>
> ➤ Inviting you to participate in an *Achievement Addiction Self-Assessment* along with other *Achievement Addiction Exercises* that you can use as a point of reference throughout the rest of the book.

➢ Guiding you through each of the **7 Steps of Achievement Addiction DETOX:**

1.	AWARENESS	Wake up!
2.	MINDSET	Make a shift.
3.	EMOTIONS	Honor your feelings.
4.	SUPPORT	Ask for help.
5.	BODY	Move a muscle.
6.	FAITH	Widen your perspective.
7.	ALIGNMENT	Trust yourself.

In this section, you will come to understand the full impact of Achievement Addiction as you read the stories of numerous real-life coaching clients, each presented through the lens of one of the 7 Steps.

➢ Challenging you to work each of the 7 Steps using the **IMAGO Coaching Questions** listed at the end of each one of the 7 Step-chapters. You can then go on to coach yourself further by visiting my website, www.achievementaddictiondetox.com, and downloading the free **Achievement Addiction DETOX Worksheets.**

How to Use This Book

Here are four final suggestions on how to read and use this book:

1. **Read through each of the 7 Steps in sequence.**
   The book, the steps and the stories are sequential. What does that mean? It means that the 7 Steps are listed in order for a reason. And it is my experience that clients benefit most when they move through each of the 7 Steps in sequence. Achievement Addicts often race their way through things preferring the finish line over the journey. But there's no hacking your Achievement Addiction recovery. Although you may be tempted to skip ahead to begin working the steps, please don't. It's

important to have a full understanding of how the DETOX process works using the 7 Steps. Questions that follow each of the 7 Steps will help you understand the DETOX process. Stories will help you "see" the DETOX process in action.

So my suggestion is this: Read through each of the 7 Steps in order and immerse yourself in each client story as if you were a fly on the wall in my office. Watch how each session unfolds and notice what, if anything, resonates for you. Let the stories carry the message and the method. My wish for you is to really feel, not just understand, how insidious, and destructive Achievement Addiction can be. Why? Because it has been my experience as a therapist and coach that memorable storytelling has a "sticky" quality and deepens our learning.

2. **Silence the voice of perfectionism as you read through the 7 Steps.**
For Achievement Addicts it is tempting to have an all-or-nothing, "gotta be perfect at this" approach to any self-help book. See what resonates, what arises. You might learn something new about yourself, you might surprise yourself, or you might become more motivated to take on some much-needed change. Take what serves you and leave the rest behind.

3. **Take advantage of additional resources.**
This book is a compilation of my years of experience, training, and research as a therapist and executive coach. I am a lifelong student, and I have spent decades immersed in the writings and teachings of executive coaches, self-help luminaries, rabbis, priests, Eastern monks, philosophers, etc. I owe them all a debt of gratitude and hope that my understanding does them justice. To the extent possible, I have made that list of literature available to you in the References and Resources section.

4. **Coaching is not a substitute for psychotherapy.**
Many of the stories that follow tell tales of real people in absolute crises. The suffering is heart-wrenching, and the crises are life-threatening. Our stories—my clients' and mine—are a testament that the 7 Steps can be

applied to anyone's life and that the 7 Steps work. My personal story and transformation beyond Achievement Addiction is no different from many of the client stories I share here. The 7 Steps offer a proven system for lasting transformation.

Lastly, it is important to emphasize that coaching (whether career coaching or life coaching) can never serve as a substitute for psychotherapy, psychopharmacology, or any other medical or psychological support needed for those suffering from mental illness or those in a genuine life-or-death crisis. The References and Resources section of this book also offers clinical resources, telephone numbers, and relevant contact information for use by individuals in need of support or medical intervention. It can never be emphasized enough that if you or someone you know is in immediate danger, please call 911.

Try to keep an open mind as you read this book. The 7 Steps you'll read about have saved my life and have helped many of my clients detox and thrive *beyond* achievement addiction.

A Final Personal Note

I believe that we teach what we need most to learn, and we write what we need most to remember. I am in recovery from Achievement Addiction, and boy, do I relapse! Despite the many positive and remarkable changes I have made over the past fifteen years using the 7 Steps I'll be sharing with you in this book, it's been humbling to notice that Achievement Addiction is still alive in me and still quietly trying to pull strings in the background. There is no question in my mind that Achievement Addiction was why it took me nearly two years to leave my fancy Chief Marketing Officer job, even though it was compromising my physical and mental health. And admittedly, even in the last stages of editing this book, I could feel myself slipping back into my old Achievement Addicted habits of obsessiveness, negative self-talk, and merciless perfectionism.

But alongside my triumphs, my relapses keep me humble. So, if you are seeking perfection in me, or yourself, I can guarantee you disappointment.

I want to make one final thing very clear. Despite the many changes in my life and career, I remain ambitious and driven to manifest the vision of success that I have for my life. The only difference now is that my definition of success and how I live my life have nothing to do with achievement. My sense of worth no longer revolves around the next promotion, title, raise, public speaking gig, accolade, degree, award, or recognition. And I am no longer chasing that next shiny achievement in the hope that it will be the one to save me. Instead, these days my sense of self-worth is directly tied to my ability to manifest my God-given talents, skills, and abilities in a way that aligns with my values and beliefs.

And here's the great news: **what I am offering here is not a radicalizing process**. My hope for you in reading this book and working the 7 Steps is not for you to abandon all material gains or goals. And this book is not intended as a subliminal invitation for you to join the monastic life in Assisi or to embark on a magical, mystical tour of asceticism in Tibet.

I haven't had to drop out, shave my head, live in a tree house, or join an ashram to detox and overcome Achievement Addiction. And neither have any of my clients. Instead, my hope in writing this book is to offer another paradigm for your success beyond the destructive cycle of Achievement Addiction.

This book asks that you keep an open mind, open your eyes, and start making small changes to guide your life away from Achievement Addiction. And as you will read in the stories that follow, this process is doable and within your reach.

This book will show you how.

A vibrant life awaits you beyond the counterfeit, Achievement-Addicted life that has you chasing someone else's definition of success in search of your own self-worth.

Finally, what I want most for you as you read this book is that you

- know that you are not alone.
- know that your achievements do not define your true worth.
- know that authentic, joyful success beyond Achievement Addiction is possible and within reach.

I wish you Godspeed, courage, and compassion as you embark on a transformation that will bring you closer to knowing your true self and closer to that healthy, grounded, more joyful life you long for and that is your birthright. I am always here for you. Visit my website, www.achievementaddictiondetox.com, to get in contact.

The next chapter will describe the Achievement-Addicted Personality, and from there you'll be introduced to the IMAGO Coaching Method. IMAGO will help you work the 7 Steps with a process that's easy and intuitive. Think of it as a new success paradigm designed just for Achievement Addicts, because it is!

Let's get started.

UNDERSTANDING THE ACHIEVEMENT-ADDICTED PERSONALITY

"Tell me the facts, and I'll learn. Tell me the truth, and I'll believe. But tell me a story, and it will live in my heart forever." —Native American proverb

L et's dive in and start with Jack's unforgettable story so you can experience what Achievement Addiction looks and sounds like.

Jack with the Long Eyelashes

Jack sat in the small waiting area outside my office, dressed in a bespoke pinstriped blue suit and a tailored, light pink shirt with the letters "J. K." monogrammed on each shirt cuff, with a cup of coffee in one hand and a buzzing cell phone in the other. He was very slim and unusually tan for that time of year in New York City, and the pair of vintage red Bakelite glasses he was sporting made him look more like a Hollywood movie producer from the 1940s than an international corporate lawyer.

As if this image wasn't striking enough, as I walked toward him, I noticed that this man had the eyelashes of a runway supermodel or an Arabian camel. Jet black, long, curled upward, super thick, and nearly touching his well-groomed eyebrows. At the time, I remember thinking he looked a little bit like a virile Betty Boop. But I quickly put the comparison out of my head and walked closer to his seat to introduce myself and show him to my office.

"Hang on a minute, okay?" he said curtly, not looking up at me. "I'm responding to a client emergency. Okay? Hang on, okay?"

And there we were. He was seated and typing furiously into his cell, and I was standing over him at a handshake's distance, silently waiting for him to finish. Finally, after several long seconds, he stopped texting, put his phone in his suit jacket pocket, stood up as if he had just gotten off at the wrong subway station, looked right through me, and said in a very distracted, slightly awkward and disoriented tone, "Okay. Right. Okay. Now I'm ready. Okay. Wait? Who are you again?" This encounter was getting ruder and odder by the second.

"I'm Elena," I said slowly. "Executive coach? The law firm sent you here to—"

I had started to walk him down the hall to my office, and he was trailing behind.

"Oh yeah, yeah, yeah. Now I remember. Right. I'm here to work on . . . work on—"

He couldn't even remember why he was there. This was going to be fun.

"Coaching," I said flatly. I was glad he was walking behind me and couldn't see the less-than-impressed expression on my face.

We walked into my office, and he sat down in the chair across from mine.

"Right, right . . . sorry. Coaching. Right. I don't really even know what that is, to tell you the truth." He laughed nervously. "I mean, the only coaching I know has to do with soccer. I coach my son's soccer league, and this year his team—"

It was now my turn to cut him off.

"Right. Jack. So, okay. The firm didn't tell me much about what the focus of our coaching would be. So why don't you fill me in a little. Why do you think the firm thinks you could benefit from career coaching?"

Jack shifted a little in his seat, cleared his throat, and then got very quiet. No answer.

I waited.

"So the firm didn't tell you *anything* about me?" he asked. He was buying time and trying to see what I knew. And all I knew was that one of the most elite and prestigious law firms in the world had reached out to me and really wanted me to work with him, saying that he was a superstar and very valuable to the firm but that he was "going through a rough patch." They thought coaching might help him. That was it. When I had probed the HR director, she'd been cryptic and had just said, "I think it's best if Jack tells you himself." So I knew next to nothing about why this man with the very long eyelashes was sitting in my office.

"No," I answered honestly. "All they said was that you are very valuable to the firm, and they thought you could benefit from executive coaching. So why do *you* think *they* want you to be sitting here, Jack?"

Jack was now visibly uncomfortable as I watched him start to sweat. He was also rubbing his temples.

"It's my . . . well, I don't know how to put this . . . the problem is . . . it's my brain," he blurted out. I still had no idea what he was talking about, but whatever was going on was upsetting him. And I was concerned for him.

"I'm sorry, Jack. I don't understand. Help me here. Your brain is the trouble?" I asked.

"Yes. My brain," he whispered to himself.

I waited for him to go on.

"So, about eight months ago . . . I was having awful headaches, blurry vision, and I just thought it was the long hours and stress at work. I've always had headaches, migraines, stress headaches, cluster headaches . . . you name it. And, well, I've just learned to deal with it and take enough meds to block the pain. But then they got worse. I had this, I don't know what you'd call it . . . an episode . . . at the firm. The headache got worse and worse, but I was in the middle of a big merger, and I couldn't just up and leave the team, my client, my senior partners. . . . But then . . ." He paused and got quiet again. He was reliving something, and whatever it was, it wasn't good.

He was still rubbing his temples as he spoke, and now he was looking pale and nervous.

"Jack, are you feeling okay? Help yourself to some water . . . and take your time. This is rough stuff." I was now very concerned about Jack's physical well-being.

Jack poured himself some water and drank the whole thing in one shot. He then poured himself another glass. Then, for the first time, he looked up at me through his dark curtain of eyelashes and said calmly, "I passed out at my desk. Right there in the middle of the closing. Right there at my desk." He sounded so angry . . . and pretty ashamed.

"And then the next thing I remember, I'm in the hospital, and they're doing all these tests on me," he continued, "but all I could think about, even in the hospital, was the deal, the merger, and what a fuckup I was . . . and my client and how this bullshit, nonsense headache was going to cost me my partnership track. . . ." That's when Jack got pensive.

I just listened.

"They found a tumor," he said calmly. "A fucking huge tumor."

I was speechless.

He went on telling the story as if it had happened to someone else. He was detached and almost indifferent.

"But it was operable. So the next thing I know, my deal, my big deal, is yanked out from under me. After almost a year of working with my very important client, they give the deal to my frenemy . . . who is also up for partnership soon. Anyway, so they operate. Remove it. Test it. And it's benign," he said in a deflated tone.

Wow. Jack had gone through quite an ordeal, and I was genuinely happy for him and was waiting to hear how relieved he and his family were. But what followed was the real shocker.

He paused to collect his thoughts, and then he just yelled, "Benign! Can you believe it? I mean, the deal that was going to pave my way to partnership gets yanked out from under me because of a brain tumor, and it ends up being benign?! What a waste of everyone's time, right? Here this tumor goes and messes up my whole life's planning, and the fucking thing isn't even the real deal? You know what I mean? Just a cyst or something. That's just my luck. . . . I'm glad I'm okay and all . . . but can you believe how derailing this whole thing has been for me? And for no good reason. No good reason at all." He collapsed back into his seat, defeated.

I was confused by nearly everything he was saying to me. It was like watching a person fervently nod their head yes while yelling no. Everything he communicated—his word choice, tone, emotional affect, and body language—was disjointed. But here's what I ultimately came to understand:

Jack wasn't upset or worried that he had suffered months of debilitating headaches, or that he had passed out, or that they had found a tumor, or that he had to have brain surgery. Nope. He was annoyed that his tumor wasn't cancerous. That it wasn't, as he called it, "the real deal." In fact, I am sure some part of Jack resented his tumor for being so damn mediocre. For Jack, his close call with death was nothing more than a nuisance. And his newfound health certainly wasn't something he thought he should celebrate. Jack was so singularly consumed with the way the tumor had compromised his career and delayed his partnership chances at the law firm that he couldn't grasp or feel how lucky he was that it was benign. All he could focus on was the next achievement.

The firm had referred him to coaching because they planned on delaying partnership consideration for eighteen months (and Jack knew this). However, his overt disappointment with that delay was beginning to grate on the partners' nerves and threatened to undermine the partnership's faith in his overall good judgment.

Even more worrisome was that Jack was in denial that he was suffering some temporary cognitive and emotional regulation issues related to the brain surgery. The firm was worried that his compromised health might invite a liability risk to the firm. They wanted him to take the necessary time to heal and recover before putting him in front of clients again or pushing him through the partnership process.

When Jack stood up, his balance was off. His hands sometimes shook uncontrollably. The medication he was on gave him headaches and nausea. His sleep pattern was disrupted, his sentences were sometimes jumbled, and he admitted to me that he was often confused and lost many times during the day. During one of our sessions, he admitted that he had spent nearly an hour one afternoon trying to find his way back to his office after a client meeting in a conference room. But all Jack could focus on was making partner at his law firm—the next epic achievement in his career.

Jack's Achievement Addiction

➢ blinded him to the realities of his life-threatening medical condition;

➢ induced an Achievement Trance that had him chasing achievement even though doing so threatened to compromise his full recovery from brain surgery; and

➢ nearly killed him, figuratively and literally.

Achievement Addiction DETOX

➢ helped Jack develop some insight into the self-destructive nature of his unchecked Achievement Addiction;

➢ allowed him to realize that he needed to take a leave of absence to heal and focus on his health even if it meant a delay in making partner; and

➢ showed him how to define success as a lawyer on his own terms and in a way that aligned with his newfound health priorities.

In my twenty years of practice as a psychotherapist and executive coach, Jack remains the poster child for self-destructive Achievement Addiction in full bloom.

It might help to repeat the following:

Achievement Addiction is characterized by the singular delusion that achievement is worth complete and utter self-annihilation.

That is what Achievement Addiction does to us.

But now let's paint the whole picture. From what I have studied and observed over the years and from what I've personally experienced, Achievement Addicts share the following common characteristics:

1. We feel exclusively defined by what we have achieved.
2. What we have achieved or accomplished is never good enough.
3. We are always looking for our next achievement to make us feel whole, happy, worthy, grounded, and valued.
4. We define our self-worth, self-esteem, and value exclusively by our achievements.
5. We surround ourselves with people and choose environments that demand we continue our Achievement Addicted behaviors.
6. The prospect of a life without that next achievement fills us with despair, confusion, or panic.
7. We believe that only our achievements make us worthy of love.
8. Failures, disappointments, and setbacks cripple us.
9. We compulsively compare ourselves to others.

For Achievement Addicts, what we do is never enough; what we have is never enough; what we achieve is never enough, because fundamentally, we believe that *who we are*, as human beings, is not enough.

In essence, for Achievement Addicts, the equanimity of both our inner and outer lives is exclusively dependent upon and wholly defined by our achievements.

Take a moment to read that again.

What does that really mean?

Simply put, "equanimity" refers to our basic sense of "okay-ness" with ourselves and the world. **It is our sense of self-worth**. This means that for Achievement Addicts our whole sense of being ok with and within the world hinges on our achievements!

In essence, as Achievement Addicts, everything—and I mean EVERYTHING—depends on our achievements. For many of us, our achievements not only define us but validate our right to exist. Without our achievements validating our existence, many of us are not certain we deserve to be alive.

So how do we manage these terrible thoughts about our self-worth?

We compulsively pursue the next achievement (and the next one after that one and so on) in the hopes of numbing ourselves from *feeling* as worthless and inadequate as we believe we are.

Is it any wonder why we are addicted to achievement?

Understanding how Achievement Addiction offers us a psychic anesthetic for painful beliefs about our self-worth goes a long way toward explaining why we don't even think twice about giving up our health, sanity, family, friends, and well-being for our achievements.

What Is Addiction?
How Can It Be True That You Are an "Addict"?

Let's back up a bit before I lose you here because I'm using the dreaded words *addict, addiction*, and *addictive behaviors*.

I know this: *addiction* is a word thrown around quite a lot and without much exactitude. So, I think it will be helpful for us to define some terms.

Addiction is defined in the *Oxford English Dictionary* as "*the compulsive and persistent need for and use of a habit-forming substance known by the user to be harmful, characterized by a growing tolerance and well-defined psychological symptoms upon withdrawal.*"

The American Society of Addiction Medicine defines addiction in the following way:

> *Addiction* is a "*treatable, chronic medical disease involving complex interactions among brain circuits, genetics, environment, and an individual's life experiences. People with addiction use substances or engage in behaviors that become compulsive and often continue despite harmful consequences.*"

In other words, people with addiction have an *intense focus on using* a specific addictive substance or *behavior* to the point that it takes over their lives.

So, what are the common characteristics among the various addictive behaviors? In reading this list and checking it against your relationship to achievement, I would encourage you to think of your pursuit of achievements whenever you see the word *substance* or *behavior* in the following descriptions.

- You become obsessed and continually think about the substance or activity.
- Over time, you need more and more of the substance or activity to feel the same euphoric effects.
- You seek out and engage in the behavior or activity, even though it is causing harm (physical problems, tense relationships, psychological problems, emotional problems, etc.).
- You engage in the activity over and over again.
- Ceasing or reducing the substance or activity causes you physical, psychological, and emotional withdrawal symptoms, which can include irritability, cravings, restlessness, depression, or anxiety.
- You do not appear to have control over when, how long, or how much you continue the behavior.
- You deny problems resulting or arising from your engagement in the behavior, even though the cause of the problems is clearly and increasingly apparent to others.
- You hide the behavior after family or close friends have mentioned their concerns.
- You might experience a blackout when engaging in the behavior and might not remember how much or what you did.
- Because of your addiction, you spend less time on activities that used to be important to you.
- You may be prone to depression or anxiety, both of which are common in individuals with addictive behaviors.
- You resist seeing a physical or mental health professional for fear that you will be asked uncomfortable questions, exposed, or confronted.
- You usually have low self-esteem, feel anxious about your loss of control, and may come from a psychologically or physically abusive background.

Perhaps as you were reading this list and thinking about your own relationship with achievement, some of these characteristics resonated with you. I know it was shocking the first time I read through it. I realized that in many ways my relationship with achievement was no different from a cocaine addict's relationship with their next score.

It woke me up.

Now, it is not my intention to use this checklist or this analogy to create any false equivalencies between substance addiction and Achievement Addiction. However, even though Achievement Addiction may not qualify as a diagnosis in the *Diagnostic and Statistical Manual of Mental Disorders* (DSM-5), it is essential to realize that it is a real addiction and shares many of the same qualities that characterize other addictions.

As you will read in the client stories that follow, the harmful impact of Achievement Addiction on these individuals' personal lives, physical health, and mental well-being can sometimes be *as life-damaging as any other substance or behavioral addiction.*

Workaholics vs. Achievement Addicts

Let's also clarify something else that might be nagging at you, and that was nagging at me as I was writing this book:

Is this just another recycled book about workaholics?

I asked myself that same question throughout the writing process, and the ultimate answer is no. This is not a book about workaholics. It is bigger than that. It identifies an *addiction* that is, in my opinion, more elusive. While some similarities exist, addiction to work is very different from Achievement Addiction.

From what I have researched, experienced, and observed, here is the best formulation I can come up with:

Not all workaholics are Achievement Addicts, but Achievement Addicts are usually also workaholics.

Let's break this down. First, workaholics are addicted to the behaviors and activities of work itself: going to work, working a lot of hours, taking work home, taking work on vacation, sneaking in work calls during family events or celebrations. They use the activity of work itself and all its trappings as their drug of choice. The work itself gives them a sense of euphoria and allows them to escape uncomfortable feelings, complicated home dynamics, family commitments, conflict, health problems, and so on.

Workaholics work endless hours at the expense of their physical health, mental health, and family health. Many workaholics work endlessly *whether or not* there is a raise, promotion, bonus, or partnership forthcoming. Workaholics are not in it for the prize, the accolade, the bonus—nor for the achievement itself. In fact, many of them work overtime even when they are not getting paid more. It is work and work only that is their addiction of choice. Nothing else.

By contrast, Achievement Addicts are addicted to the euphoria of the next win, the next accolade, the next title, the next degree, the next client, the next project, the next interview, the next award, the next acquisition, the next house, the next million, the next car, the next wife. You get the point.

The drug of choice? THE CHASE FOR MORE ACHIEVEMENT. More praise, more applause, more respect, more approval, more promotions, more accolades, more degrees, more clients, more money, more lovers, more homes, etc. For the Achievement Addict, becoming a workaholic is usually the unfortunate cost of doing business to get the genuine high—the imagined "happiness," "recognition," and "self-worth" that they believe in their heart of hearts will finally be theirs when they land *that next achievement.*

I believe that many Achievement Addicts would be okay if they didn't have to go to work.

If they won the lottery, I have no doubt many would instantly quit their jobs—because work isn't what drives them. But very quickly, something inside them—emptiness, boredom, worthlessness—would start gnawing. In no time, many would feel the need to chase something else—usually something *big*—to feel worthy, alive, and happy. They might start a second or third company, launch a nonprofit, earn multiple advanced degrees, or write a book or two or three. And I am not condemning any of these grand ambitions or goals. Rather, what I question are the motivations and consequences. Would the next achievement project arise out of choice or compulsion? And more importantly, what's the price paid to satisfy that achievement compulsion, over and over again?

The point is this: Most lottery-winning "I don't need to work" Achievement Addicts would end up once again imbuing their next lofty achievement with all the power to control their health, sanity, and happiness. And many might easily slip into compromising and self-destructive behaviors to see that next achievement accomplished. Only to embark on another. And another.

Unfortunately, despite all evidence to the contrary, Achievement Addicts remain deluded that true happiness is just out of reach and wholly dependent on their next big achievement. As Achievement Addicts, we are not too different from one of King Arthur's Knights of the Round Table. Each of us is obsessively addicted to a lifelong and self-destructive crusade for the Holy Grail of Achievement—a futile crusade that has us sacrificing everything in pursuit of that one elusive achievement that will finally give us the lasting happiness we so desperately long for. As Achievement Addicts, we are on the hunt for that one supernatural achievement that will finally save us from feelings of worthlessness, once and for all.

And, not too unlike the Arthurian legend, Achievement Addiction ends badly for everyone involved. Invariably, Achievement Addicts work themselves to death, sacrificing health, family, and sanity only to discover, time and again, that the achievement payoff falls short of their hopes and that the afterglow is short-lived. We are crestfallen again when we discover that lasting happiness has eluded us once more, despite all the effort and sacrifice. We become deflated when we realize that our last hard-earned achievement is a rusty, tin replica of the Holy Chalice we thought we were chasing. And just before the old familiar feelings of worthlessness and inadequacy start to engulf us, we embark on a new crusade chasing the next new achievement that might be the one to finally save us from ourselves. And the cycle goes on. And on.

When you boil it down, the Achievement Addict is really addicted to *the chase of an imagined future happiness that is authentic, enduring, and everlasting.*

So, if achievement rewards consistently feel middling to disappointing, what keeps people in the Achievement Addiction game? To answer that question we need to delve a little deeper into understanding the more complex psychological drive underlying this Achievement Addiction compulsion.

Here's my best understanding of what's *really* driving Achievement Addicts.

It is **The Chase** that keeps us going, not the actual achievements or accolades—not even the material goods. Sure, we love the applause, attention, and recognition. But that's not what keeps us addicted to achievement.

As Achievement Addicts, we are addicted to **The Chase**. Why? Because **The Chase** offers us an escape from the present and the past. The time spent chasing our next achievement allows us to create and inhabit an idealized and futuristic fantasy world where our deepest longings for lasting happiness and self-worth are still alive, possible, and as yet untainted by reality.

In other words, the pursuit of a future achievement creates a hologram moment in the present that transcends the heartbreaking disappointments associated with our present condition and our past history. Achievement Addiction—like any other addiction—offers us an escape from the chaos, disappointment, and emptiness of our present reality and existence. And as you will read in each client story, the Achievement Addict is left hopeless, desperate, and lost without **The Chase** for the next achievement.

Once again, is it any wonder why **The Chase** for more achievement is so alluring?

So, even though our long-forgotten past achievements somehow didn't make good on their promises, and even though the most recent achievements we live with now somehow also seem to disappoint, we still mindlessly embark on the next achievement and the next—at the cost of health, family, and sanity—because **The Chase** allows us to numb-out and escape into a world where true happiness somewhere in the future is still possible.

So, while it may appear at times throughout this book that we are talking about workaholics, we are not. My clients and I were not addicted to work. Work is the dosing device; it is the means to an end. The end being all the idealized rewards, both inner and outer, that we believed endless high achievement promised us—decades before it went on to betray us.

Healthy Ambition vs. Achievement Addiction

Okay, so I'm sure many of you are asking yourselves at this point, "So, what's the big deal? I mean achievement doesn't hurt anyone. I'm not harming anyone if I want to work myself into the ground because I am ambitious and want more for my family and myself. It's my damn right and ability to do that. So why should all that be *pathologized?*"

I know that argument very well. It's one I frequently hear from clients and struggle with pretty regularly myself.

So here is the answer: addiction is addiction is addiction is addiction. What does that mean?

It means this:

There has always been a fine line between acceptable, non-pathologized behaviors and addiction.

And the line is as thin and treacherous as a razor's edge. You know as well as I do that there is no harm in having two glasses of wine once in a while, but there is a problem with needing a bottle of wine (or more) every night to fall asleep. One behavior allows for choice and moderation and is not a compulsion. The other is a need that robs you of choice and makes you feel like your life and well-being depend on it.

Same thing with achievement. There is no harm in healthy, grounded, purpose-driven ambition designed to help you fulfill a dream or aspiration. There is no harm in ambition that resonates with your true self, that manifests the best version of yourself. In fact, showing you how to design that type of joy-based success is this book's real purpose. However, *Achievement Addiction is not joyful, healthy, balanced ambition.* Achievement Addiction *will rob you of choice* and the joy you used to feel when you accomplished something meaningful and challenging.

Instead, Achievement Addiction will have you chasing achievement after achievement *out of compulsion.*

Why?

Because Achievement Addiction creates something called "**Achievement Tolerance.**" For alcoholics, the more you drink, the higher your tolerance for alcohol, so you need more and more alcohol to get drunk and get your original "happy buzz." A similar phenomenon occurs with Achievement Addicts. No matter the achievement, many Achievement Addicts report that they can no longer feel joy or sustain an improved feeling of self-worth for more than a moment. By chasing achievement their whole lives, many Achievement

Addicts have developed a super-high *achievement tolerance.* Meaning that for many Achievement Addicts, it takes many more and/or bigger achievements to get them feeling anything close to the achievement-euphoria they used to experience in the past. It can be said, that as Achievement Addicts we are in a futile cycle that has us "chasing the Achievement Dragon"—trying with each achievement to experience the same high we experienced the first time a big achievement left us feeling ecstatic and unstoppable.

So, this book is anything but a condemnation of ambition or success. Rather, it is a rallying cry for each of us to redefine success on our terms, an endorsement for us to pursue those goals and dreams rooted in a value-based and more holistic foundation within us and not from a place of addiction.

This brings me to two more terms that will be referenced again and again throughout the book.

Allow me to introduce you to the two-headed, evil offspring of unchecked Achievement Addiction—the *Achievement Trance* and *Achievement Amnesia.*

Understanding The Achievement Trance and Achievement Amnesia

The *Achievement Trance* is my term for the half-conscious, dream-like mental state that many Achievement Addicts experience when they either embark upon or are in the midst of chasing their next achievement. Many of my clients report that when they are in the process of striving for that next achievement—getting into law school, graduating from business school, working as an associate, shooting for partnership—they feel as if their lives are on autopilot; robotically moving through all the stress, and sacrifice without much self-reflection or concern for their health, families, or mental well-being. Many describe it as "being on a treadmill" and not knowing how to get off.

When you read the stories of "Gustav and His Go-Go Girls," "Immovable Mark," and "Omar the Somnambulist" you will become intimately familiar with the Achievement Trance and understand how living in a semi-dream state propelled exclusively by achievement can ruin lives.

And here's the real problem. The Achievement Trance seems to induce a type of *Achievement Amnesia* that leaves many of my clients, like Omar, saying, "I don't even remember when or why I decided to [fill in the blank], and I don't really know how I got here to this situation either." For many, their focus on achievement was so single-minded and self-sacrificing that they lost sight of *what* they were chasing and *why*.

Others develop another type of Achievement Amnesia, one that I experienced myself.

This type of Achievement Amnesia has more to do with forgetting or obliterating any achievement's value or meaning. You will begin to understand the impact of Achievement Amnesia when you read the upcoming stories of "Joan, the Million-Dollar Winner," "Oh Sweet, Sweet Betsy," and "Blake, the Choirboy." The fixation on the next achievement is so heightened that we consciously or unconsciously devalue the former achievement itself, to the degree that some of us forget we ever achieved it, to begin with. We shrug our shoulders with a kind of indifference when we talk about attending a great university, obtaining a professional degree, or starting a business. We never allowed that achievement to integrate into the fabric of our selfhood because our addiction had us all jacked up and excited about the *next* achievement.

Does any of this resonate with you?

With this type of Achievement Amnesia, some subconscious part of the mind has you believing that no achievement is worth integrating into your sense of self-worth because (and here is the kicker) some voice inside asks you in its quiet, snarky voice, "If *you* accomplished it, how valuable can it really be?"

The tragic logic inside the Achievement-Addicted mind goes something like this:

- You fundamentally believe you are worthless.
- You believe only achievement can make you feel like you are worth anything.
- But you also believe that whatever you have already achieved is worthless, too.
- Because deep down, you fundamentally believe that you are worthless.

It is this flawed logic that leaves us indifferent to and disconnected from our past achievements. And it is why none of our past achievements ever fill us up or feel like "enough."

Over the years, I have encountered too many newly minted young law partners who never took the time to celebrate the culmination of their life-long effort to become partners. Most of them are so numb or exhausted by the process that they find themselves unable to enjoy the final achievement. Years later, many of them share that they cannot recall the joy of reaching that pinnacle or associate any real sense of satisfaction with their herculean accomplishment. I have worked with law-firm partner after law-firm partner whose success in landing or winning a significant litigation matter or a corporate deal was short-lived and immediately eclipsed by the pressure of having to land a million-dollar book of business. And then I'd work with a million-dollar partner whose enormous success was eclipsed again by his drive to grow his book to $5 million. And the cycle continues.

The *Oxford English Dictionary* defines *trance* as a "*half-conscious state characterized by an absence of response to external stimuli*" and defines *amnesia* as "*a partial or total loss of memory, a form of 'forgetfulness.'*"

In truth, many of my clients' experiences don't rise to the pathological symptoms associated with somatically induced amnesia or somnambulism. However, as you read this collection of stories, the subjective residual impact of Achievement Addiction offers more than a few striking parallels. As one client once put it, "The Achievement Addiction has us sleepwalking through our lives until we wake up and don't recognize ourselves or where we are, what we've accomplished, or how we got here."

The Achievement Accomplice: Your Achievement Avatar

So, on a practical level, what really keeps us running from achievement to achievement? Of course, we all know that high achievement of any kind requires disciplined focus, staying power, and motivation. So, where is that coming from? What force drives the trance and keeps us going?

For many, the inner voice that drives us is our *Achievement Avatar*. This Avatar is what many refer to as the "inner critic" in your head. It's that inner chatterbox persona whom you allow to push you around and verbally bully you, whose number one job is to make sure you never feel "okay" or too satisfied with yourself so that you keep chasing achievements at all costs. The Achievement Avatar's job is to induce Achievement Amnesia. The Avatar does it primarily by devaluing you and robbing you of the pride and joy of your most recent achievement so that you never rest and never feel sated.

The Achievement Avatar will have you convinced that
- Your last achievement was no big deal.
- Anyone could have done it.
- You shouldn't rest on your laurels too much because you still have a lot to prove.
- You shouldn't celebrate any win too much because disaster is around the corner.
- There are other achievements that are bigger, better, shinier, and newer that will really make you happy.
- You owe it to your family to keep achieving.
- You owe it to yourself to keep achieving.
- You have a lot to prove to yourself, to your family, etc.
- You are invincible, and you deserve more.
- Other people want more for you.
- Other people with less talent have achieved more than you.
- You are superhuman and can do anything without being harmed.
- You need to toughen up and set your sights on the next big thing.
- You aren't entitled to rest or settle or give up.
- Not continuing to achieve makes you dull.
- Not continuing to achieve means you are not successful.
- Not continuing to achieve makes you a loser.
- Being content with what you have means failure.
- You are a loser if you don't take up the next challenge.
- You are a disappointment to others if you don't leverage all the opportunities available to you.
- You are spoiled, selfish, weak, and entitled if you don't embark on the next achievement.

And so on. It's exhausting and meant to wear you down, so you keep moving compulsively from one thing to the next without overthinking.

Let me share a little about my own Achievement Avatar.

Like the coxswain at the helm of a rowing scull, my trusty Achievement Avatar, "Leona," has always been at the ready with her blowhorn, poking me with her nasty, negative self-talk, guaranteeing that I stayed in the Achievement Addiction race. No matter the achievement, there stood Leona with her arms folded, rolling her eyes with bemusement, tapping one foot impatiently, waiting for me to get over myself so that we could move on to the next *real* achievement she had schemed up. And if Leona ever had the slightest inkling that I might be resting on my laurels too much, she was ready to whip me into shape, abuse me, tear me down, jack up my fear, and devalue what I had just accomplished. For most of my life, Leona has tried to make happiness a moving target. With her coaxing, it was always "when I finish my master's degree . . . when I land my first Am Law 100 client . . . when I get my company to scale . . . when I have thirty clients . . . no, fifty . . . when I become CMO!" then I would be happy and could relax. Leona even reared her head as I was writing this book about Achievement Addiction!

But this is not atypical for Achievement Addicts. For many of us, our Achievement Avatar has us on a compulsive chase to nowhere, believing each and every time that the next achievement fix will finally be the one to bring us what we long for most. So when you read the stories of "Just-Fine-Thanks Luisa" and "Anna-Maria, a Girl from Brooklyn," you will get to know two brilliant women who allowed their Achievement Avatars to control their thoughts, emotions, and actions to the point of abject misery. And when you read the stories of "Joan, the Million-Dollar Winner," "Immovable Mark," and "Melody and Her Sweet Potato Pie," you will learn how clever our Achievement Avatars can become in inducing real Achievement Amnesia.

So, what does your Achievement Avatar tell you? How does your Achievement Avatar keep you chasing achievement to the point of self-destruction? You can learn more about your Achievement Avatar by completing the Achievement Avatar exercise at www.achievementaddictiondetox.com.

And once you become more familiar with your Achievement Avatar and its voice, language, and strategy, you will be able to start choosing another path for yourself beyond Achievement Addiction.

The Origins of Achievement Addiction

So, now that we understand the nature of Achievement Addiction, the characteristics of the trance and amnesia, and the role that your Achievement Avatar plays in perpetuating this cycle, let's try to understand the root causes of this addiction.

What are the origins of Achievement Addiction? Where did it start? Were we born this way? Is it biochemical, or is it learned behavior? Is change possible, or is it hopeless? And what, if anything, can you do to rejigger your relationship with achievement?

These are all critical questions. My need to understand the underlying forces at play led me to complete a master's degree in clinical social work and a psychodynamic, psychoanalytic fellowship.

And while this book isn't an in-depth psychological study of the psychosocial history or psycho-familial dynamics underlying the Achievement-Addicted personality, I believe it is helpful to look at Achievement Addiction through the lens of our past. Perhaps by reflecting on our personal history, we can better understand what we might *really* be chasing when we are in the throes of Achievement Addiction. With understanding, we can then seek out other, healthier ways to fill those voids, different ways that don't have us killing ourselves or sacrificing our lives.

As you might expect, much of the research in this area focuses on the family system because it is the primary socializing environment for most of our early years. Our family system's stability, how our parents treated us, and our socioeconomic circumstances are critical variables in determining whether our needs for safety, sustenance, and security were adequately met.

Some of the research in this area has found the following familial similarities among individuals who demonstrate behaviors also associated with Achievement Addicts:

- We were often raised in less-than-ideal or non-nurturing environments that poorly satisfied our basic security and safety needs.
- We were often raised in emotionally non-expressive and non-nurturing environments, which diminished our self-esteem and self-worth.
- We were often raised in environments where receiving affection, love, attention, and resources was contingent on meeting or exceeding certain external standards, such as success, earning good grades, winning, etc.
- We were often raised in environments where we did not feel listened to, we did not feel free to express our own opinions, thoughts, or feelings, and we did not feel we had many choices.
- We were often raised in strict, punitive, or highly structured environments with many rules and a hierarchy in which we felt we were not allowed to be ourselves.
- We were often raised in environments where our parents led us to believe that we were their investments.
- We were often raised in highly evaluative or competitive environments where our performance and behavior were continually scrutinized for "goodness" and "badness."
- We were often raised by parents who suffered from addictions.

In other words, many Achievement Addicts were raised in environments that fostered what Tim Kasser, in his book *The High Price of Materialism*, calls *"contingent self-esteem."* Contingent self-esteem means that our feelings of self-worth are fundamentally unstable, fragile, and highly *contingent* upon meeting certain specific external standards.

Kasser explains that many of us learn to depend on materialistic values (i.e., external achievement) for our self-esteem very early in childhood. Eventually, our achievement/materialistic values are not only *"a symptom of the underlying insecurity [but also] the coping strategy that we use in an attempt to alleviate the problem and satisfy our needs."*

It's worth taking a closer look at that quote: Achievement is both the symptom of and the coping strategy for our unstable and contingent self-worth. A preoccupation with achievement results from our low self-worth and is also how we soothe the negative feelings around our low self-worth.

Kasser helps us understand the cycle of Achievement Addiction discussed above in the following passage:

"When such individuals are successful at meeting their goals, they experience positive feelings. Such positive feelings tend to be short-lived, however, and the sense of worth is fairly unstable, as new challenges and threats quickly arise that can easily deflate their self-esteem."

To simplify this, growing up in these types of environments may have taught us that our

- lovability
- value
- worth
- importance
- safety
- security, and
- receipt of limited resources

were all *contingent on achieving certain specific external standards.*

Kasser helps us understand what many of us have been quietly aware of our whole lives: namely, that our whole sense of self-worth is contingent upon our achievements! And that without our achievements, or without another achievement to pursue, we as Achievement Addicts feel worthless. **In essence, the root cause of Achievement Addiction is contingent self-worth.**

So, whether we knew it or not, psychically, we grew up determined to jump as high and as often as was expected of us so that we could survive, and feel worthy. Many Achievement Addicts chase achievement at the expense of everything else because something in their early childhood experience created a hardened, core belief that has them convinced that if they do, they will then, have all their needs met and they will be safe so they can thrive.

But it is the corollary to that core belief that explains a lot more about how the Achievement Addict understands achievement.

The core belief and its corollary go something like this:

If I achieve then I will have all my needs met and I will survive.

If I don't pursue achievement, I will not get my basic needs met and I will not survive.

Psychically, this core belief about achievement that lives in many Achievement Addicts translates into existential danger. So, as alluded to before, achievement is not really about obtaining or having more things. Instead, for many of us, achievement is a "life or death" psychological construct deeply rooted in our fragile and contingent self-worth.

That's some pretty heavy hardwiring to recognize, much less try to disentangle and defuse.

But, while we may not be able to undo that hardwiring instantaneously, I am here to tell you that from what I have experienced and what I have witnessed in working with others, we can do a "workaround." The stories about "Trevor and the Princeton Club," "Jonathan The Supreme Court Clerk Chased By a Tiger," and "Julia, the Singing Lawyer" show that we each have it in us to DETOX; using the 7 Steps we can connect with our **non-contingent, innate self-worth** and go on to transform our lives beyond Achievement Addiction. That's what this whole book is about!

If we can find a way to access your innate self-worth you are on your way to Achievement Addiction DETOX. And as you will read in the stories that follow, working the 7 Steps offer a proven way to access your innate self-worth.

The 7 Step method I present here works and helps you DETOX, precisely because the method goes to the heart of what drives our Achievement Addiction: our primal longing to feel a sense of self-worth that is stable and enduring.

If we can reconnect with our **innate and non-contingent sense of self-worth** we can dislodge the chokehold that Achievement Addiction has over our lives.

And working the 7 Steps offers a proven method for doing just that.

So, now that you have an understanding of the Achievement Addict personality, I invite you to take the self-assessments in the next chapter.

ACHIEVEMENT ADDICTION
SELF-ASSESSMENTS

Achievement Addiction Self-Assessment

Now, let's talk about YOU. You picked up this book for a reason. Maybe something about the title intrigued you; perhaps you thought to yourself, *That's me!* or *That's my wife!* So before we go any further, I invite you to take this self-assessment. For this personally conducted assessment, make a note of your **Yes** or **No** answer for each item; you'll tally the total of each at the end.

1. Is achievement very important to you?
2. Do you tend to overinflate or exaggerate, to yourself and others, the importance, significance, or impact of the achievement you're working on while you are working on it?
3. Do you tend to "empower" the achievement you're working on with the ability to "change everything" or "make everything better"?
4. Do you believe that attaining a specific achievement will make you happy?
5. Do you believe that attaining a particular achievement will prove you worthy?
6. Do you believe that attaining a certain achievement will make you better than other people?

7. Do you believe that attaining a certain achievement will solve many of your problems?
8. Do you believe that attaining a certain achievement will make you more peaceful?
9. Do you believe that attaining a certain achievement will make you more respectable?
10. Do you believe that attaining a certain achievement will guarantee you more money?
11. Do you believe that attaining a certain achievement will insulate you from pain?
12. Do you believe that attaining a certain achievement will insulate you from generalized danger?
13. Once you attain a particular achievement, are you frequently disappointed with its real impact on your life or happiness?
14. Once you attain a specific achievement, are you surprised to discover that it isn't all it was cracked up to be?
15. Once you attain a certain achievement, are you surprised when you are still uneasy/unhappy/sad/restless?
16. Once you attain a certain achievement, do you devalue what it took to achieve it?
17. Do you believe that once you attain a certain achievement you will then be more worthy of love?
18. Once you attain a certain achievement, are you disappointed to discover that it doesn't make you worry less?
19. Once you attain a certain achievement, are you already looking for another achievement to attain?
20. When you are close to attaining a certain achievement, are you already starting to focus on finding the next achievement?
21. When you look back on your past achievements, do they leave you feeling empty, numb, or indifferent?
22. When you look back on some of your achievements, do you wonder why you did them?
23. When you look back on some of your achievements, do you feel as if someone other than you did them?

24. When you look back on some of your achievements, do you have a secret sense that it wasn't you who accomplished them?
25. When you look back on some of your achievements, is it difficult to recall the actual time and effort you invested in attaining that achievement?
26. Do you have a hard time recalling some of your significant achievements?
27. Are you more comfortable talking about the next achievement you are working on than your past achievements?
28. Does the next achievement excite you?
29. Does the next achievement energize you?
30. Does the next achievement take up your whole focus, to the exclusion of your other achievements?
31. If someone else has attained a similar achievement, does it diminish in value in your eyes?
32. Do you measure your self-worth as a human being through your achievements?
33. Do significant lifelong achievements leave you feeling less than fulfilled?
34. When you finally attain a certain achievement, do you feel significantly different than you did before reaching it? If so, does that new elated state dissipate quickly?
35. Do you feel uneasy, restless, or guilty if you have nothing "achievement-oriented" to do?
36. Do you ascribe "meaning" to everyday hobbies, games, social gatherings, or friendships?
37. Do you fundamentally believe that you are special, better, or more unique than other people?
38. Do you think less of people with fewer achievements than you have?
39. Do you replay failures in your past?
40. Do you replay criticizing conversations in your head?
41. Can you recall humiliating or criticizing conversations that may have happened decades ago?
42. When you recall them, do they still have a lasting "sting"?
43. Are you afraid of failing?

44. Are you restless, impulsive, and easily bored?

45. Do you drive yourself into the ground with exhaustion, self-deprivation, not eating, or not sleeping in order to attain a certain goal or achievement?

46. Do you get a sense of pride or virtue and/or a sense of superiority from your ability to go without meals, sleep, or breaks?

47. Do you find it harder and harder to take long vacations?

48. Do you often feel rushed or hurried, or have an exaggerated sense of urgency?

49. Do you regularly work on the weekends and while on vacation?

50. Do you worry if you have not been in touch with work or your achievement project while on vacation?

51. Once you attain a certain achievement, do you avoid celebrating?

52. Do you find celebrating your achievements "silly" or "pointless"?

53. Are you working on achieving more than one achievement project at a given time?

54. Do you like things done "just right"?

55. Do you tend to see things as black or white/right or wrong? Or all or nothing?

56. Are you competitive, even in family games or fun social environments?

57. Is it essential to you to be "right" and "win" every conversation, debate, game, or sport?

58. Are you overly critical, almost abusive of yourself when you make a mistake?

59. Do you avoid thinking about planning for retirement?

60. Are you very responsible and accountable concerning work or matters related to achieving your goal but not in personal or family matters?

61. Does what other people think of you really matter to you?

62. Do other people's actions or words have the power to ruin or "make" your day?

63. Do you believe that your moods and feelings are strongly impacted by what others say or think about you?

64. Do you believe that your moods and feelings are strongly impacted by how much you feel you have achieved on any given day?

65. Do you beat yourself up if you feel that you haven't achieved enough on any given day?
66. Do you fear criticism and rejection but find it easy to criticize and reject others?
67. Do you get upset if plans don't work out as you expected?
68. Do you create artificial deadlines that create pressure or "fire drill" situations at work? At home?
69. Do you find yourself focusing on the future or future events or future achievements instead of enjoying the present moment?
70. Do you believe that your achievements make you worthy of joy, happiness, and love?

Number of **Yes** answers: _____

Number of **No** answers: _____

If you answered Yes to more than **fifteen** of these questions, then you have picked up the right book. Most likely, you have an addiction to achievement that is and has been running the show in your life, health, and career.

If you answered Yes to more than **twenty-five** of these questions, it is very likely that your addiction to achievement not only has been driving the bus for some time but also is at the heart of some of your present unhappiness, numbness, sense of disorientation, or general malaise.

If you answered Yes to **thirty** or more of these questions, it is very likely that you have been and still are sacrificing your physical, mental, psychological, spiritual, and interpersonal well-being on the altar of achievement. *Welcome to the club!* And I am happy you picked up this book.

Achievement Trance Self-Assessment

In this last chapter, we learned about the Achievement Trance and how it manifests as obsessive striving, loss of control, and self-numbing. The Achievement Trance has us trapped and experiencing our lives and the people around us exclusively through the lens of our Achievement Addiction.

Here are some questions designed to help you understand the nature of the Achievement Trance and whether you are presently experiencing one or have in the past. Make a note of your **Yes** or **No** answer for each item; you'll tally the total of each at the end.

1. Has attaining your latest achievement occupied most, if not all, of your waking life and thoughts?

2. Has attaining this achievement regularly kept you up at night, preventing you from falling asleep, or intruded on and interrupted your sleep in any way?

3. Do you believe that attaining this one achievement will "fix" everything that feels wrong or broken or disappointing in your life?

4. Do you become hostile or belligerent toward people, places, circumstances, or things that in any way impede, inconvenience, or delay attaining your achievement?

5. Has attaining this achievement caused the rest of the world to "fade into the background"?

6. Has attaining this achievement caused other people who are important to you to also "fade into the background"?

7. Do you have difficulty remembering the details of specific chapters of your life or certain family celebrations because you were obsessed with attaining a particular achievement?

8. Do the people in your life—friends, family, colleagues—ever feel like the supporting cast to your quest for any given achievement?

9. Do you value, categorize, or appreciate others almost exclusively through the filter of how they endorse, further, or diminish your attaining a specific achievement?

10. When you are not doing things associated with attaining this achievement, do you blame, shame, feel bad about, or feel guilty about yourself?

11. Do you measure the value of any given day, week, month, year, or decade in terms of how productive you were in furthering your achievements?

12. Have friends and family confronted you more than once about the negative impact of your singular focus on your achievement?

13. When you tried to set aside your thoughts about attaining an achievement and engage in other thoughts, activities, or events, were you easily bored, restless, detached, and/or numb?
14. Did you promise to change that behavior in the past only to fall into it again?
15. Do you regret your past behavior but also feel that you had or continue to have limited control over those choices?

If you answered Yes to zero to five questions, then you probably haven't experienced the full impact of an Achievement Trance.

If you answered Yes to six to ten questions, it is very likely that your Achievement Addiction has lured you into a temporary Achievement Trance that has you living your life singularly focused on your achievements and that sometimes everything and everyone else in your life is background noise.

If you answered Yes to more than ten questions, you are very familiar with the Achievement Trance. Most likely, you have an obsessive focus on achievement, and your health, sanity, friends, family, and the rest of the world have been taking a backseat for most of your life. This trance-like state probably is, more often than not, your way of being and existence—so much so that you may also have experienced the fallout of Achievement Amnesia. Take the assessment that follows to see if Achievement Amnesia might be something you have experienced as well.

Achievement Amnesia Self-Assessment

Achievement Amnesia can frequently accompany the Achievement Trance. Sometimes it takes the form of not remembering what was going on around you while in the heat of chasing your achievements. And sometimes it can take the form of "undoing" or disowning your past achievements altogether. I know that sounds a little extreme, but for many of us, the intensity of our Achievement Trance induces a low-level form of dissociation (non-clinical), which, later on, makes it very hard for you to believe that you actually were responsible for that achievement.

The assessment that follows doesn't distinguish between these two types of Achievement Amnesia, mainly because it has been my experience that if you have one type of Achievement Amnesia, you probably suffer from elements of the other because they are so intimately tied.

For each statement below, circle the answer that best reflects your experience.

1. You discover that you have done things in pursuit of your achievement that you do not remember today.

    Never   Sometimes   Often   Usually   All the time

2. It's not clear whether you have completed an action or task related to that achievement or just thought about completing it (e.g., you're not sure if you made that phone call to a client or only thought about making it).

    Never   Sometimes   Often   Usually   All the time

3. You arrive somewhere and can't recall how you got there.

    Never   Sometimes   Often   Usually   All the time

4. You struggle to work out whether a memory associated with that achievement actually happened or you just made it up.

    Never   Sometimes   Often   Usually   All the time

5. You "lose yourself" in an activity related to attaining a particular achievement and completely lose awareness of what is going on around you.

    Never   Sometimes   Often   Usually   All the time

6. You cannot remember important moments in your life or moments leading up to those moments, like getting married, having a baby, graduating from college, etc.

    Never   Sometimes   Often   Usually   All the time

7. Daydreams about this achievement feel so vivid and real that they feel like they are actually happening.

    Never   Sometimes   Often   Usually   All the time

8. When you disconnect from activities related to chasing your achievement, people or things around you seem very far away or unclear, as if you were seeing them through a mist or fog.

    Never   Sometimes   Often   Usually   All the time

9. You don't really feel or are able to ignore things that would normally be painful or uncomfortable to others, like a burn, a cut, a broken limb, or a high fever.

    Never   Sometimes   Often   Usually   All the time

10. You feel as if you are in someone else's body or that your body is not your own.

    Never   Sometimes   Often   Usually   All the time

11. You see your reflection and don't recognize yourself.

    Never   Sometimes   Often   Usually   All the time

12. You feel as if people and things around you are not real, or they might be imaginary.

    Never   Sometimes   Often   Usually   All the time

13. Your overall reactions to things are inconsistent; sometimes it can feel like you are two or three different people reacting in a completely different manner to people or things.

    Never   Sometimes   Often   Usually   All the time

14. You talk to yourself out loud when you are by yourself, focused on attaining your achievement.

    Never   Sometimes   Often   Usually   All the time

15. You have an out-of-body experience, like being able to see yourself as if you were a different person.

    Never   Sometimes   Often   Usually   All the time

16. You discover notes, work products, doodles, emails, texts, etc., that you must have created but do not remember writing or completing.

    Never   Sometimes   Often   Usually   All the time

17. Places you have been many times before feel as if you are seeing them for the first time.

    Never   Sometimes   Often   Usually   All the time

18. You hear a person speak and realize that you did not hear much of what they said.

    Never   Sometimes   Often   Usually   All the time

19. Most nights, you go to bed not remembering much about what you accomplished or ate, or what other people said, unless it was directly related to activities connected with attaining your achievement.

    Never   Sometimes   Often   Usually   All the time

As you tally your results, eliminate all those you circled as "never" from the final count.

Now count all those questions for which you answered either "sometimes," "often," "usually," or "all the time."

If you have a score of less than five, then Achievement Amnesia isn't something that characterizes your Achievement Addiction.

If you have tallied a score of six to ten, it's fair to say that not only are you an Achievement Addict, but your hyper-focus on achievement most likely has induced a trance that now causes you to either forget or completely disown many of your achievements.

If you have tallied a score of eleven or higher, Achievement Amnesia is actively present in your life and a key indicator of full-on Achievement Addiction. And if you are really truthful, you've probably wondered quietly to yourself about these odd lapses in memory or moments of disconnection from your achievements.

ACHIEVEMENT ADDICTION DETOX

THE 7 STEPS

Working the 7 Steps

Now that you understand more about Achievement Addiction, Achievement Tolerance and the Achievement Avatar, Trance, and Amnesia and have taken the assessments, it's time to start talking about the DETOX part of the book—how do we experience Achievement Addiction DETOX?

By working the 7 Steps!

These 7 Steps were not handed to me on a platter, and I did not learn them as part of my coaching, clinical social work, or psychoanalytic training. Instead, I learned almost everything I write about here from my clients. My clients imparted these collective insights to me during hours and hours of one-on-one sessions over nearly twenty years. They taught me that self-directed, joyful success beyond Achievement Addiction could best be accessed by working these 7 Steps:

1. AWARENESS   Wake up!
2. MINDSET   Make a shift.
3. EMOTIONS   Honor your feelings.
4. SUPPORT   Ask for help.
5. BODY   Move a muscle.
6. FAITH   Widen your perspective.
7. ALIGNMENT   Trust yourself.

Working the 7 Steps helped all the clients you will read about in this book DETOX and go on to transform their lives and define success on their own terms beyond Achievement Addiction.

And working the 7 Steps helped me do the same.

But how and why do the 7 Steps work in bringing about Achievement Addiction DETOX?

Here's the short answer:

By working the 7 Steps we ignite a radical chain reaction within our mind, body, and spirit that changes our fundamental relationship to achievement.

When we change our relationship to achievement and strip it of its power over our self-worth we experience Achievement Addiction DETOX.

It works like this.

- By working the 7 Steps you'll start waking up from your Achievement Trance.
- By working the 7 Steps you'll start shaking off your Achievement Amnesia.
- By working the 7 Steps you'll start recalling your multitude of innate talents, skills, and abilities.
- By working the 7 Steps you'll start reintegrating those long-forgotten skills and talents into the fabric of your identity and sense of selfhood in a permanent way.
- By working the 7 Steps you'll start ignoring your Achievement Avatar along with all the other abusive voices—internal and external—that diminish your value in your own eyes.
- By working the 7 Steps you'll start connecting with your true self.

And ultimately, when you start connecting with your true self you are well on your way to rediscovering your **innate and unconditional self-worth** that is not and never has been . . . DEPENDENT ON ACHIEVEMENT!

Take that in for a minute.

What I know for certain is that there is another way to embolden your innate self-worth that does not hinge on any achievement—past, present, or future. And working the 7 Steps has worked for me and countless others.

Here's another way to understand why this 7 Step method works:

The 7 Steps offer a way to disprove the core fallacy that drives your Achievement Addiction.

And what is that fallacy? That you are worthless without your achievements.

And what challenges that core fallacy? Your reconnection with your *true self—which can be accessed by working the 7 Steps!*

Time and again I have witnessed how Achievement Addiction DETOX kicks into overdrive once a client has truly connected with their true self. Why? Because when you reconnect with your true self, you can start to uncover and listen to all the wisdom your true self has to share with you about your non-contingent, innate self-worth, your hidden talents, buried passions, and ultimate purpose.

That's the moment when the magic happens.

Because that's the moment when ACHIEVEMENT ADDICTION no longer has a death grip on your sense of worthiness and no longer controls your choices, beliefs, emotions, and behaviors. That's the moment you can start making career and life decisions from a place of agency and not from a place of compulsive addiction fueled by fear and feelings of inadequacy and worthlessness.

That's what happened to me. And that's what happened to all the clients you are about to read about.

All the clients you will read about worked the 7 Steps, reconnected with their true selves, rediscovered their innate self-worth separate and apart from achievements, and went on to transform their lives and careers. In the process, they regained sanity, health, joy, and a sense of renewed control over their lives and careers.

But telling isn't selling. Showing is. That is why I've illustrated these 7 Steps with a collection of more than twenty tell-all client stories that reveal each of the 7 Steps in action.

These stories of super-smart, talented, ambitious, creative people who are driven to self-destruction by Achievement Addiction are not necessarily unique to the executives, bankers, and lawyers who make up most of my coaching practice. The demographic details could easily be swapped with those of an Achievement-Addicted surgeon, accountant, Olympic athlete, high school student, tenured professor, artist, investment banker, self-made entrepreneur, salesman, stay-at-home mom, or C-suite type

So, how can the 7 Steps be applied to your life?

By working each of the 7 Steps using The IMAGO Coaching Method. The very same coaching method I used in each story you'll read in this book.

As I have mentioned before, this book and its DETOX approach is practical.

This book not only outlines the 7 Steps through client illustrations, but it also walks you through each of the 7 Steps allowing you to coach yourself using the method that worked for so many others.

Let's get started!

Introducing The IMAGO Coaching Method

The IMAGO Coaching Method is a transformational coaching method I invented and use with my clients. It has its origins in the traditional five *C*s of coaching: clarity, commitment, co-creation, change, and celebration. However, the IMAGO Method refines these basic coaching concepts and is designed *to help you create a stable and unconditional sense of self-worth that is separate from your achievements.*

The IMAGO Coaching Method helps you apply to your own life the 7 Steps you will read about, through a process of

- INQUIRY
- MAGNIFICATION
- ACTION
- GROWTH
- OWNERSHIP

This is the very same method I use with all my coaching clients and that helped all the clients you will read about in this book. But it's not enough to understand the 7 Steps. I want you to work each of the 7 Steps using the IMAGO Coaching Method as if you were a client sitting across from me in my office.

So, after you read about each of the 7 Steps, you will be asked a series of IMAGO Coaching Questions designed to help you work that particular step and immediately apply it to your life. And if you want to go deeper into the DETOX process you can download The Achievement Addiction Worksheets for free at www.achievementaddictiondetox.com.

This is a practical book designed to help you DETOX from Achievement Addiction.

As the age-old adage reminds us: the plan works if you work the plan.

Achievement Addiction DETOX starts right now with the 7 Steps.

Your Achievement Addiction DETOX Game Plan

Read the stories, familiarize yourself with the 7 Steps, start working the steps by answering the IMAGO Coaching Questions after each of the 7 Steps, and apply what you have discovered to your life. To continue working on the DETOX process you can download more of the in-depth Achievement Addiction DETOX Worksheets at www.achievementaddictiondetox.com.

What follows is a collection of real-life stories of real people, like you and me. People who had dramatically veered way off course by barreling down a gilded but dangerous Achievement-Addicted path that left them teetering on the verge of self-destruction. Their stories are my story. And most likely, if you have picked up this book and gotten this far, their stories, or parts of them, are your story, too.

Your journey through the 7 Steps starts with the first step of AWARENESS and one of my very first coaching clients, Jay.

THE 7 STEPS

STEP 1

AWARENESS

Wake Up!

Time To Open Your Eyes

So, how well do you think you know yourself?

The truth is that most Achievement Addicts haven't taken the time to understand themselves. Their motivations, aversions, passions, values, or priorities are murky. As Achievement Addicts, we are extremely others-oriented and preoccupied, even obsessed, with external approval. That preoccupation with what others think about us doesn't typically allow much time or space for focusing on our own preferences, beliefs, and values.

Developing awareness requires that we intentionally and actively become curious about our inner workings—our feelings, thoughts, compulsions, and motivations so that we can shift our focus away from others and back onto our own lives.

But for many Achievement Addicts, close self-examination poses too much of a risky undertaking—one potentially laden with unknown, messy results that may generate disapproval from others. In fact, many Achievement Addicts intentionally dodge self-awareness because they believe that "too much self- awareness" has the potential to threaten the drive for more achieve-ments. We have all heard the cautionary tales of those high achievers who one day took a detour off the treadmill and went to "find themselves" but got lost in the process. Better to keep our heads down, we tell ourselves, stay the course, do what is expected of us, and keep striving for the next achievement, even if it kills us.

Eventually, this lack of self-awareness catches up with us. And not always in the most attractive ways.

Jay was one of those clients who had side-stepped self-awareness for most of his adult life.

Jay's Awakening

Jay was a client of mine who found his way to me through a referral from the head of professional development at a large law firm that had a reputation for grinding and burning out its young associates. This firm was also known for its loud, abusive, and nasty partners.

Upon receiving the referral, I pressed the professional development director to find out more about what the firm wanted Jay's coaching to focus on from a skills perspective. She shared with me that Jay was one of the hardest-working young associates she had seen in her twenty years on the job.

"He never goes home," she told me. "He never takes vacation, and he works nonstop, but he will never make partner."

"Why?" I asked.

"He's . . . weird," she said apprehensively. "On the rare occasion he isn't completely mute," she went on to explain, "he speaks in this eerie, robotic tone that creeps his coworkers right out."

Jay apparently made people very uncomfortable, so much so that the partners of the law firm decided he would never advance to the partnership. But the firm wanted him to continue working as hard as ever in the back room, even though a promotion to partner would never be in the cards for him.

I invited Jay to meet with me for a chat. The moment he walked into my office, I understood what the HR director meant.

Jay was tall, in a Lurch-y way. He was bald, cadaverous white, and sweating profusely. His hand was dripping wet when I shook it, and I quickly realized Jay was having a full-on panic attack at the prospect of having to speak to a stranger. I ran to get Jay a glass of water and returned to my office to find him frozen in the exact spot I left him. I handed him the water; he slowly drank it without saying a word.

I asked him to take a seat. He did, and we were silent for what felt like ten straight minutes (although I'm sure it was only a few seconds).

"The firm has asked me to work with you on some career development topics, which I am happy to share with you," I began. "You should know everything we talk about here is completely confidential. So, I'm curious about what you think brings you to coaching and what you want to get out of our engagement."

"I am dying," he said, eerily calm.

My immediate thought was *Oh my God, why didn't the firm tell me he was ill?*

"If I stay and continue the way I am working," Jay droned in a monotone, "I will most likely drop dead at my desk one day or just shoot myself. If I leave, I will feel so lost and empty that I might also just shoot myself."

"Do you have a plan?" I asked.

Suicidal ideation doesn't shock me. Treating people with chronic suicidality was my area of expertise as a psychotherapist. And treatment protocol indicated that the first thing I needed to assess was whether Jay had a specific suicide plan in place. If he did, I would be dialing 911 before his next sip of water.

"A plan?" he echoed, confused.

"Yes. A plan for killing yourself. Do you have a plan, Jay?" I repeated calmly.

A look of surprise crept across his face, and he began to ponder my question.

"Sure I do," he said calmly. "At the rate I'm going, I will most likely drink myself to death."

Okay. No specific plan in place, I thought as I breathed a sigh of relief. But Jay was definitely in crisis.

"What rate is that?" I inquired.

"Well," he began, "I have no life. I worked almost 4,000 hours last year, and I'm on track to do the same this year. If I get home before 11 o'clock, that's an early night. I work weekends. Every weekend, actually. And I haven't taken a vacation in over five years. And whenever I do have downtime of any sort, well, I drink."

Things were starting to make sense.

"I drink to fall asleep every night," he continued, his head hanging in shame. "I drink until I black out. But somehow, by the grace of God, I have the kind of constitution that allows me to drink and still be able to get up and be in the office by 10 a.m. to start the process all over again."

Jay painted a picture of a very isolated, chaotic, and sad life that revolved around billable hours and alcoholic binges.

"Jay, I'm starting to get a picture of what's going on," I said. "But let me ask you, what's the point of all this self-abuse and self-sacrifice?"

"Making partner!" he said. "I am killing myself to make partner. Once I do that, then I can start rebuilding some semblance of a life."

Clearly, Jay had no idea how his firm viewed him. My heart ached for this man.

"At least I know that if I continue to work this way, I will make partner. They need me!" he exclaimed. "No one works the hours I do. No one else has the expertise I have. At least I have the comfort of knowing that all this hard work and sacrifice will pay off when I make partner."

It took all my energy to stay quiet as he rationalized this slow path to death in the hopes of achieving a pipe dream that only I knew was extremely unlikely.

"And what do you envision for yourself once you make partner?" I asked. I knew I had to continue down this path with him to get him to let me in and have a chance at helping him.

"More of the pie. More pie for the winner of the pie-eating contest," he chuckled.

"So, what would you like our coaching to focus on?" I asked, hoping to steer him back on track.

"I want to know what I need to do so I can make partner," he replied, his focus unwavering. "That is the only thing that matters to me. Being a lawyer is the only thing I know how to do well. Everything else, well, I've screwed up."

Jay was killing himself both figuratively and literally, and he wasn't even aware that the firm had eliminated him from partnership consideration years prior because of his awkward interpersonal ways. Jay was a "worker bee" and would be for the remainder of his career at this firm, but no one at the firm had ever had the decency to let him know. Why? Mostly, Jay's billable hours were making his partners wealthy, and they had no vested interest in letting him know the truth. The partners were using Jay, cajoling him, and stringing him along, and Jay was on the verge of self-destruction because of it.

Jay and I worked together for quite a long time, and I can assure you that our focus was on everything but making partner. The first thing we unpacked was his crisis-level alcohol addiction. Jay explained that he isolated himself from family and other loved ones because of his fear of what they might think of him and his alcoholism. Once he trusted me, he also confided in me that in addition to alcohol addiction, he had developed a chronic sex addiction to prostitutes that was putting his health and life even more at risk. Jay's life had become chaotic and unmanageable, and he needed help, and fast.

Within the first several weeks, Jay enrolled in his first AA meeting, which got him on a sobriety path. Despite his initial objections, he committed to attending one AA meeting every day for the first month of our work together. As I got the sense that he was actively addressing his addictions to alcohol and sex, we slowly began unraveling his job at the firm and his addiction to achievement.

In our coaching work together, AWARENESS—the first of the 7 Steps —was Jay's portal to realigning his life and career. Jay and I discovered that he had no real idea of what being a partner entailed, and in fact, he realized that he actually didn't want to become a partner. After I consulted with the firm's professional development director, we both felt a responsibility to let Jay know and help him understand that he would never make partner at the firm. He was very disappointed, but there was a part of him that was visibly relieved. This realization led Jay to investigate in-house opportunities that offered regular hours, a predictable life schedule, respectable compensation, and an environment that would not fuel his addiction to achievement, alcohol, or anything else. He was attending daily AA meetings and picked up swimming after a long hiatus from his competitive swimming career. He also learned how to play tennis and began spending more time connecting with his spiritual practices. The work we did together was successful because of Jay's heightened awareness of himself and his surroundings, his change of mindset, and his willingness to get help for his many addictions. Developing his awareness in one area of his life had a positive domino effect on other areas of his life.

Awareness is listed as the first of the 7 Steps precisely because it helps break through the dulling Achievement Trance that has you robotically chasing achievement for the sake of achievement. Developing awareness about your achievement addiction both catalyzes and sustains many of the other significant changes you may want to make.

In Jay's case, the Achievement Trance had him chasing something he didn't even really want! He just didn't know it.

Achievement Addiction

➢ blinded Jay to the realities of his circumstances at work and the impact that his single-minded obsession with achievement was having on his mental and physical health;

➢ induced an Achievement Trance that had him chasing an achievement that he ultimately didn't want, or appreciate; and

➢ made Jay so miserable that he turned to other addictive substances and behaviors as a way to cope.

Achievement Addiction DETOX helped Jay

➢ look at the multiple addictions that were destroying his life;

➢ discern whether the achievement he was pursuing was something he really wanted or simply a function of his Achievement Addiction; and

➢ recognize that he could define success as a lawyer on his own terms and in a way that aligned with his newfound self-care priorities.

Alcohol and Achievement Addiction

Jay is far from the only high-performance professional who drinks.

When I was a first-year attorney at a big law firm, I worked on a mind-numbing discovery request for an insurance defense case that required me to review endless insurance policies. For those of you unfamiliar with this particular type of litigation, it requires that you read thousands upon thousands of documents in the hope of finding a needle in the haystack. I was locked in a small, windowless "war room" with boxes of documents stacked to the ceilings (back when documents were still reviewed on paper and not online) and told to come out when they were all reviewed. I saw no one for days. Then weeks. I worked at a fancy, prominent law firm, but I felt like I had been sentenced to an isolation cell in a federal penitentiary. Then one day, John, the senior attorney managing the litigation discovery process, stopped by around 10 p.m. as I was preparing to leave the office and head home. He came in and sat down at the conference room table.

"How's it going?" he asked, leaning back in his chair, making himself comfortable.

"Fine, I guess," I mumbled.

He chuckled and put his feet up on the boardroom table. "It gets better, Elena. . . I promise. Every associate has to pay their dues with discovery and due diligence. That's how we separate the men from the boys. I mean, who can hack it. You know what I mean. . ."

I was still rubbing my eyes from exhaustion while packing up my stuff, so I didn't know what he meant, and at that point, I didn't really care.

"Yeah . . . I know." I wanted him to leave me alone so I could go home.

"Hey, where are you heading?" he asked.

"Out . . . was heading home. . . . My boyfriend and I . . ." He perked up, cutting me off mid-sentence.

"How about you come out and join us?"

"Us?" I asked.

"Yeah, Tom and Larry and the team head out for drinks every night around 10:30. We talk about the cases, firm gossip . . . It'll be good for you to get to know the partners. That's how you get noticed as an associate." He was now practically giddy at the idea.

"Well, thanks, I would love to, but I have plans tonight, and if I don't get a decent number of hours of sleep, I'll be useless tomorrow."

I suddenly felt the mood in the room shift. Silence. I looked up at John.

"Elena," he said seriously.

"Yes?" I was now thoroughly confused.

He swung his feet off the table and leaned forward with an avuncular look on his face. "Listen," he said earnestly, "I wish someone had told me this when I was a young associate. The sooner you know how law firm life works, the better it will be for your future in making partner one day. . . ."

He had my attention. He was telling me the secret to winning the next round of prizes on the achievement merry-go-round I had just boarded.

"I'm listening."

"Elena, you seem like a tough chick, so I don't need to mince words. The bottom line is, if you can't shoot the whiskey with the boys, you will never make it as a good litigator. Understand?" He was quietly pleased with himself. This was his idea of attorney mentoring. And in his mind, he was doing me a solid. I just stood there quietly stunned, and I have no doubt that, in that moment, he interpreted my silence as gratitude.

I had gone to a university where drinking was a vital part of the culture. But I didn't expect that learning to drink regularly with my teammates would also be crucial to my success as a big-firm lawyer. This was the first warning sign that I had worked my ass off to land somewhere culturally misaligned with how I wanted to live my life. I went out with them that one night but quickly realized that my episodic drinking would not be enough. These guys drank. A lot. Almost every night. For a long time. And then woke up and went to work. Even at a younger age, I knew high-functioning alcoholism when I saw it.

Even after I changed firms, drinking was a big part of the culture and pivotal to bonding with team members and partners who could ultimately control your future at the firm.

Flash forward twenty years later. As CMO of a large, well-known law firm, I could easily see that the culture had not changed much. Every event was driven by alcohol, and some partners still showcased their "bar" of top-shelf bourbons in their offices. One firm had weekly cocktail hours that rivaled the top-shelf bars at some of the best restaurants in NYC. And at another firm, particular floors were known for their informal Friday bourbon tastings; being invited to that event meant you were well-regarded by the partners.

Booze. Cocktails. Wine tastings. Beer flights. Whiskey tastings. The list of corporate, banking, or law-firm-sponsored events that were and still are centered on alcohol is staggering.

But I don't care what you call it or how you spin it or sanitize it—alcohol, and the ability to consume and tolerate lots of it, is intricately woven into what I call "make it big" Achievement Addiction culture.

It is encouraged and endorsed at every stage.

In our Western culture of growing interpersonal and social isolation, alcohol remains the ubiquitous and socially accepted currency for access to the best opportunities, off-hours training, client development, and success. My Achievement-Addicted clients all understood that they needed to learn to shoot the whiskey to get on the right deals, gain access to mentoring, and bond with the power brokers who controlled their destiny. Rainmaking high achievers regularly need to drink round after round with clients for business development. Young up-and-coming high achievers watch their bosses and mirror their values to fit in and be considered worthy of promotion. Achievement Addiction culture isn't subtle in its endorsement of alcohol abuse. The power brokers use it as just another performance benchmark of endurance, conformity, and strength. Alcohol tolerance becomes just another notch in the Achievement Addict's belt. And where there's smoke, there is fire.

In the prevailing corporate culture that continues to stigmatize mental illness, many clients I've worked with turned to alcohol as a way to self-medicate and cope with the soul-crushing stress and demands of modern working expectations. It is no wonder that at least 50 percent of the high-performing professionals who have come to me for coaching struggled with alcoholism and the evil brood of children that unfettered alcoholism bears. Likewise, many clients turned to alcohol to avoid the pain associated with the deterioration of their health and relationships and help them cope with work stress.

The bottom line is that alcoholism, like any other addiction, blunts self-awareness. And as you will read, the damaging impact of alcoholism is only redoubled among Achievement Addicts, who already have a preternatural aversion to self-awareness.

That's another reason why AWARENESS is the first of the 7 Steps.

Achievement Addiction, Awareness, and the False Self

At one point or another, many of my clients come to me and say that they feel numb or they don't know how they feel about anything anymore. Some describe a chronic feeling of being lost, disconnected from themselves, or disoriented in their lives. Others feel paralyzed by chronic "imposter syndrome"—a gnawing inner belief that has them convinced that they are phonies, living a con artist's existence on borrowed time.

Here's a simple explanation of the psychodynamics underlying these chronic feelings of disconnection and numbness: When we chronically bypass awareness, we increasingly run the risk of abandoning our true self while reinforcing what the shrinks call a *false self.*

Familiarity with how the false self manifests and its relationship to Achievement Addiction is key to understanding Step 1: Awareness.

Here's how the false self feeds Achievement Addiction:

- The false self allows you to portray someone other than your authentic true self.
- For Achievement Addicts, this false self always places achievement and a very narrow definition of "success" at the center of all other values and beliefs, at the expense of everything and everyone else.
- Over time, what starts out as a temporary personality construct ends up eclipsing the true self until the person no longer recognizes their life, interests, behaviors, values, or beliefs.
- Eventually, the person's connection to the true self becomes increasingly threadbare, and all they are left with is a highly choreographed false self-focused exclusively on achievement.
- Eventually, the false self becomes habitual but feels foreign and counterfeit.
- The end result is internal dissonance between the true self and the false self.

- Dissonance is a psychologically uncomfortable state that needs resolution.
- So the person resolves this dissonance (unconsciously) by distancing, objectifying, or dissociating completely from the true self.
- And by doing so, the person further identifies, strengthens, and solidifies the false self to the point of hollowness, numbness, and disorientation.
- The false self seeks out more achievement to escape the numbness, disorientation, and dissociation from the true self.

Needless to say, this cannot be good.

Not good for the individual and not good for their friends and family.

At this point, if you haven't already tossed the book across the room in annoyance, you might be thinking to yourself, *This all sounds like psychobabble to me. What's the real harm in all this? How I choose to live my life is my business, and whatever persona—true or false—that best serves me and furthers my achievements is what works for me.*

In principle, I would tend to agree. You are correct. Your posture or persona in the world is your choice and prerogative. How you show up—true or false—is entirely up to you. However, in my experience, the problem arises for individuals when they lose that power of choice. When we make a habit of sidestepping self-awareness, we impair our ability to discern our true self from our false self. Without discernment, we lose our ability to choose. That's when things start to get tricky for Achievement Addicts and where the trouble can begin.

For many of my Achievement-Addicted clients, decades upon decades of accommodating others' expectations and demands at the total expense and obliteration of their true selves created a challenging internal dissonance. That true self/false self dissonance was largely responsible for their professed numbness, disorientation, dissociation, and misery. How they chose to mollify that numbness and pain became the core problem. Achievement Addiction was one way. Alcoholism or other addictions were usually the most favored choice.

Why? Because the Achievement-Addicted person who has their false self running the show heartily welcomes a shot or two or three of vodka as a way to "feel something" in an otherwise numbed-out or disoriented existence. The tough question of "how the f$#k did I get here?" can be quickly muted and dissolved into the background for another day by a couple of well-chilled martinis. Or prescription drugs or illicit drugs.

But here's where things get even more thorny. Addictions of any kind demand a talent for compartmentalization. And as you might expect, compartmentalization comes easier to the individual who has been living with a false self for a long time. So it would make sense that a highly compartmentalized life would emerge as a natural extension for the person already disconnected from their true self.

What's the harm in one more lie or half-truth when you've allowed your false self, premised on false values and beliefs, to dominate and dictate your life for decades anyway?

A highly compartmentalized life driven by a false self can often create a dangerous breeding ground for harboring multiple secret addictions and sometimes even cultivating an entire second life. Many of my clients invested tremendous psychic energy into keeping these second and third lives (usually filled with addictions of every nature) sheltered from one another. Invariably, these individuals suffered devastating fallout once the truth came out.

Gustav was one of those cases.

Gustav and His Go-Go Girls

Gustav was a partner in New York who hailed (as his name might suggest) from Europe. He came to me for business development coaching to grow his book of business from $2 million to $5 million. Gustav had a very icy, impenetrable, transactional way about him.

He made it quite clear early on in our relationship that he was not interested in any personal inquiry of any sort.

"Create a business plan for me, and I will execute it. I need to double my book of business. I'll be damned if I end up at the whim of one or two clients or even one particular industry. . . ."

"Makes sense to me, but just for the record, I don't create the plan, Gustav. You do. I—"

He cut me off abruptly with an impatient wave of his hand as he adjusted his seat.

"Yes, yes, yes, whatever. Very well. I know you have to say things like that as a coach. I get it. Yes, sure, I will create a plan. You will review it, and you will make sure I do it, agreed?"

I felt overly managed and put in a box by this conversation, but I didn't make much of some of my clients' idiosyncrasies. Part of my job as a coach is to determine whether a client is coachable and decide whether I am the right coach for the client.

Gustav was bossy, imperious, and slightly full of himself. But he was coachable. So long as we established mutual respect, I believed that I was the right coach for him.

And yet . . . there was something about the sentence, "I know you have to say things like that as a coach," that stuck with me, and I filed it away. It was a giveaway of sorts. Gustav assumed that I was playing a role—perhaps even a disingenuous role—that required me to say things I didn't mean. To me, that suggested that Gustav, too, was accustomed to "playing a role," and he assumed the rest of the world also interacted that way.

I tucked that sidebar into my notes, saying, "Sounds good to me."

Together we started outlining goals, identifying market opportunities, making a list of existing clients that needed more attention, and drilling down into what action items needed to happen over the next ninety days, sixty days, and thirty days. We were on our way, and in the first month, Gustav proved at first to be an "ideal coaching client." He would complete all assignments and connect with me between sessions about progress or roadblocks. And while the relationship seemed very transactional to me, Gustav was making progress, and it felt like we were forging a productive coaching alliance.

But that dynamic quickly shifted after the first month.

First, Gustav started showing up late to our sessions. Then, over time, sessions frequently got postponed or canceled. And when he did show up, he wasn't prepared with completed action items and was growing increasingly distracted and impatient with the coaching process.

Gustav was used to immediate gratification, and coaching is a process that takes time, commitment, and accountability. I would only learn the extent of Gustav's need for immediate gratification later on in our coaching relationship.

Gustav had rescheduled with me two weeks in a row and then was a no-show.

He was on his last leg with me when he called me one day, very intoxicated. I couldn't tell right away if it was drugs, alcohol, or both, but the slurring was tough to ignore, and he seemed out of it (to put it nicely).

"I don't think this coaching thing is working. . . . I mean, I'm not a child. I mean, I don't take orders from anyone; I'm a partner and a super-successful one at that. This whole bullshit coaching thing doesn't seem to be working; you know what I mean? Fuck it. Why should I be taking advice from you, anyway? You weren't even good enough to make partner, so what do you know? Wow . . . I'm sorry, I don't mean to offend you. Goddamn it, I'm such a fuckup! I'm sorry, truly, I really, I mean, I didn't mean . . ."

I was sidestepping the insults being hurled at me and was more focused on Gustav's speech.

"You're slurring your words, Gustav."

Silence.

"I'm so sorry, Elena. . . . I just . . ."

"Gustav, are you okay? Where are you?" I asked calmly.

After a pause that felt like forever, he finally fessed up.

"The strip club," he said flatly. "I'm at a strip club. A fucking strip club. Again . . ."

It was just after the lunch hour, and I know that daytime strip clubs aren't exactly an elegant experience. I became tenacious to the point of annoying and managed to convince Gustav to come straight to my office.

Nearly an hour later, he stumbled into my office, his bespoke suit disheveled, smelling like cigarettes, mouthwash, and yesterday's dive bar.

He sat with his head in his hands and wouldn't make eye contact with me. Without looking up, he started to explain what was happening.

"This is what I do. I thought I could stop. I did stop for a while, for about six months. That's when I thought I would come to you for help. But then . . . then it just all falls apart again."

Gustav visibly unraveled right there in my office, and over the course of the next hour, he shared with me that he was addicted to going to strip clubs. He would go for large chunks of the day, nearly every day of the workweek.

He had racked up a significant amount of debt and was abusing alcohol and cocaine, and his family was none the wiser. This big-shot, multimillion-dollar ogre of a partner had truly mastered the art of the double life.

And it was on the verge of ruining him.

Gustav needed help in getting his addictions under control before we could focus on his grandiose goal of doubling his book of business. So I worked with him to find a therapist who could help with his addictions, and I suggested that Debtors Anonymous might be a helpful framework for him to look at his addiction to strippers and debt.

Because Gustav didn't trust many people, he wanted to continue working with me as a career/life coach at the same time. He wanted to understand "how the f$#k [his] life and work got so out of control." We agreed that he needed to retrace his career steps to figure out what actions he needed to take to move forward. This wasn't psychotherapy; this was a stealthy, surgical, and strategic inquiry into Gustav's past career choices designed to give him the insight needed to take action and correct his course.

One afternoon after discussing how he had decided to go to law school and his path to partnership, I asked bluntly, "What do you think went wrong? Can you think of a day or event or conversation that might have triggered this whole detour?"

Gustav looked at me coldly and said, "No. It wasn't one thing or even one event. This shit show has been a long time coming."

I said nothing.

"Truth is, I was never supposed to be a lawyer."

Silence.

Gustav then started to tell me about his life before law school.

"I come from a very long and distinguished lineage of classically trained violinists. Some famous, some not, but all brilliantly accomplished violinists. I was also classically trained and on my way to following in the family's footsteps . . . but I copped out. My family was accomplished, but there were always money struggles. Coming from a family of artists can be glamorous, but it doesn't always pay the bills or the mortgage or tuition."

I wanted to tell Gustav that I was very familiar with artists and their financial struggles, but I kept quiet.

"My father was a famous concert violinist, and my mother was a prominent music teacher, but despite the appearances, we always struggled financially. And no one could know about it. It was a dark secret. My family had multiple mortgages on our ancestral home and on our priceless heirloom violins in order to keep up appearances and make sure I went to the right schools, etc. So I got sick of it . . . sick of the lies, and sick of the struggle.

"My best friend's father was a wealthy lawyer, and one day I asked him about what it meant to be a lawyer. All I cared about was that it promised me a way out of financial struggle and the shame of being so culturally sophisticated yet financially deprived. So . . ."

Gustav finally exhaled.

"So?"

"So? So you know the drill. . . . I sold out. I left the conservatory, to my parents' great outrage. We didn't speak for almost six years. But once I started making money as a partner, they conveniently overlooked their disappointment in me, and we reconciled. And I helped them with some bills. Then some more. And so . . ."

"What about the violin?"

"What about it?"

"Do you still play, or . . . ?"

He looked at me oddly and then started laughing.

"When exactly? Between flying from deposition to deposition? Between endless conference calls with clients and GCs? I don't have the time . . ."

I cut him off fast.

"But you made time for strip clubs?"

He looked at me sidelong.

"What's your point, Elena?" he asked, slightly peeved.

"I don't know exactly. But do I have your permission to talk bluntly with you?"

"Do you do anything else?" he winked.

"Okay, I'll take that as a yes, and I might make a mess of what I'm about to say, and if I upset you or offend you, I will clean it up later. It seems to me that you left a huge part of your identity and passion locked up somewhere in a black, beat-up violin case in some music school or conservatory in Europe."

"Go on." I had his attention.

"And I don't think it is a coincidence that you were searching for something visually or musically stimulating to fill the gap years later," I added.

"Elena, have you ever been in a strip club?" he chuckled. "It's not exactly Lincoln Center."

"Yes, yes, I have, and I know that, but follow me here for a minute. Is it possible that you're too proud to admit that you miss your days playing the violin? Let me put it another way. What do you feel when you think about picking up the violin?"

Gustav was silent for a long time. He then took out his perfectly ironed handkerchief from his pocket and wiped his brow. It took him a long time to look directly at me, and when he did, his eyes were very emotional.

"The violin was my universe. I was a hotheaded, proud, impatient, impulsive kid, and I wanted to solve my problems and my family's problems. I haven't played violin in over ten years, not since making partner."

"And yet your first sentence to me was 'I was never supposed to be a lawyer.' What were you supposed to be?"

"A concert violinist, of course." He smiled.

"Of course." I smiled back.

Gustav and I continued to work together on finding a way to reintroduce his passion and love of the violin back into his life. Slowly, with the help of a therapist, I worked with Gustav to address what he felt was missing in his life and why he felt the need to fill those voids by spending his days in a dank strip club. Gustav didn't leave the law or leave the firm to go back to Europe to pursue the violin, but he did make playing music a priority in his life. He also started investing in music-related charitable causes that were important to him.

Gustav had left a huge part of himself back in Europe. That void needed to be filled. Reconnecting with his lifelong passion and talent for music filled his soul in a way that practicing law did not.

Gustav wasn't evil, crazy, or depraved. He was lost, disconnected, unaware, and living a hollow life dominated by a false self.

Gustav taught me that finding a way to connect with your true self through purposeful awareness building is not an indulgent luxury. It is an imperative for thriving beyond Achievement Addiction.

Achievement Addiction

➢ propelled Gustav into a highly destructive Achievement Trance that had him obsessively chasing achievement after achievement at the expense of his sanity, health, and family;

➢ allowed Gustav's false self to dominate and eclipse everything else that mattered to him leaving him feeling numb, purposeless, and disconnected from his true self;

➢ made him so miserable that he turned to other addictive substances and behaviors as a way to cope.

Achievement Addiction DETOX helped Gustav

➢ recover from the multiple addictions that were destroying his life;

➢ reconnect with his true self and his love of music;

➢ recognize that he could define success on his own terms.

My False Self/True Self Story

The corrosive power of living with a false self that is misaligned with your values, passion, and beliefs is potent and bigger than any person's intellectual determination to suppress, it. A false self will not hold forever without fallout.

I should know. My false self had been running the show for nearly ten years before I realized what needed to change.

Here is my personal story about Awareness.

I wanted to be a doctor. And a poet. A brain surgeon by day and a published poet laureate by night. I told that to anyone who would listen by the time I was six years old. William Carlos Williams was my heartthrob hero crush, *Jane Eyre* my personal bible, and the Beatles my religion. For my twelfth birthday, I asked for a copy of the book *Gray's Anatomy*. And the *White Album*. I lived for the sand, sun, and sea and spent nearly every summer in a tiny fishing village in Sicily in a one-room apartment that was our family's ancestral home. I was pre-med in high school and spent the summer between my junior and senior year of high school studying virology at the Weitzman Institute of Science in Israel. I was the editor of our high school's literary magazine and had the proud, early distinction of having my poems censored for sexual lewdness. In celebration of that day, I got my hair buzzed off at Astor Place in New York and promptly added Grace Jones to my altar of idol worship. By the age of eighteen, I was on a four-year disciplined streak of writing "one poem per day no matter what," and I had been accepted into a six-year pre-med program straight out of high school. I was one intense and driven girl.

So, what happened? How did I wind up becoming a lawyer and then an executive life coach?

People ask me that all the time.

And the best answer I have been able to cobble together after all these years is that coaching others to transform their lives and manifest their passions, dreams, and values is my professional and spiritual calling. A calling that found me at my lowest point in life after a series of unexpected and unwelcome events in my health and career forced me to reevaluate my life's path. A calling that has gone on to heal me as much as it has helped others.

But clarity about my life's purpose did not come to me in one revelation. Instead, the road has been long, convoluted, and muddy. And the journey, like its traveler, has been *complicated*.

But here is the uncomplicated version of my story.

I never made it to med school. And I never became a published poet. Somehow, along the way, I ended up in law school. When I got my first C in college chemistry, my lifelong plans for medical school were suddenly dashed. All-or-nothing thinking dominated my view, and a C meant lifelong failure as a doctor. I was in crisis. I needed a backup plan, and I needed one fast. My boyfriend came from a long line of attorneys and judges and was hell-bent on becoming an attorney. So, without much self-reflection, I pivoted.

Even though I didn't know any lawyers and had no idea what lawyers did, becoming an attorney suddenly made complete sense.

Why? Because I am a first-generation Italian-American woman whose family struggled financially. Because I was the first person in my extended Italian family to go to college and a big-deal Ivy League college at that. There was no financial support system for me to dawdle or experiment with various careers. My father had been a struggling NYC artist for most of my childhood, and I experienced the financial hardships that came along with following your passion and creativity. And even though writing was my lifelong passion, I decided I wanted no more part of it. It was too risky.

In my mind, I needed to make money, lots of it, pay off my student loans, and embark on a career train that would take me fast and far away from financial struggles. I was told that all lawyers made boatloads of money. So, for that scared, achievement-driven eighteen-year-old, becoming a lawyer made total sense. By the time I was a sophomore in college, without forethought or regret, I had neatly extinguished my lifelong dream of becoming a doctor and writer. Looking back now, I am horrified to admit that I gave up my deepest longings and professional dreams with a level of detachment akin to mindless fly-swatting on a hot August afternoon.

There was no way I could have foreseen that my breezy decision to go to law school would end up taking me down an ever-darkening path that carried me further and further away from my true self and my calling. Ultimately, that eighteen-year-old's panicked decision would later send me into the first of several full-blown depressive episodes.

Fast-forward seven years.

I hated practicing law. Even though I was a relatively talented lawyer, I spent my nights and days fighting with people. I was exhausted and drained. I felt that my work had no meaning and no relation to my strengths, talents, and abilities. I was lost, in debt up to my eyeballs, stuck.

Then I got pregnant. It was the perfect storm. I was a new mother, I was suffering from undiagnosed postpartum depression, my newborn was born prematurely, he suffered from colic, and when he wasn't howling around the clock, I was crying every day as I boarded the subway to work. At the age of twenty-seven—only nine years after that fateful, impulsive decision—I hated my work, my career choice, and myself. In my mind, I was a total failure. My false self had taken the reins and elbowed out any trace of my true self, and I was paying the price. I was in the depths of a full depressive episode, and I couldn't see a way out.

So, in the haze of my depression, I made the only decision I thought I could. With no other career plan or job prospect in place, I just quit and left law practice. After speeding at 120 miles an hour through every aspect of my education and career for nearly the whole of my twenty-seven years, I crashed headlong into a brick wall at full speed.

I needed guidance. I needed help. I needed someone to listen and help me figure out my next step. And the only resource for that in the marketplace was the headhunting industry. Or a shrink. My one short experience with a college psychology intern at the Student Health Center had me scared of shrinks and the stigma I associated with needing them. (Never could I have predicted that I would go on to become a psychotherapist only seven years later!)

But at that moment in time, I skillfully dodged therapy, along with the whole self-help trend.

That touchy-feely stuff was for weak-minded, self-indulgent losers, I told myself. I was a leathery, award-winning high achiever. In my mind, what I needed was a new path, a new direction, and maybe a new career where I could put my high-achievement muscles to work before they atrophied.

So, I shimmied my post-baby body into an ill-fitting suit, marched my sleep-deprived, self-loathing personhood to the first legal headhunting company I could find, collapsed in their chair, and bawled my eyes out for about an hour. I didn't realize that I was, in fact, their worst nightmare client because I wasn't sellable. And little could I have known then that most headhunters were infamous for having all the human empathy of a black-hooded executioner.

But I was lucky that day, and the account exec listened patiently. And she listened some more. Despite herself (and bless her!), she helped me clear my thoughts. She helped me identify what I needed as a new mom with a career. She helped me understand that my legal practicing options were limited, despite my platinum credentials. After about an hour, she then went in for the kill: "Elena, have you ever thought of maybe becoming a legal recruiter? You could use your legal knowledge and contribute to the business of law and law firms. We have hours from 9:30 to 5. You can work a little from home. You can use your legal education, network, and knowledge of the law firms to make a lot of money without a lot of long hours."

Then she said the magic words that spoke to my dormant true self: "*You would be helping other attorneys like you who are lost and struggling in their careers to find clarity and direction and meaning.*"

That was it. The next month I started with a headhunting company in NYC.

And, at my husband's insistence, I started seeing a therapist.

Flash forward another five years.

I was now a managing director at a major headhunting company; my children were five and two years of age, I was very successful, and I was on my way to making partner at the company. But once again, something was off. Something about the recruiting business and my role in it just didn't sit right with me. Somehow along the way, my true self had been elbowed out again. My Achievement Addiction had me focusing on the money, the success, and the promotion at the expense of my true values and purpose.

Once again, I felt like a complete loser. I was lost and numb. I was disconnected from anything that gave me meaning, joy, or purpose. My outside didn't match my inside. I was successful on the outside but hollow on the inside. And once again, the depression started creeping up behind me. So, again, I felt a deep need to correct my course once more.

That's when I quit and gave up a chance at partnership with the recruitment firm. (You can imagine what my family had to say about it.)

Now everyone *knew* I was nuts. I had just bought a dream house in a super-ritzy NYC suburb that was under renovation, and I was on a clear path to making partner at a very successful firm, and, oh! right, we had also just bought a beach house.

Here I was again, at age thirty-two, about to achieve the ultimate American dream after years of hard work, and I was derailing myself. My inner thoughts plagued me:

What is wrong with me? How many more times am I going to self-sabotage all my hard-earned success and achievement? Why am I never happy with anything I've achieved when everyone else is applauding? Why do I keep chasing achievements that only end up making me feel empty, depressed, and crazy? And why do I keep making career and life decisions that look and feel "right" on the outside but feel so wrong and disconnected on the inside? How much longer will my family and friends put up with this madness? Is it possible that I'm one of those people who can never be satisfied or happy? And if so, should I just settle for a career, job, or life that looks great on the outside but is soul-crushing on the inside?

The self-abuse that came along with my depression was merciless. But on this go-round, I was fortunate to have been working with a great therapist. With his help, I developed some deep and much-needed self-awareness. In my work with him, I realized that there lived in me an inextinguishable, fundamental desire to help and heal people. And that the very same desire that had fueled my dream of becoming a doctor at age eighteen was still quietly smoldering in me at age thirty-three. I realized that I could not keep that part of myself buried any longer. It was time for me to take bellows to those embers. Going back to medical school was logistically out of the question. Instead, armed with more awareness about my true self, I became a psychoanalytic psychotherapist while also getting trained as an executive career coach. Within the same year, I enrolled in the NYU School of Social Work, completed a career coaching training program, and launched my coaching business, LawScope Coaching. Helping people transform their psyches, lives, and careers brings deep, meaningful holistic healing. It was finally clear to me that life and career coaching was my truest professional and spiritual calling.

So, as you can see, the road to reconnecting with my true self and becoming a coach was messy. My path was fraught with wrong turns, dead ends, disappointments, and frustrations. But my path was equally propelled forward by an intense awareness that developed over time about what felt true, inspired, and meaningful. My drive to design a life and career aligned with my true self has sometimes felt like a mixed blessing, but ultimately, pursuing my life's work has allowed me to thrive professionally, personally, and spiritually. I would do it all over again.

Awareness—the first of the 7 Steps for breaking through Achievement Addiction—is fundamental. It allowed me and my clients to reconnect with our true selves to make better choices that are in keeping with our values and beliefs.

STEP 1: AWARENESS
The IMAGO Coaching Questions

Now it's time for you to work on this first step, AWARENESS, using some powerful and exploratory questions (IMAGO Coaching Questions) derived from my IMAGO Coaching Method. Each question below is designed to help you work the first step and deepen your awareness of how Achievement Addiction shows up in your life.

Following each question, I offer you a way to summarize your insights in the form of a declaratory sentence. These summarized insights will be essential to refer to should you choose to download and complete the Achievement Addiction DETOX Worksheets accessible at www.achievementaddictiondetox.com.

To recap, the IMAGO Coaching Method invites you to INQUIRE, MAGNIFY, ACT, GROW, and OWN.

The questions below can help you work this first step.

INQUIRE

What challenges, if any, are you facing currently in your work? What problems can you trace back to Achievement Addiction?

The present-day problems, issues, or challenges that I can trace back to my
Achievement Addiction are . . .

_____

_____

_____

_____

_____

MAGNIFY

Review your list. Which challenge stands out for you and warrants your
immediate attention and magnification?

_____

_____

_____

_____

The biggest challenge or problem Achievement Addiction has caused in
my life is . . .

_____

_____

Because of my Achievement Addiction, I suffer in the following way:

_____

_____

_____

_____

. . . and the people around me suffer in the following way:

_____

_____

_____

_____

Act

Think about the one big challenge you identified in your life right now that warrants your immediate attention. If there were no obstacles in your way and you knew you couldn't fail, what actions would you be willing to take right now to improve that situation?

I want to take the following action steps toward improving my present challenge with _____:

_____

_____

_____

_____

_____

Grow

Let's turn to the idea of a false self.

Does the idea of having a false self and a true self resonate with you? In what ways are the values and characteristics of your false self dissonant or out of sync with those of your true self?

_____

_____

_____

_____

_____

I want to grow and improve my connection with my true self because it would mean that . . .

_____

_____

_____

Own

Hopefully, answering these questions has increased your awareness about your relationship with achievement and has opened your eyes to the price you have been paying because of your Achievement Addiction. So, let's turn to owning that newfound AWARENESS.

When it comes to my level of awareness about my Achievement Addiction, I acknowledge and own that . . .

_____

_____

_____

_____

_____

. . . and that if I could take the steps to change and improve my level of awareness of my Achievement Addiction, it would mean . . .

_____

_____

_____

_____

_____

FINAL THOUGHTS:
Awareness and Achievement Addiction

✓ Focusing on Awareness (Step 1) can be a decisive first step toward overcoming Achievement Addiction and is a gentle invitation to investigate, inquire about, and invest in yourself.

✓ As Achievement Addicts, we are others-oriented and preoccupied with external approval, respect, and acceptance.

✓ Developing awareness requires that we intentionally and actively become curious about our individual circumstances, feelings, thoughts, habits, motivations, preferences, choices, and actions so that we can shift our focus away from others and back onto our own lives.

MINDSET
Make a Shift

Thoughts Create Matter, So Our Thought Life Matters

Most clients who come to me for executive coaching express a baseline sense of malaise. They are not alcoholics or addicts. They are not medically depressed or anxious. In fact, on the outside, their lives look pretty perfect. They are just chronically unhappy and stuck.

Many of these clients start solving the problem by changing their external environment or circumstances. Many change jobs, change practice areas, change states, change spouses, and so on, yet they find that the malaise resurfaces within several months.

Others look for relief in another form. They don't necessarily make external changes but instead turn to material objects for solace and comfort. They turn to the power of "moreness"—more achievement, more business, more skills, more networks, more money, more degrees, and more prestige. They're convinced that unlimited acquisitions will make them happy.

And, oddly enough, many of my clients seek out my coaching right after buying a new home or a new car or returning from an exotic vacation. Many say they are left with an even more acute sense of disappointment, particularly after the surface changes don't live up to their expectations. For many of us, including me, the afterglow of acquiring the most recent shiny toy is short-lived and leaves us feeling unhappier than before.

A lot of research has focused on the relationship between material excess and a sense of happiness. The research shows that while material well-being definitely can increase emotional well-being, there is a leveling off, and the law of diminishing returns starts to kick in. So, over time, the joy factor of material excess flattens out, and we find ourselves back where we started.

I have learned firsthand and from my clients that while making external changes and acquiring more can offer a temporary panacea to the laundry list of situational complaints, there is a more profound, more elusive force at work that contributes to our misery.

The one thing that has not changed for many of us is our mindset. Throughout this book, I use the term *mindset* to describe the *habitual set of cognitive thoughts and patterns of thought that characterize a person's worldview and response to internal and external stimuli.*

Mindset is personal. It is your private collection of thoughts that make up the baseline of how you view the world. Mindset informs and shapes your perspective, attitude, emotions, and actions. I like to think of our mindset as our mental set point—that loop of thoughts we habitually turn to again and again because of familiarity. Just like a home's thermostat, your mindset is your mental comfort zone, regardless of whether that zone makes you miserable. Our self-talk feeds our mindset. So, to change our mindset, we first need to change our self-talk.

Achievement Addiction: A Distorted Mindset

It has been proven time and time again that our mindset—or our habitual way of thinking—affects our emotions for both good and bad.

Along with many of the clients I have worked with, I am relentlessly plagued by chronic, habitual, nasty, defeatist, abusive self-talk. As a result, we habitually embrace a mindset that is disproportionately negative and devaluing.

These types of chronic, unreasonably negative thoughts are called *distortions.*

So here are some of the top **thought distortions** typical of Achievement Addicts.

- Flaw fixation
- Dismissing the positive
- Assuming
- Labeling
- Overgeneralizing
- All-or-nothing thinking
- Unfavorable comparison
- Catastrophizing
- Emotional logic
- "Should" statements
- Personalizing
- Blaming

On any given day, my mindset can be a constellation of several of these distortions. But, ultimately, it is nearly always my distorted mindset coupled with my negative self-talk that causes me to feel miserable, "less than," and defeated.

Mental distortions and negative self-talk impact our emotions and behaviors in the following way:

- Chronic and unchecked negative self-talk (thought distortions) generates our habitual thought-life designs and casts the mold for our mindset.
- Our mindset, in large part, modulates our emotions and feelings in response to external and internal stimuli.
- And our feelings and emotions often influence, if not control, our ultimate affect, actions, and behaviors.

Bottom line: What I describe here is a simplification of a very complicated neurological and biochemical process. In essence, though, if you want to make any meaningful change in your habits or behavior and if you're going to improve the quality of your emotional life, you need to work on your negative self-talk, thought distortions, and overall mindset.

But the reality is that many of us have learned or inherited our distorted thoughts, negative self-talk, and mindset through our families, education, social systems, culture, and religion.

In his book *Negative Self-Talk and How to Change It,* Shad Helmstetter sets forth some basic principles about negative self-talk that have helped me and have informed much of the mindset work I do with clients.

Here are the six basic principles of negative self-talk:

1. Everyone has been "hardwired" from inception on, and whether we like it or not, we all end up living out (consciously or unconsciously) the hardwired programming we received.
2. Everything we believe, think, say, and do results from the programming that we received both from others and from ourselves over time.
3. Our self-talk is the automatic replay loop of the dominant programs we have that are the strongest.
4. Negative self-talk is the combined result of the unconscious negative programming we received from others and ourselves.
5. We can undo negative unconscious programming because of the brain's neuroplasticity, which is designed to allow for rewiring and reprogramming continually throughout our lifetime.
6. Negative self-talk can be changed; it can be rewired and replaced with different, more positive, and more empowering programming.

In short, a distorted mindset can be altered by intentionally correcting the negative self-talk that strengthens the mindset.

The good news is that you can control and change the thoughts that feed your mindset. Your brain can be rewired so that different thoughts can replace less useful ones and become strengthened over time. Change your thoughts, change your mindset. And the method is simple in design, although less simple to implement. Catching our distorted mindset, labeling it, identifying the negative self-talk that feeds or strengthens the mindset, and then intentionally replacing it with less-distorted self-talk is where the day-to-day work is for my clients and me.

I know, easier said than done. But taking micro-steps using this "catch and switch" process is the key to changing your negative self-talk. And the cumulative impact of this process can go a long way. Just as it did for Luisa. . . .

Just-Fine-Thanks Luisa

Luisa was always "just fine, thanks." She was an immigrant who had come to the United States from Nicaragua when she was four years old. She was an IvyLeague–educated lawyer who worked for one of the most prestigious firms in the US. She was beautiful and graceful and fluent in several languages, along with her native Spanish. She spoke the Queen's English and was impeccably dressed when she arrived at my doorstep.

But Luisa was miserable. She didn't know why. She had been to a therapist who, as she put it, "wanted to vivisect my psyche without anesthesia. Huh! No, thank you!" She wasn't depressed. She just wasn't happy. The only word she used was "melancholy," a deep, unsettling malaise about her work and life. She said she had friends, a fiancé, a great apartment, a great job. So, what was the problem?

She came to me to help her put together a business development plan for her partnership dossier, but in our first meeting, she also wanted some insight into why her life "was feeling gray and bleak." Luisa was on the brink of making partner at a prominent law firm, and she felt nothing.

Luisa wanted to work on her partnership plan but also wanted to spend time figuring out how to improve her attitude about her life in general. She didn't want to leave the law; it was "fine." She didn't want to leave her apartment; it was "fine." She didn't want to leave her fiancé; he was "fine."

In the shrink biz, I was taught that "if it ain't on the outside, it must be on the inside."

With her permission, our coaching focused on both business development and life coaching. Together we started to look at the impact her mindset was having both on her business development efforts and her view on life. We needed to understand her thought-life "set point" before we could make any course corrections.

Once we started to look at the quality of her thought life and how her mind was filtering and reframing events in her work and life, it was becoming evident to me what wasn't fine.

Luisa had a very well-developed and entrenched *pessimism filter*. Better put, Luisa lived in fear. Of everything. She was fearful of losing everything. All of it: her job, her looks, her life, her health, her fiancé, her license, her car, her apartment. At any given instant, Luisa's thought life was a terrorizing amalgam of distortions that included flaw fixation, ignoring the positive, all-or-nothing thinking, and catastrophizing. The end result was that Luisa's set-in-stone mindset was: nothing was good, nothing is good, and nothing could ever be good.

Every beautiful achievement in her life automatically went through the "Luisa pessimism filter," which turned anything and everything good, joyous, and celebratory into another item that she risked losing.

This endless loop of torturous thoughts stole her joy and left her world colorless.

- When she was assigned a new high-profile case, she said, "Yeah, that's great; let's hope I don't screw it up."
- When she was given a beautiful ring for her birthday, she said, "Yeah, it's beautiful; let's hope it doesn't slip off my finger and I don't lose it."
- When she was told she was on track to make partner, she said, "Yeah, that's good news; let's hope I don't miss the billable hour requirement this year."
- When she was on her way to Europe for a well-deserved vacation, she said, "Yeah, I guess it will be fun; let's hope I don't drink the water and get sick the whole time."

No matter what happened in her life, Luisa's pleasure and joy were immediately put in check by her distorted mindset and the avalanche of negative self-talk that smothered her happiness before it could even begin to surface.

But something about this joylessness gnawed at Luisa's psyche. She wanted more. A healthier part of her knew that she should feel, enjoy, and be happy. It just seemed out of reach. And what was keeping it out of reach was her automatic pessimism and fear. Her fear of loss prevented her from fully enjoying and embracing the abundance in her life.

Luisa's family history and culture had contributed to this fear-fueled pessimism.

Her family had been landowners and manufacturers in Nicaragua, and over a period of several months, they had lost everything and arrived on US shores with next to nothing. Over time, her family rebuilt its wealth and business in America, but as a very young girl, Luisa learned two things: you can lose everything in a moment, and don't draw attention to your happiness because someone will always want to take it away. She had inherited a mindset premised on fear and loss, and she saw everything in her life through those two darkened lenses.

Many cultures have that formulation: the evil eye, *k'en ahora, malocchio*—the idea that you should not celebrate too much or too loudly because it will draw the attention of the "devil," and jealous people will try to take it away from you.

But Luisa had taken this cultural superstition, incorporated it as her core mindset, and built a wall around herself so that she couldn't feel joy or happiness. And this mindset also prevented her from gathering up enough optimism to take action steps on her business development plans.

Luisa and I worked together on identifying the critical belief system that was creating her mindset. At the heart of her pessimism was the singular, fear-fueled belief that "everything that gives me joy and pleasure and happiness will be ripped away from me."

Together we focused on working with Luisa's strengths. She was a litigator, and a good one at that. So she understood and also believed in the persuasive power of strong evidence. So she and I teamed up and went to trial against her negative mindset and belief system. And we collected evidence that pointed to the staying power of her success and resilience.

She was eventually able to reframe her family's history and focus on how she and her family had been able to persevere and thrive, even after their tremendous losses.

Together, using her words and culture, we were able to develop for her a more positive mindset fueled by positive, faith-based thoughts and self-talk.

- "Yeah, it's great legal work; let's hope I don't screw it up" turned into *"I have faith I can do this because I've done it before."*
- "Yeah, it's beautiful; let's hope I don't lose it" turned into *"Yeah, it's beautiful; I know I'll enjoy it for many years to come."*

We worked to identify all the things she was grateful for that had not been ripped away. Then we made a list of the things in her life that had real "stickiness."

The list was long.

One day, Luisa came into my office beaming. It was as if she'd been carried to my office on a ray of sunshine. I was justifiably concerned.

"Wow!" she started when she threw herself into the chair. "Wow, wow, wow," she repeated, shaking her head from side to side with enthusiasm.

When she looked up, I discreetly tried to monitor her pupils' size to determine whether her contagious joy was natural or substance-induced.

"You seem really energetic, Luisa. What's going on?"

"Things are really good. I mean, really exciting. I handed in a brief to a very demanding client yesterday, which would usually cause me to lose a night's sleep. I'd be up worrying about a comma or sentence or whether I submitted the right appendix with the right supporting documentation. I would normally be a wreck, expecting that I had screwed up or missed something. But last night I slept! Like, I went to bed at ten and woke up at seven and slept the whole night."

"That's terrific to hear," I said. "You actually look different, too; your whole energy level is higher."

"I know! I can't tell you how different it feels to . . . I don't know . . . to be able to finish a project and feel okay, almost good about it, and just feel . . . I don't know . . . safe, I guess."

"Safe. That's a great word to hear from you."

"I know. . . I never feel safe. Or safety. I'm always waiting for the next shoe to drop. But something shifted last night."

"What changed?"

"I caught myself. I caught myself mid-sentence as 'Scary Sister Miranda' entered the room in her habit, with her stick in her hand, and started with her litany of why I am not good enough," Luisa started laughing, "and I just smacked her . . . smacked her hard in my mind. That's when I heard myself say to her and myself, 'I am safe to enjoy my life and my talents. I trust myself.'" Now Luisa began to tear up.

"Can you believe it?! I was actually able to finally say that I am safe and that I trust myself. I never feel safe, and no matter what the achievement,

I always feel shaky and unsure and doubt my talent and ability. But not yesterday! Nope. Scary Sister Miranda took it right on the chin, and that's when, I don't know . . . I was able to think about something other than her mantra of negativity."

As you've guessed, "Scary Sister Miranda" was the name Luisa had given to the nasty, unkind, and sabotaging Achievement Avatar that embodied all her negative self-talk and that stole her joy time and time again.

In my work with clients, I ask them to identify and describe their Achievement Avatar using the same Achievement Avatar exercise available for download at www.achievementaddictiondetox.com.

But let me offer a quick refresher: The Achievement Avatar is that inner critic and slave driver in your head that simultaneously forces you to work yourself to death to pursue endless achievements but will also turn on a dime to devalue those very same achievements to guarantee you never rest. Our Achievement Avatars usually embody all our thought distortions, fears, and doubts. For many of us, our Achievement Avatars intrude on and interrupt our more positive, hopeful, creative, optimistic, and joyful moments . . . and beat us down . . . and send us back to chase the next achievement.

By identifying their Achievement Avatar, giving it a name, a face, a body, a caricature, a voice, a script, or a storyline, my clients learn how to spot the negative self-talk when it arises, challenge it, and reject it. Suddenly they realize that they do not need to listen to, believe, or act on all the stories and thoughts being fed to them by their Achievement Avatars. Suddenly, they have a choice.

Luisa's ability to identify Scary Sister Miranda and her negative thoughts and distorted mindset freed her up to reject the negative noise and those mental distortions that were robbing her of joy.

That afternoon, Luisa slapped down Scary Sister Miranda hard, and as a result, Luisa allowed her more positive self-talk and mindset to surface. She decided that one of her positive anchoring mantras was "I am safe to enjoy my life and its gifts, and I am grateful for my abundance." At our next session, she shared that she had bought herself a small pinky ring with the words "I am Safe. Trusting. Grateful." inscribed on the inside.

I am sure Luisa continues to have pessimistic moments and a negative mindset that intrudes on her thought life. But she did the work and had an amulet of optimism—an amulet to remind her that she could change her thoughts, her mindset, and her feelings of fear to feelings of enjoyment and gratitude. Her happiness was a choice and a deliberate practice, one that she felt more equipped to embark upon with the help of some mindset tools.

Achievement Addiction

➢ robbed Luisa of any sense of joy or pride in her accomplishments;

➢ caused Luisa to be riddled with merciless negative self-talk that undermined all sense of self-worth; and

➢ induced a form of Achievement Amnesia that essentially obliterated or devalued all of Luisa's prior achievements.

Achievement Addiction DETOX helped Luisa

➢ overcome her Achievement-Addicted mindset and negative self-talk;

➢ identify her Achievement Avatar along with the power it had over her overall mindset and sense of worth;

➢ develop new skills that allowed her to replace her chronic negative self-talk with more positive, self-affirming thoughts.

Resilience and Achievement Addiction

Part of the profile of an Achievement Addict is that we struggle when faced with setbacks, failure, and rejection. As a result, many of the Achievement Addict's choices and behaviors are driven by the single-minded need to create impenetrable safety and security. Achievement Addicts deliberately create a life and lifestyle designed to insulate themselves, at all costs, from the unknown and the unpredictable. Unfortunately, that level of over-insulation can seriously impair a person's resilience, leaving them dangerously vulnerable to the blows imparted by life's less-than-welcome events.

So, what is resilience? Simply put, resilience is bounce-back power. And it is a skill that can be learned. But, more importantly, it is a skill intimately tied to and dependent on a nimble, positive mindset.

Resilience has been defined as the collection of inner strengths of mind and character—both inborn and developed—that enables a person to respond well to adversity, including the capacity to

- mitigate or reduce symptoms related to stress-related conditions such as depression or anxiety or their recurrence;
- recover faster and more completely from stress and stress-inducing conditions; and
- optimize mental fitness and functioning in various areas of life.

So, what are the practical qualities of a resilient person?

You don't give up, you are scrappy, and you find a way back on your feet; you always have a plan and a backup plan; you don't allow yourself the luxury of wallowing, paralysis, or self-pity. And if you do, something deep inside you reminds you and says, "Wake up! You are talented, smart, hardworking, and creative, and you *will* find a way out of this mess!"

And, as the definition suggests, resilience is something we are all born with. However, some have strengthened it more than others.

Many elements contribute to a person's resilience, but one of the key elements is the ability to replace *thought distortions* with calmer thoughts that result in less emotional disturbance and overall better health and functioning.

But Achievement Addiction can sometimes result in compromising a person's resilience to adversity. Decades of uninterrupted achievement and success insulated many of my clients from dealing with the difficult emotions associated with rejection, disappointment, and failure. As a result, it can be said that the Achievement Addict's mindset—already prone to obsessive negative self-talk—is even more fragile and highly vulnerable to any type of disappointment or failure. Resilience in the face of failure is simply foreign territory for the Achievement Addict. As a result, during the economic downturns of 2008 and 2020, many of my clients were caught blindsided and emotionally unprepared to deal with their new and unwelcome reality.

Trevor was one of those clients.

Trevor and the Princeton Club

During the economic crisis of 2008, many top-tier law firms, investment banks, and corporations implemented massive layoffs of their employees almost overnight. And the law-firm landscape was a virtual bloodbath. No one was immune to this massacre—legal staff, associates, contract partners, and even once-profitable equity partners were all being escorted out of their Class A buildings within hours of receiving their dreaded "pink slips."

I met Trevor in the spring of 2009. Trevor was dressed in a very expensive, European-tailored soft gray suit and crisp white shirt, cufflinks, a gold Rolex, soft Italian leather loafers, a camel hair cashmere coat, an Hermès tie, and designer spectacles à la Philip Johnson. He looked more like one's idea of a European architect than an international corporate mergers and acquisitions attorney. Trevor had a very smooth forehead that alluded to monthly facials and manscaping, along with quarterly Botox injections.

He was the embodiment of metropolitan breeding and grooming.

Trevor shook my hand firmly, made soft and authentic eye contact with me, smiled, nodded, and, with a tasteful witticism, declined my offer of a beverage. He had been groomed in the finest boardrooms in the world, dined in only the chicest downtown restaurants, supported wildlife funds and self-taught arts, played golf well enough, was on his second marriage and second family, and spoke several languages fluently. He had spent his life cultivating and honing this aesthetic persona of achievement and success that stood before me.

His efforts to build this persona were as tireless as his insistence that no one ever pierce that well-armored persona.

Trevor sat down in my office and started asking all kinds of authentically curious questions about me, my training, my background, my last name, my heritage . . . anything and everything to prevent me from asking anything about him.

So, I went along. For a while. Then I just stopped answering his questions.

"Have I offended you with all my questions? Sorry about that, you don't have to answer them all. I'm just so curious about other people's lives and decisions. I didn't mean to overstep."

"Trevor, why are you here?"

He laughed uncomfortably, coughed, shifted a little in his seat, and then cleared his throat.

"They warned me that you don't tolerate bullshit." More laughter. "Well . . . I'm here to sort out my life, figure out my passions, next steps, what options I have, where to go next with my skills and abilities," he explained with all the breezy and remote intonation of a five-star restaurant sommelier pointing out the various notes in my breathing cabernet.

"Sort out your life? What needs sorting out?" I asked.

"Well, you know I'm a partner at *blah, blah* firm and have been there for ten years . . . youngest attorney ever to make partner, and focused on *blah, blah, blah, blah.*" Trevor went on verbalizing his professional résumé with that same patiently remote tone for quite a while. The details of his answer were less important than the fact that Trevor had just told me in no uncertain terms without saying it explicitly that being a partner was his "life."

"Sounds to me like your career and life don't need sorting out at all. In fact, it sounds like a success dream come true. So, I still don't hear what needs sorting out," I pressed.

Trevor looked at me with slightly troubled eyes. This was a man who knew how to keep his composure and hold his cards close to his chest.

"Elena, can I please trouble you for some water?" he asked.

I handed him the pitcher of ice water and a glass and watched him slowly pour the water, place the pitcher back in its place, wipe the table of droplets, sip the water, clear his throat, and swallow hard.

He was now leaning forward with elbows on his knees, playing with the droplets of water that had condensed on the glass and not looking at me.

"I'm here because . . ." More throat clearing.

Deep inhalation. "I'm here because I was let go by my firm."

He was now staring at the rim of the glass of water. "Yup, I was let go." Long pause. "You are the first person I have told."

"I'm truly sorry to hear that . . . " I began.

"I mean, you are really the *first* person I have told this to. Not my wife, not my kids, not my friends . . . No one knows." The pace of his speech had increased, and he was visibly unnerved.

"This is hard stuff," I offered. "Painful stuff. So, when did this happen?" Silence.

He took another sip of water, placed the glass carefully on a perfectly ironed linen handkerchief he pulled from his pocket, put his elbows on his knees so he could lean forward, and then cradled his whole face in his palms. He was massaging his forehead.

"December," he mumbled into his hands.

"December?"

"Yes. December," he repeated flatly.

"Wow. That's hard stuff to carry by yourself for so long."

"Yes."

"So, what have you been doing for the past six months?"

Trevor hadn't told his wife he'd been fired. Not for six months.

"Nothing."

"So, where do you go in the mornings?"

"I get up. I get dressed. Everything has remained the same, except instead of getting into the limo that takes me to Sixth Avenue, I take the 6 to Grand Central and walk to the Princeton Club and spend the day in the library drinking coffee and reading the paper until it's time to go home."

"And then?"

"And then I do it all over again the next day. No one asks me about my day. My wife hasn't asked me about my work in years, and the kids are occupied with their lives, so I . . . so I . . . just don't tell them anything."

"Why not?"

Silence.

"I don't want to worry them," he said stoically.

"And what about your worry?"

"I'm used to that," he rebounded. "I'm used to always being in a quiet panic about work, the deal, the client, the partnership. So, in many ways, my worry about not having a job is kind of normal for me."

"So, why are you here?" I asked again.

"I know I have to tell my wife and kids, but I can't cross that line. . . . I can't actually believe this is happening to me. I mean, maybe the firm is reconsidering their decision, and maybe if I wait it out, they'll rehire me, so then what would be the point in worrying the family if it all works out and it turns out that the firm just made a big mistake?"

Trevor needed a reality check.

"Trevor, it's been six months. That firm is still doing layoffs, from what I read. Have they reached out to you about taking you back?"

"No."

"Have you been in touch with your partners to see if there is any inclination to take you back?" I continued.

"No."

"So . . ." I paused and allowed the silence of finality to conclude my sentence and fill the room.

Trevor sat silently in quiet turmoil for some time.

"I just can't accept that this is happening, okay? I just can't. This isn't and shouldn't be happening. Not to me. God . . . what is going on?! I can't even wrap my head around this having happened, much less tell my family about it. How do I even do this?!" he exclaimed, throwing his arms up.

"What do you mean, 'how do you do this?'"

"Exactly what I asked: how do I do this? *This*!! This *failure* thing! How do I do *failure*?! How do I do being a loser?! This isn't supposed to happen to people like me, people who do everything right, keep their noses clean, don't make waves, work their asses off for years. . . . What the fuck do I know from failure?! Some people are just better at that shit than I am," he grumbled miserably.

"What shit?" I genuinely didn't understand what Trevor meant.

"Well, you know, giving up, not making the grade, not cutting it, letting themselves and others down. I was one of the guys who was responsible for letting those losers go, giving them a thumbs-down for partnership. I am the guy on top making decisions about others, you know what I mean? I'm not one of the guys who gets cut from the team, for Christ's sake! All I know is that I can't believe this is happening to me, and I have no idea how to tell my family, and I have no idea what happens next." He crossed his legs, crossed his arms over his chest, shifted his body and gaze away from me, and sat back in his seat, quietly fuming.

I didn't have any wise solutions or advice for Trevor. I knew from firsthand experience that sometimes life just blows up in your face, and all you can do at first is sit with it until you get your bearings. But it seemed that this was Trevor's first real encounter with unwelcome change, and he was rudderless.

"I don't know what happens next, Trevor, but I'm glad you're here. And I'm glad you told me. That's the first step. I'm happy to help you try to figure out how you 'do failure' and still live to tell about it." I imagine what I said wasn't much consolation to him, but a compassionate reality check and some validation were all I had to offer him at that moment.

After a deep breath, he said, " 'Do failure.' Wow. I have to learn to 'do failure.' Dear God, how did I end up here? This wasn't supposed to happen to me. This just wasn't supposed to happen to me," he repeated incredulously.

Trevor and I worked together for about six months. During that time, we worked on his mindset about what had happened to him at the firm so that he could accept the reality without the stigma of "failure." We also worked on ways to talk about what had happened to him in a more resilient and less defeatist, all-or-nothing way. Ultimately, Trevor and his family moved out of New York and to London, where his wife's family lived. The last I heard from him, he was a partner at a major London-based law firm.

Achievement Addiction

➢ compromised Trevor's resilience to failure and disappointments, leaving him shocked and paralyzed when he experienced his first significant career setback;

➢ made it so impossible for Trevor to accept the reality that he had been fired that he spent six months living a lie to himself, his family, and his friends; and

➢ induced a form of Achievement Amnesia that fueled extreme and self-destructive denial.

Achievement Addiction DETOX helped Trevor

➢ identify his Achievement-Addicted mindset that was steeped in self-destructive denial;

➢ develop resilience to this career setback by recognizing that his self-worth was more than the sum total of his professional achievements;

➢ control his Achievement Avatar and the paralyzing negative self-talk that prevented him from being honest with himself, his family, and his friends.

More on Resilience and Achievement Addiction

We can develop resilience to failure, disappointment, criticism, tragedy, unfairness, difficult people, and other curveballs life throws at us by learning to manage our mindset and negative self-talk. A resilient mindset helps you handle your emotions better, feel physically and mentally stronger, maintain a sense of autonomy, think rationally, and gain strength through self-esteem, optimism, and adaptability.

But developing our resilience doesn't happen overnight. It takes self-awareness and effort precisely when you feel most defeated, deflated, or disappointed. But it is my belief and experience that the power of resilience is innate in each and every one of us—innate and waiting to be uncovered, honed and strengthened.

Joan was someone who needed to learn that for herself.

Joan the Million-Dollar Winner

Joan was a large woman. A very, very large woman. It wasn't something you could avoid noticing the first time you met her. And when she sat in the waiting area, it was clear that the seat holding her was making her very uncomfortable.

Joan was also a genius. For real. She came from a family of geniuses. Her father was a renowned nuclear physicist, and her mother was a theoretical mathematician. Joan had graduated from high school at the age of thirteen, gone to Harvard undergrad on full scholarship, graduated at seventeen, attended Yale Law School, clerked for a federal judge in Illinois, and been fortunate enough to secure a Supreme Court clerkship.

In her spare time, she was a trivia maven. However, the HR director who'd referred her had explained that Joan was always thought of as "arrogant and off-putting," partly because she had the annoying habit of correcting people's grammar and peppering every other sentence with obscure references under her breath as other people spoke. Ultimately, Joan's social idiosyncrasies were enough to get her fired when the economy nose-dived in 2008.

On our first visit, Joan followed me down the hall to my office in complete silence. No hello, no "how are you?" Just a nod and downcast eyes. She stepped into my office and stopped at the doorway, staring at the chair I was pointing at for her to sit in. Again, silence.

"Joan? Is everything okay?" I asked.

"*Okay* is a very relative term, don't you think?" she snarled back at me. Joan was still looking at the diminutive chair.

Oh man, this is going to be fun, I thought to myself.

But I didn't take the bait.

"Are you feeling well? Or is there something bothering you that I can help you with? You don't seem to want to sit down," I observed.

"I *want* to sit down, but *can* I sit down is the real query, Elena, don't you think?"

Once again, she was rhetorically asking me, "don't you think?" But in that moment, she had a point. I wasn't thinking, and smarty-pants actually had a good visual-spatial point.

"Here," I offered. "You can have my seat, or we can stand. Or we can go to the coffee shop down . . ."

"I'll sit here," she said, cutting me off.

She moved into the room and shimmied herself into my slightly larger chair.

I leaned on the desk and didn't fully sit down.

Joan was sweating, breathing heavily, and moving her knee up and down at a furious pace. She was gazing at the floor and shaking her head no, quietly murmuring to herself, not looking up at me once, and I couldn't make out what she was saying.

I was beginning to get slightly unnerved by this one. The silence seemed to drag on. It seemed that I had stumbled with every step in the course of ten minutes, and every time I opened my mouth, stupidity and incompetence seemed to emanate from my lips. But my sudden insecurity felt foreign and not my own. Lord knows I'm not immune to moments of extreme self-doubt and feelings of incompetence, but it just wasn't like me to doubt myself so quickly with a new client.

Like a lightbulb going on, it occurred to me that perhaps these feelings had more to do with Joan than they did with me.

"Joan? I really want to help. Tell me . . ."

"I am useless," she burst out.

Silence.

Then she launched into a rant.

"I have no skills, zero . . . less than zero. In fact, I can't do anything right. I am supposed to be smart, but who cares?! Nobody cares that you're smart.

Forget smart. Nobody cares if you're a genius when the world is coming to an end. And the world has definitely come to an end." This rapid-speed, machine-gun fire of words came hurling at me with enormous force. She wasn't just telling me how she felt. I could feel her rage like a hot javelin from across the room. My head was starting to throb.

"What world has come to an end, Joan?" I was struggling to draw her out, but admittedly, I was still slightly unnerved by her tirade.

"I got fired! Those imbeciles, those intellectual dwarfs, those overpaid pseudo-legal minds, those inferior minds in their $5,000 suits had the nerve to *fire me*! *Me*?! *ME*?! The genius child, summa cum laude Yale law grad, and Supreme Court clerk . . . and . . . and the fucking all-time million-dollar winner of *Jeopardy! Me*?!"

She was bright red, sweating, breathing hard, and her eyes were bulging out.

She just kept yelling, "*Me? Me? Me?*"

I offered her some water. I sat back in my chair and let her tirade wash over me. I have learned that sometimes decades of suppressed rage needs a contained, safe space to cut loose and expand. This was now Joan's space, and I was a bystander. A benign witness to the injustice and deep well of grief she felt.

She was finished. Breathing hard, sweating profusely with tears streaming down her face, she was quiet now. And she looked like an infant after a temper tantrum: calm, pale, exhausted, scared, and helpless.

"You won a million dollars on a game show?" I asked flatly.

I don't know why I asked that or why that was the thing that stuck with me during her rant, but sometimes you follow your instincts and hope for the best.

She looked up at me and smiled for the first time. "Yes. A million dollars. It was the happiest day of my life."

"Wow" was all I could muster.

She grabbed a tissue, blew her nose quietly, and continued.

"Truly, the happiest day in my life because I showed the world that I was more than a fat smart girl. I could actually do something no one could have ever imagined with my brains and do it in front of a million people and for the first time really, really *win* something and feel . . . I don't know, feel . . . seen." She paused. "Yeah, that was quite a moment for me. For one short moment in my life, I was finally someone everyone envied." Her smile quickly faded, and that cloud of anger was appearing across her face again.

"So, Joan, when you think about that moment, on stage, with cameras, everything in the balance, and your realization that you had just won . . . what comes to mind?" I was genuinely curious.

Long pause.

Silence.

"I feel happy when I think about that moment, I guess. But seriously, who cares? I just got fired, and no one is hiring, and what skills do I have, really? How am I going to live? How am I going to survive? Who needs my kind of brain in this economy? Nobody! So what if I won a million dollars as a freak on a TV show? The reality is that I am worthless and useless."

More clouds were gathering as we sat silently.

Joan broke the silence.

"Elena, I just don't know what to do next. Or how to live or make a living or survive if . . . if I'm not just being . . . I don't know. Smart. That's all I'm good for, you know? Being smart." Joan felt betrayed by her intelligence, and it was painful to listen to her helplessness.

This woman was a genius, but she couldn't see how strong and capable she truly was. I felt her resentment and the injustice of it all as if it were happening to me. What she needed was a reminder.

"I don't know what you are going to do next or how you're going to make a living either, but I know one thing that you just taught me and that you may not know about yourself," I started.

"Oh really? Please, do enlighten me," she quipped.

I took her playful, somewhat condescending sarcasm as a good sign that she felt more herself again. Perhaps now she could listen.

So I went on.

"I know that anyone who was scrappy, ballsy, calculating, and just damn driven enough to outsmart a game show rigged against the players . . . that person also has some deeply embedded survival instincts and untapped skills that can come in mighty useful in a shit time like this."

She stared at me.

"You may not know this, but you have some seriously kick-ass survival skills and intuition that are going to be at the heart of any next step you take. And those skills have nothing to do with your book smarts."

Joan just looked at me hard with a blank expression on her face. I couldn't tell if she was going to hurl a chair at me and storm out of my office or hug me. I was prepared for both or neither.

She sat thoughtfully for quite a while, and at one point, she rolled her eyes upward as if she were tracking a fly on the ceiling tiles. It was more than a little weird to watch, but I knew something was cooking in that brain of hers, and by then, I had developed a high threshold for weird. So, I waited patiently for her brain to finish.

"So, kinda like Pooh?" she asked, looking at me expectantly.

"Excuse me?" I was confused.

She started to smile.

"Like Winnie the Pooh? ... You know, Christopher Robin says to Pooh, 'You are braver than you believe, stronger than you seem, and smarter than you think.' Few people know this little bit of trivia, but that quote actually wasn't in A. A. Milne's book, but it was in the 1997 movie." Joan was now smiling to herself with great satisfaction and a little more ease.

In that moment, I was overcome with respect for Joan. Not just because of her uncanny ability to quote the perfect line at the perfect moment from a children's story that meant something to her, but for her courage to try something new at a difficult moment in her life. I smiled to myself, thinking about Winnie the Pooh and how good-natured he was, no matter how many times he got his head stuck in a honey jar or tumbled down into unexpected trouble. Winnie and Christopher Robin would be proud of Joan in this moment, too, I thought.

"Yes, Joan," I said. "Just like Pooh."

Joan and I worked together for about a year to develop and magnify her resilience when it came to her work. Our efforts focused on identifying her multitude of skills, and we also devised a game plan to help her transition out of the practice of law and look into becoming a law school professor. With some more exploration, it became clear that Joan was cut out for academics, both intellectually and strategically. She was an astute survivor who previously had never needed to develop her resilience or understand the power of her survival and intuitive skills.

Achievement Addiction

➢ compromised Joan's resilience to failure, leaving her shocked and deflated when she experienced her first significant career setback;

➢ induced a form of Achievement Amnesia in her that had Joan forgetting all her strengths, talents, and brilliant achievements; and

➢ left Joan feeling so worthless and powerless that she could not envision any career or life for herself beyond this setback.

Achievement Addiction DETOX helped Joan

➢ identify her Achievement Amnesia and its self-destructive impact on her ability to move on with her life and career;

➢ reconnect with her talents, skills, and abilities and develop resilience to this career setback by recognizing that her achievements did not exclusively define her self-worth; and

➢ develop a new vision for her career and side-step the distorted mindset that prevented her from moving on.

STEP 2: MINDSET
The IMAGO Coaching Questions

Now it's time for you to work on Step 2—MINDSET—using several IMAGO Coaching Questions. All the questions below are designed to help you work the second step and deepen your understanding of how Achievement Addiction shows up in your daily mindset and chronic negative self-talk.

In addition, after each question, I offer you a way to summarize your second-step insights in the form of a declaratory sentence. These summarized insights will be essential to refer to should you choose to download and complete the Achievement Addiction DETOX Worksheets accessible at www.achievementaddictiondetox.com.

To recap, the IMAGO Coaching Method invites you to INQUIRE, MAGNIFY, ACT, GROW, and OWN.

The questions below can help you work this second step.

INQUIRE

How would you describe your typical mindset about achievement?

_____

_____

_____

_____

_____

What does your negative self-talk say to you about your self-worth and value? About your past achievements? Your future achievements?

_____

_____

_____

_____

_____

_____

My mindset and/or negative self-talk about my self-worth and achievements tells me that . . .

_____

_____

_____

_____

_____

Magnify

What recurring mindset or negative self-talk stands out for you and warrants more attention and magnification?

_____

_____

_____

_____

_____

The most recurring negative self-talk I have about my self-worth, value, and achievement is . . .

_____

_____

_____

Because of my mindset and/or negative self-talk, I suffer in the following ways:

_____

_____

_____

. . . and the people around me suffer in the following ways:

_____

_____

_____

Act

Think about the most challenging mindset or negative self-talk that you are struggling with right now. What action would you be willing to take to improve that situation?

_____

_____

What might the opposite mindset/negative self-talk say to you?

_____

_____

When I find myself believing this negative self, I will take the following steps toward reframing and improving my negative self-talk:

_____

_____

_____

Grow

If you could wave a magic wand and improve your mindset and/or get rid of your negative self-talk about achievement, what would it mean to you emotionally? To your self-confidence? To the way you feel about yourself day in and day out?

_____

_____

_____

I want to grow and improve my overall mindset and negative self-talk about achievement because it would mean that . . .

_____

_____

Own

Hopefully, answering these questions has increased your awareness about your mindset regarding achievement and the negative self-talk that feeds it. So, let's turn to owning that newfound awareness around your MINDSET.

When it comes to my mindset about achievement and the negative self-talk that feeds my Achievement Addiction, I acknowledge and own that . . .

_____

_____

_____

. . . and that if I could take the steps to change and improve my mindset, it would mean . . .

_____

_____

_____

_____

FINAL THOUGHTS
Mindset and Achievement Addiction

✓ Focusing on Mindset (Step 2) is a powerful step toward overcoming Achievement Addiction. Overhauling our negative mindset not only is possible but is a pivotal step toward challenging our Achievement-Addicted thoughts, beliefs, and self-talk so that our thought life can mirror and support any changes we may want to introduce into our life.

✓ Achievement Addicts live with crippling, defeatist, and devaluing negative self-talk, which creates a negative mindset that robs them of joy, happiness, and a sense of self-worth.

✓ When we start to change our negative self-talk through reframing techniques and cognitive-behavioral prompts, we allow change to be possible by correcting many of the habitual mental distortions that previously guided our choices and actions.

STEP 3

EMOTIONS

Honor Your Feelings

How Feelings and Emotions Contribute to Achievement Addiction

The truth is that this chapter almost didn't make it into the book. Not intentionally. During a group therapy meeting I attended, I came face-to-face with my glaring blind spot. It hit me when I listened to one of the members talk about her nervousness and her feelings of inadequacy in speaking publicly to the group. Here I was, an experienced therapist/coach writing a book about how to overcome Achievement Addiction, and yet the vestigial Achievement-Addicted part of me had conveniently sidestepped writing about the messy topic of feelings and emotions! In my desire to write this book, I had my eye on the prize, and somehow, automatically, when I wanted to get something done, the first things I threw overboard were my emotions and feelings.

It was a very humbling moment.

Like so many Achievement Addicts, I had come to believe two things about feelings and emotions:

1. Feelings and emotions "get in the way" of achievement, and
2. Achievement is a great way to avoid, bury, numb, and sublimate difficult and unwelcome feelings.

In the process of escaping from feelings and emotions, many Achievement Addicts struggle to understand the distinction between the two, why they are important, and how they impact our experience of life.

So, let's define some terms.

Feelings and emotions are fundamental to our human experience, and it is through our feelings and emotions that we navigate and interface with the world and get a sense of our place in it. Emotions and feelings are two interrelated concepts, and volumes have been written about the distinctions between them. But for our purposes, let's just say this:

Emotions are automatic, physical bodily reactions to external stimuli. Emotions are aroused consciously or unconsciously before feelings arise. Feelings are the collection of our day-to-day conscious, subjective mental associations with and interpretations of an emotional experience.

Here are a couple of simple examples of how emotions and feelings are different but related:

We see a Labrador retriever. We automatically experience happiness (an emotion) and feel love (a feeling).

One of our superiors criticizes us at work, and we experience fear (an emotion) and feel shame or anger (feelings).

As Achievement Addicts, many of us are fundamentally uncomfortable with our emotions and feelings, for reasons too numerous to count. For the Achievement Addict, feelings and emotions are human inconveniences that get in the way of what we want to achieve. The common denominator is that Achievement Addicts either were taught or learned later in life that emotions and feelings can make us vulnerable to disapproval and that engaging them can compromise our ability to achieve.

Bottom line: Our feelings and emotions are impediments to our next achievement "fix."

So, we learn to tell ourselves that our emotions and feelings are unnecessary, compromising, a sign of weakness, and an overall waste of time and energy better spent achieving more. Therefore, for many of us, whenever an uncomfortable emotion or feeling arises, our Achievement Avatar quickly pipes up and minimizes the feeling. Our Avatar tells us to either ignore, bury, or sublimate that feeling. The result is that over time, by ignoring or pushing down our feelings and emotions, we develop a dissonance between how we present ourselves to others and how we actually feel. This only strengthens and solidifies our false self. And, as we discussed, it is our false self (with some help from our Achievement Avatar!) that keeps us stuck in our destructive Achievement Addicted cycle.

But at some point, our emotions and feelings catch up with us.

Anna-Maria learned this lesson the hard way.

Anna-Maria, a Girl from Brooklyn

Anna-Maria came to me the day after her firm asked her to put together a dossier supporting her promotion to partner. She had been a litigator with a prominent Los Angeles–based law firm, based in its large New York City office, for nearly twelve years. Since her eighth year at the firm as an associate, the firm had told her that she would be "up for consideration," but she had been passed over every year for the past four years and deferred for partnership consideration. And each of those four years, the firm had told her that she "needed to keep doing what [she] was doing, keep [her] hours up, network more, speak more, get more visible." And every year, she'd done exactly what had been asked of her.

Anna-Maria was billing between 2,300 and 2,500 hours a year; she'd rarely spent a weekend to herself in more than five years. When on vacation, she worked at least two to three hours a day responding to calls or emails. She and her husband had decided to delay having children until she made partner so she could dedicate her time and energy to pursuing the partnership. When Anna-Maria arrived in my office, she was sweaty and very agitated, and she had her cell phone to her ear as she followed me down the hallway to my office and sat in the chair.

"Yeah, I got it. Yeah. Uh-huh. Yup. I hear ya. I got it. Yes. I don't think so . . . but I . . ."

I sat across from her, watching. She was a nervous mess.

"Yeah, I don't know. . . . I'm sorry, yes. I will handle it; I got this. . . . I'm in the middle of another meeting, so I have to . . . Hello? Hello?"

Whoever Anna-Maria was speaking to had just hung up on her mid-sentence.

She closed her phone, threw it violently into her designer satchel, and looked up at me with eyes that were frightened and angry at the same time.

"This is the fourth time this week he's hung up on me," she said to no one in particular.

"Hi," I said slowly.

She was still in her private inner world. "This is the shit I put up with. Day after day," she said, staring blankly through me.

"Want to tell me what's going on?" I said.

"Max. That's what's going on. Fucking Maxwell . . . the man who controls everything in my life. My work, my life, my sleep, my partnership shot . . . everything. He just yells and yells and calls me names, and I put up with it," she explained with exhaustion.

"Names?"

"Yeah . . ." I immediately recognized that Anna-Maria had the vestiges of a tough Brooklyn accent peeking out like a black silk slip from underneath her tight, couture pencil skirt. I smiled to myself, thinking she was a Brooklyn girl like me. "Yeah, this asshole likes to call me an idiot pretty regularly and to my face." She laughed bitterly and shrugged her shoulders. "It doesn't bother me anymore."

"It doesn't?" I asked.

"Nah. At first, he would just hint at it, like he'd say, 'Even an idiot would know . . . blah, blah, blah.' But since he agreed to put me up and endorse me for partnership a couple of years ago, he's dispensed with the politeness, and now he just calls me an idiot." Anna-Maria was doing a good job of acting like it all didn't bother her, but I could tell that her avoidant, darting eye contact and nervous fidgeting belied a different story.

As I would later find out, Anna-Maria had worked as this partner's right hand for more than twelve years, and Max had a nasty habit of screaming expletives when things went awry with a case. He didn't think twice about calling her an idiot, a "waste of breath," "stupid," and "moronic" on a relatively regular basis. He phoned her at all hours of the night, expected her to take his calls at all times, and hung up on her pretty regularly. Maxwell Whitfield was verbally and emotionally abusive. And Anna-Maria was "okay" with it because, as she put it later on in another session, "Max controls whether I make partner or not." He was her ticket to achievement, and absolutely nothing—even abuse—was going to get in the way of her winning her next achievement.

Anna-Maria was now bent down and rummaging around for something in her satchel. She took out a red enameled makeup mirror, opened it, removed something small, popped it in her mouth, and washed it down with a gulp from her water bottle.

I said nothing, but Anna-Maria felt like she needed to explain.

"I see a psychiatrist, and he's prescribed me something to calm my nerves so I can get through my day without falling apart," she blurted out defensively as she eyed me from behind the water bottle.

I remember thinking that that was an odd way of putting it, but I didn't comment and just tucked that away for another discussion.

"Anyway," she continued as she smoothed out her skirt, "I *need* to make partner this year. I mean, like, I *need* to. They passed me over a couple of times, and I guess each time they had their reasons, but this is *it*. I have to put together a solid game plan and business case for them making me partner. Can you help me?"

Anna-Maria was retaining my services to help her formulate a compelling argument for her promotion to partnership, refine her business development plan, and outline a more robust visibility strategy. As a coach, you start where the client is. There were many warning signs about Anna-Maria in that first session, but she had herself and me somewhat convinced that she would deal with the other things in her life after she got promoted.

Anna-Maria and I were making some good progress. Throughout our sessions, I heard more and more detail about Max's abusive rants, digs, and all-out explosions. Anna-Maria seemed immune to his nastiness and slights; she had her eye on the prize, and nothing was going to get in her way.

One afternoon, I got a call from her about an hour before our regularly scheduled session.

All I could hear was sobbing on the other end of the line. "Hello? Hello?"

"Elena, it's me. It's Anna-Maria." And she burst into tears again. "I'm sorry, I'll get it under control. . . . I just, I just . . ."

The sobbing broke into full-on, muffled howls of hysterical crying as she tried to cover the phone.

"Anna-Maria, are you okay? Where are you?"

"I'm in my car, waiting for AAA. God damn it, why am I such an idiot?!"

"Anna-Maria? Are you safe?"

"Yes. My car broke down. I went to see my mom in the hospital, and now my car broke down. I've been meaning to take it in for service, but then this case exploded. And Max . . . and this whole promotion thing . . ."

The sobbing started again.

"Nothing works for me, nothing. My mom is in the hospital again. Maybe Max is right after all, I don't know. . . ."

"Anna-Maria, can you talk while you're waiting for AAA?"

"Yeah, I can talk," she sniffled.

We talked for a while, and when she regained her composure, I asked her the question that was really on my mind.

"I know you are frustrated and upset right now. What do you think is causing this level of upset and crying?"

Anna-Maria blew her nose, and I heard the ruffling of things in the background. She had stopped crying, and her voice was calm but still shaky.

"It's Max. Max and then my mom, and my dad and my crazy brother . . . I just can't anymore," she sobbed.

"Hold on a minute, I get it, but it seems like you have been managing Max for over ten years, and your mom has been ill for some time. What happened *today* to bring on this meltdown?"

"They are all the same, all exactly the same, all three of them, my dad, my brother, and Max. Nasty and mean and just cruel. My dad, I understand. I mean, he's had a really tough life, taking care of my younger brother, Paulie, who's been in and out of group homes because of his schizophrenia, and now my dad is taking care of my mother with Alzheimer's. But I got used to my dad's rants and Paulie's episodes, in one ear and out the other, and that's how I put up with Max all this time. Dad and Paulie were good training grounds for Max's antics. I was a pro at handling this kind of BS from my family, but damn it! Max just crossed a line this time. My God! How could he say that to me?" Her sobbing was now louder.

"Say what? What did Max say?" I was almost afraid to hear what cruelty he had come up with this time.

"I was in the office and got a call from my dad that for the second time this week, my mom had wandered outside lost and in her PJs. When Dad tried to coax her back into the house, she started to yell and get violent, so he had no choice but to call the cops. My dad called to tell me that the ambulance was taking her to the hospital. So I grabbed my stuff and laptop, walked over to Max's office, and told him I was dealing with a family emergency, and I would need to work from home tonight, but that I would be available by email and phone."

"And?"

"And he didn't even look up from his papers. He just mumbled something under his breath, so I said, 'Max, what did you say?' I thought he was saying something about the hearing I was scheduled to attend the next day. That's when he looked up at me with a cold stare, put his pen down, and calmly said, 'What I said, you idiot, was that it's a damn good thing you don't have kids. You're totally incompetent and a hot mess. Fuck. No kid deserves that kind of a mother.'" Anna-Maria was now sobbing uncontrollably like a small, wounded child.

I was shocked.

Once she caught her breath again, she said forcefully, "This doesn't work. I can't take another day of this . . . this *abuse*! I just can't hack it anymore."

"You're right," I said. "This is abuse, and no one should have to put up with it. Anna-Maria, when you get this car thing all sorted out, would you feel comfortable stopping by or talking again by phone? I think—no, I know—that what happened to you today is shocking and painful. And before you decide that somehow you should be redoubling your efforts to be tough enough to 'hack it,' as you say, maybe we can see what other options are available to you?"

"Yeah. I'm feeling like a complete wuss and loser for not being able to let that one slide. But everyone has their limits, right? I mean, what kind of person would put up with that kind of abuse?"

"It seems to me you are the kind of person to put up with that kind of abuse. Until today."

"That's me all right . . . my whole life. I used to think that I was Teflon, I could feel no pain, and no emotion could get to me. For years, I've been just toughing it out, shaking it off, and moving on. Success was the best revenge, I thought, and that kept me going for years. But today . . . I don't know. Something just snapped. And I don't think I can do it this way anymore. . ."

Anna-Maria had done a brilliant job of pushing down her feelings and making believe she was impervious to pain and abuse. But she, like many of us, had just met her breaking point, and when that happens, decades of ignored emotions can come flooding in. Anna-Maria's exchange with Max that day had opened the floodgates to decades of repressed feelings of humiliation, anger, sadness, and trauma.

Anna-Maria and I continued to work on her dossier for promotion, but she had now started to look for another law-firm job with better promotion opportunities. And she found a therapist who could focus on talk therapy and dealing with her feelings and emotions around the abuse she experienced at home and work, along with her abusive treatment of herself.

In coaching, we focused a lot on her negative mindset and self-talk. We identified the ways her negative perspective was impacting her professional presentation to other firms and even to other partners at her firm. Years of repressing her true feelings and ignoring her emotions had left Anna-Maria with a false self that came across as hardened, sarcastic, bitter, and cynical. She had become a caricature of her real self. It was a clear turnoff to others at the firm and had been brought to her attention in multiple performance reviews. Eventually, Anna-Maria conceded that her prickly demeanor might have been one of the obstacles to her being promoted to law partner.

When I last connected with Anna-Maria, she'd had several interviews with smaller national firms in New York. She seemed pleased to learn that there were some law-firm environments with a clear "no asshole tolerance" policy that were very interested in her. I lost touch with her, but I recently came to learn that she had made partner at a smaller firm in NYC that has a reputation for treating its employees very well.

Achievement Addiction

➤ caused Anna-Maria to put up with abusive, compromising, and devaluing colleagues to obtain a specific achievement;

➤ convinced Anna-Maria that earning a promotion was worth minimizing and ignoring her feelings and emotions in working with a boss who was abusive and devaluing; and

➤ landed Ann-Maria in an Achievement Trance that had her mindlessly chasing a promotion that would only result in more abuse and powerlessness.

Achievement Addiction DETOX helped Anna-Maria

➤ recognize the impact that minimizing her emotions was having on her career aspirations;

➤ identify the particular nature of her Achievement Trance and the self-destructive impact it was having on her health, life, and career; and

➤ regain her dignity and sense of self-worth which allowed her to move on to a better career environment.

Underneath the veneer of success, feelings of being chronically over-whelmed, disappointed, disillusioned, anxious, stressed out, panicked, sad, grief-stricken, depressed, angry, enraged, unworthy, humiliated, and devalued make up only a short list of the many responses that regularly plague most Achievement Addicts.

A variety of secondary suffering and pain arises from not processing, honoring, and feeling our emotions in real-time. Some of us eat our feelings and suffer the illnesses that come along with obesity. Others drink or use substances to manage and regulate their emotions and suffer the consequences of addiction. Still others of us have full-on emotional breakdowns after years of ignoring or minimizing our feelings and emotions.

The point here is this: Emotions will manifest themselves either directly or indirectly, but like any other energy force, they will find a way to be expressed. Finding a way to process challenging feelings and emotions is fundamental to restoring health, sanity, and well-being.

Getting the Brass Ring Feels Like . . .

In law, making partner is the great reward for all those years of self-sacrifice and deprivation.

In corporations and banking, becoming a VP, managing director, or CEO is the prize for years of dedication and sacrifice. For doctors and academics, becoming chair of a particular department or getting a research funding grant is the reward. Every profession has its own desirable brass ring that every Achievement Addict is jockeying for and coveting. And you would think Achievement Addicts would feel some sense of ease, relief, and accomplishment once they finally snag that brass ring. But the absolute opposite is true. Once Achievement Addicts succeed in bagging that one big brass-ring achievement, most of them are either numb or *even more panicked than before*. Why? Mostly because Achievement Addicts only know how to chase achievement, and most of them have spent the prior decade pushing down emotions to survive the trials and tribulations of securing that brass ring—so much so that for many of these newly minted law partners, chairs, VPs, CEOs, and managing directors, any feelings of joy, delight, ease, self-worth, or happiness are either fleeting or thoroughly inaccessible. Out of habit, many Achievement Addicts are unfazed by their most recent accomplishments. Instead, many automatically focus on the next daunting achievement ahead of them.

The result of this Sisyphean undertaking is the not-so-hidden secret that my most unhappy coaching clients were million-dollar partners or executives at big law firms, banks, or corporations. They had spent their lives chasing achievement after achievement only to find themselves paradoxically both disillusioned by the empty promises of their recent milestones and at the same time hungering for more goals to conquer. But, even for the best of us, there comes a time when the music stops, and we cannot go on at the speed or rate of achievement that was the hallmark of our heyday. For some, that wake-up call may come in the form of a tragedy, a death, an illness, or a family crisis. Others find their achievement trajectory suddenly disrupted because of office politics, layoffs, or a downturn in the economy. The absence of the next achievement or identified goal can leave a lifelong Achievement Addict with a boatload of feelings that they are not equipped for or accustomed to handling.

Doug was one of those superstar, multimillion-dollar law partners who showed up at my door one day with a yachtful of unwelcome events and emotions.

Doug and the Odd Couple

Doug had been the managing partner of a large international law firm in NYC. He had attended a presentation I had given at the NYC Bar Association on networking and business development and walked up to me after the presentation and asked for my card. Doug was in his mid-sixties, bespectacled with thin blue designer glasses that matched his blue eyes. He had a full head of salt-and-pepper hair, was soft-spoken, and had a "senatorial" demeanor that reminded me of a mixture of Bill Gates and George Clooney. He called me the next morning, and we set up our first in-person meeting the following afternoon.

Doug came straight to the point: he was planning on retiring from the law firm within the next twelve months and wanted to find a way to transition his lifelong, big-shot clients to other, younger attorneys at the firm. He said he found the process "tricky and clumsy, at best," and he didn't want to risk these personal and professional relationships that he had spent a lifetime cultivating. He then pulled out a folder with his client contact list to immediately walk through each one.

Before he launched into the details, my experience as a coach and therapist told me that I needed to understand his mindset about retiring. In my experience, the ambivalence around retiring is frequently thick with intensely conflictual emotions. These pent-up emotions can manifest in weird ways and can end up blowing up long-standing relationships within the partnership and with clients as well. This was not going to be as simple as moving through an itemized checklist. Succession planning and transitioning existing clients to younger partners is more akin to neurosurgery; it is a delicate, time-intensive undertaking and potentially hazardous to everyone involved.

"Doug, that's great. We can walk through these clients and your ideas about who they should be assigned to for sure, and I will need your insight into the nature of these relationships, etc. But before we get to that . . . whose idea was it?"

"Idea? What do you mean?" he said, slightly defensively.

"Whose idea was it for you to retire? And who picked the timeline?" I asked calmly.

Power and control are the major currencies in any Achievement Addict's career, and I needed to know who was in control of Doug's destiny at the law firm. In addition, I needed to know whether Doug had the power to navigate the changes he was about to make.

Doug eyed me carefully from behind his Prada glasses, took them off slowly, looked down, and pulled a black felt square from his pocket. He then cleaned each lens carefully, put them back on his face, and looked up at me, flashing me a mischievous smile with his set of Chiclet-white enamels.

He had regained his composure and was now ready to proceed.

"Are you familiar with *The Odd Couple*, Elena?" he asked.

"The TV show or the movie?" I offered too eagerly, kind of like a *Jeopardy!* contestant. As a kid, I was a huge fan of the sitcom, and at one point I even had a slight crush on Felix Unger. It now explains a lot, but at the time, I just liked how driven and neat he was.

Back to Doug.

"Either one. As I was thinking about the answer to whose idea it was for me to retire, I thought about that opening scene where Felix Unger is standing in front of his apartment with his packed suitcases. Suddenly the door opens, and you see a woman's hand shoving a frying pan at him as the announcer says, 'On November 17th, Felix Unger was asked to remove himself from his home. That request came from his wife.'" Doug paused. And there was no indication of any emotion other than mild amusement at his answer.

I nodded knowingly, smiled, and continued, "So it was your wife's idea?"

Without missing a beat, Doug answered, "Not exactly. My wife and my mistress . . ." he said, smiling at me. *Oh boy*, I thought to myself; *this one's a professional charmer with tectonic layers of metal armor around him.* Getting to understand him was going to require a jackhammer.

"Good to hear you've been keeping yourself entertained and busy," I quipped.

He then smiled downward, somewhat abashedly.

"My mistress is my law firm, Elena. Not as scandalous as my unchecked male vanity might have you believe." He was pleased with himself. This brilliant, elegant man was a crafty wordsmith accustomed to the art of deflection, and now he was trying to use his disarming charm and witty banter to avoid talking about the real topic at hand.

Transitioning Doug's clients was not going to be as easy as going through his checklist. The man was a formidable fortress, and he had little to no intention of letting me in.

"My wife and my partners—the executive committee, to be exact. It was their idea. Actually, the word they used was 'suggestion.' Truth is, I didn't have much to say about this and still don't. It is in the firm's bylaws that after age sixty-five, partners can be asked to retire or given a year-by-year extension on a case-by-case basis." Doug was serene, but I could tell he was now quietly seething.

Doug didn't look sixty-five, and he seemed like he still had a lot of energy and stamina left in him. Retiring seemed like it was the last thing on his mind. This whole transition thing was not his choice, and you could feel the heat of his resentment filling up the room.

After nearly forty years of dedicating his life to developing his career and building a thriving practice with an enviable client roster in a competitive market, he was now being shown the elevator and told, "Thanks, but we'll take it from here."

Doug looked at me and said nothing more. His eyes told me everything. They were filled with blue-hot rage.

Sometimes a coach needs to "say what is so" to purge the room of any lingering denial that can get in the way of the client's progress. But, admittedly, I was clumsy this time.

"Sounds like you are not the one in control here. So, what's next for you?" I asked with all the delicacy of a heat-deranged trumpeting elephant. I knew I had screwed up with him, but before I could find a way to clean it up, he answered curtly.

"Adapt." He then attempted to stare me down with an unwavering and practiced steely gaze.

I had my misgivings pretty early on that Doug didn't like me, but now I was confident that he had made the affirmative decision to actively dislike me. My fumble had sealed my fate with him. I had nothing to lose, and I thought he had a lot to gain from some more honest probing, so I sidestepped the stare-down and went on with my questions.

"How long have you known about this request to retire?" I asked matter-of-factly.

Doug paused for a moment, slowly blinked, and then said, "Three years. They let me know three years ago. Conveniently, for them, at the height of the economic recovery." I was beginning to hear some emotion in his voice, even if it was sarcasm. Rage is usually the emotion that feeds biting sarcasm, and from where I was standing, it seemed that Doug had every reason to feel rageful.

"And how much progress have you made on transitioning the clients on the list you just pulled out?" I knew the answer to that question but thought it best for him to articulate it.

"Other than putting this list together three years ago? None," he said flatly.

"Sounds to me like you're pissed off and digging in your heels on this one," I summarized.

"Pissed off would be an understatement. Furious and insulted would be a good starting point," he answered, shifting in his chair and recrossing his legs.

Now we were getting somewhere.

Doug went on to calmly tell me that he'd been so shocked by the EC's request that he had simply ignored it and gone about his business, making more money for himself and the law firm as if the topic had never been addressed. That had gone on for two years, primarily because not pushing the issue with Doug served the partnership and the EC—stubborn Doug was helping to increase the overall pot of profits that the partners and he would divvy up.

But this past year, with the threat of a downturn and recession, suddenly the EC decided to revoke his request for another year of retirement deferment. His profitability had dropped, and now Doug was running the possibility of costing the firm money to keep him on at his full partnership share. So they'd sat him down and told him he had twelve months to transition his clients and move on "to the next chapter of his life."

"So, let's start over. Tell me why you're really here and what you want help with, because—and feel free to tell me I'm full of it—it sounds to me like you are more than happy to keep waving that list of client names around and do nothing about transitioning any of them until the day you walk out of the firm." It was now my turn to smile at him coyly.

Doug looked at me with a Cheshire smile. "Exactly right you are."

"So, why seek out a coach?" I continued. "Seems like you have a plan already in mind that satisfies you, at least. What would you like to work on with me?"

Doug needed to crystallize what he wanted to accomplish in this coaching engagement before we both ended up wasting our time designing a transition process that he had no intention of executing.

He eyed me for a long moment, took a deep breath, sat back in his chair, and sighed audibly.

"I understand you are also a psychotherapist, correct?" he asked.

"Yes, I am."

"And a lawyer, correct?" he continued.

"Yes, that, too." I was beginning to feel like I was in a deposition.

"Well," he continued, "my wife has been trying to get me into therapy for years, and I just can't see sitting for years and years talking about my feelings and issues with someone who has no idea what it truly means to be a law-firm partner. And besides, I'm too old and crusty for that touchy-feely shit. Don't get me wrong, I see its merits. For other people. It has helped my wife and children enormously to have someone to confide in and process difficult events in their lives."

Events. Not feelings. Not emotions. Doug was stoic, patrician, old-school, all the way.

He took another deep breath before he continued. "Look, I know that I have to transition these clients, but most of them are lifelong friends. I know myself well enough to know that if left to my own devices, I will handle this the way I have handled most difficult events in my life. I will bury it, ignore it, throw myself into my work, and happily live in denial." He now sounded a little more self-aware and real, but he still couldn't even bring himself to say the word *feelings*. Doug was only prepared to deal with facts and events. I suddenly felt a swell of empathy for him and believed I could help him.

"I know I have to find a way to deal with all the issues and complications around my retiring," he said. "So I guess I called you because I guess I want to talk about my thoughts about this whole retirement thing and how to deal with it all. It's a lot. It's taking a toll on me, mostly because I have no idea what retirement might look like for me, and I don't want to ruin my reputation with these folks by not handing them off responsibly to other competent lawyers. But I know I can't get there by myself. I've sat on this for two years because . . . I don't know . . . I'm frustrated, and in denial, I guess. But I know I need some help in crossing the line. So, I think coaching would suit me better. I'm good at following instructions. A quick study. Tell me what to do, Coach, and I'll do it." He then flashed me another one of his charming smiles.

At that moment, I felt a deep sadness for Doug. I couldn't imagine the level of shock and grief that he was burying underneath his calm, charming demeanor as his partners of thirty years were rewarding his decades of dedication to the law firm with a politely disguised pink slip and a twelve-month countdown ultimatum.

As I was processing my feelings and thoughts about what he had just shared, Doug was deep in his own thoughts and recollections, and he started to talk a little more about himself and his achievements.

"You know, I built that whole corporate department almost by myself, back during the Y2K era, and started working with telecom companies that were only beginning to envision the possibility of using our phones for entertainment. No one saw the tech boom coming, but I did. And I saw the potential in investing in those emerging company clients."

I listened intently as he continued. This man was a visionary and a maverick.

"And now, suddenly, I'm too old? I mean, I'm experienced, these clients trust me with their businesses, their estates, their kids' college recommendations—and I'm not old, damn it. I mean, until three years ago, I was being billed out at the highest partner rate at the firm and made them and myself a pretty penny. So how exactly do you go from being the most valuable asset one minute to being the one they're trying to get rid of the next? I guess . . . I don't know . . . I guess I'm just confused."

It was occurring to Doug that, just like the rest of us, no matter his past achievements, he was also expendable and fungible. And nothing in his life could have prepared him for the emotional blow that was now being dealt to his ego and his dignity.

In his worldview, he was going from being the superstar, revered, and feared multimillion-dollar partner to now being a nobody who needed to be eliminated. Even worse, he was being made to feel like a burdensome problem to the very law firm he had helped build and grow. This was sounding more and more to me like a 21st-century Shakespearean tragedy with Doug reluctantly cast in King Lear's role.

"Where will I go every day? I mean, what do I do with myself, for God's sake?! I won't be one of those old, sad former firm partners that haunt the firm's hallways and are given an honorary office to read the *New York Times*. I won't be one of those golf-playing has-beens who drink themselves into oblivion while regaling other has-beens with tales of the good old days. Jesus. Who knew? I mean, what was it all for? I have spent a lifetime building something I could be proud of, at the expense of absolutely everything else, and I haven't had a moment to think about what's next. There wasn't supposed to be a 'next.' You just keep going when you're someone like me. You just keep building. This is my life! That's all I know. The law. The firm. I gave up everything or almost everything for it, and now, *poof*, just like that, it's over?"

It seemed to me that for the first time, Doug was not only confronting his expendability at the law firm, but he was also confronting his mortality. This transition was akin to a mini-death of sorts. Doug was being asked to face his mortality, his expendability, and his regrets, and do so while he quickly and quietly exited the building.

Being a big-shot law-firm partner was Doug's entire identity. And now it was being unceremoniously stripped away. Doug was lost, and I genuinely wanted to help him. And helping him meant that I needed to be direct and honest, even if he walked away resenting me as much as his back-stabbing partners.

"Doug, this is tough, complicated stuff. And forgive me if I sound too touchy-feely right now, but there's no bypassing the fact that you need to spend some time facing and coming to terms with the feelings and emotions you are having about retirement before you'll be able to execute whatever transition plan you have in mind. This time, it isn't about following instructions. You said it yourself: you know what you need to do. You just don't want to do it because you, well, you just don't want to retire. But there's no getting around these emotions, and there's no getting around your new reality. I hate to say it, but this time you gotta go *through* it to get to the other side."

My final sentence landed with an audible thud in the space between our seats.

Doug wasn't happy about what I'd said. And he was even less happy with what he was being forced to confront. He left my office visibly flushed and annoyed. I didn't hear from him for nearly a month. Then, one afternoon, he called again, and we agreed to meet a second time.

Doug was oddly agitated and fidgety in his chair. He lacked his Cary Grant composure; he was upset and didn't care who knew it.

He started to explain.

"They gave me a real ultimatum this time. They said if I didn't start making visible, tangible progress in transitioning clients, they would need to consider reducing my draw in the coming year. They want me to create a ninety-day plan outlining the transition plan and start working with younger partners in getting it in motion. Like, *now*. Today!"

His left knee was anxiously bobbing up and down at a humming-bird's pace.

I said nothing.

I knew firsthand how harsh and heartless firms could be when money was on the line. And I was sure that in his career as managing partner, Doug had participated in that kind of indifferent harshness when it came to firing or dismissing others. But, surprisingly, it didn't diminish my empathy for him at that moment; it made me feel for him more.

Karma was having her way with Doug, and it was painful to witness.

"So, how do you feel about that ultimatum, Doug?" I intentionally posed the question that way.

"Like I just got hit in the back of the head with a frying pan, Elena."

He laughed smugly to himself, looking down at his aging hands. "Funny, isn't it? Who could have predicted that a lifetime of the highest achievement would end up like this?" He paused and then looked up at me with a resigned expression on his face. "Just call me Felix, Elena. Just call me Felix Unger."

"Sure," I said, "as long as you call me Oscar Madison, okay? I mean, you have to admit it, Doug, you and me working together? We certainly do make an odd couple, don't you think?"

Doug nodded his head while he quietly laughed to himself.

It was the first time I'd seen him shine an authentic smile.

Doug and I worked together for almost eighteen months. And while he was reluctant to "talk about his feelings" in the traditional way he might with a psychotherapist, he was surprisingly eager to sort out the internal and external challenges and obstacles that were preventing him from making progress. While he might never become fully immersed in understanding his emotions and psychological motivations, he was willing to look at his ambivalence, frustration, and anger at having to "give it all up" at what he believed was the height of his career. His developing insight into his feelings and emotions was pivotal to his correcting course, moving on, and taking action.

During our work together, a personal tragedy brought his priorities into sharper focus. Doug suffered the loss of his mother, who had struggled with Alzheimer's for nearly ten years. That was the straw that broke the camel's back, and it was during his grieving for his mother that Doug was slowly able to access his feelings of grief over a stellar career that was now coming to a close. The loss of his mother seemed to permit him to feel some compassion for himself for the first time in a long time. He was able to truly feel sadness, loss, and grief over the circumstances of his forced retirement, but over time, his ability to identify and handle these difficult emotions freed him up to start thinking creatively and envisioning the next chapter of his life.

By the time we ended our coaching engagement, Doug was less focused on the partner infighting that was going on in the buildup to his retirement. He became more and more excited about launching the new investment fund that he had formed with some other buddies from college. Doug was still able to stay connected to his lifelong client contacts, but he was also able to start designing a new chapter that allowed him to be more creative, travel more, and take the kinds of risks that fed his adrenaline needs. I lost touch with Doug over the years, but for me, he has always symbolized the very high emotional price that many Achievement-Addicted professionals pay once there is no more race to run and win.

Achievement Addiction

➢ enabled Doug to repress his feelings and emotions for decades which left him feeling paralyzed and lost in the face of an unmanageable professional crisis;

➢ caused Dough to deny the reality of his impending retirement for nearly three years; and

➢ induced in Doug a form of Achievement Trance that had him mindlessly continuing his practice as if he would be at the firm forever.

Achievement Addiction DETOX helped Doug

➢ recognize the impact that suppressing his emotions was having on his health, family, and well-being;

➢ process some of the emotions brought out by his forced retirement so that he could strategize his next step; and

➢ control the negative self-talk that partly prevented him from moving on to the next chapter in his life.

Minimization and Mental Health

Sometimes, as much as we may try, we are not entirely in touch with or in control of our emotions. The sad truth is that mental illness can rob you of control over your thoughts, emotions, and behavior.

As someone who has struggled with depression, PTSD, and anxiety for most of my life, I know firsthand how mental illness can hijack my mindset, emotions, and behaviors. Medication and therapy have certainly helped, but sometimes they are not enough. Occasionally, despite all my best efforts, depression, and anxiety still eclipse the curative remedies of my self-care routines, treatment plans, spiritual practices, and accumulated self-knowledge. In those moments, I have had to learn how to seek out more help and support.

Many Achievement Addicts lack these supports and don't ask for help. For many reasons (discussed in detail in Step 5: SUPPORT), Achievement Addicts typically reject diagnosis, therapy, medication, or support of any kind. For many, their work environments stigmatize mental illness, and they do not want to be seen as weak, incapable, or "less than."

And with any stigmatization, we invite its evil twin: *minimization*. What do I mean by that? When we are frightened to admit to ourselves or others that we are struggling with something because of stigmatization, our automatic tendency is to reject our emotions. We "push it down," "push it away," or minimize its impact on our lives. If we are really excellent at minimizing, we may ultimately enter a state of absolute denial.

Mark was a client who had mastered the art of emotional minimization to the point of complete self-destruction.

Immovable Mark

Mark was a seasoned and highly experienced trial lawyer in his early forties who enlisted my services after hearing me speak at a conference. He worked at a large, prominent law firm in New York City and had dedicated his entire life to succeeding at the firm. Unfortunately, the price of dedication to his career was that at the age of forty-something, he had "no life, no social life, and no family in NYC."

Mark wasn't clear about why he wanted to work with me or what he wanted out of the coaching process.

"I'm stuck" was his go-to phrase for describing his malaise. But even with a lot of probing on my part, Mark couldn't articulate what he wanted to change in his life.

From the first day we met, I noticed that his expressions were flat and his tone of voice hollow. Almost every probing question I asked about his career elicited the same knee-jerk response: "I don't know." Mark's body was sitting in my office, but his mind was somewhere else far, far away.

Mark was polite, appropriate, and responsive enough during our coaching sessions, but his eyes always seemed glassy and empty. He was only going through the motions of engaging in our discussions. On the surface, everything seemed normal, but something felt really off for me. After a couple of sessions of getting nowhere, he finally said he wanted to explore the possibility of a career change but had no idea where to start or whether it was even an option for him. After nearly a month of coaching, he finally admitted that his position at the firm was at a dead end. After years of Mark's dedication to the firm, the chair of the firm had told him that he would never be promoted to partner, and that he should make his peace with that. Mark was just grateful that he had a job.

That's when Mark admitted that he hadn't had a raise in five years. And that's when I learned that he had initiated some efforts to leave his job in the past, but despite receiving offers at other law firms and even a couple of corporate in-house roles, he was chronically unable to take the leap into something new. He would try to leave. He'd interview and get a new job. But then, at the last minute, he'd back out. Time and time again. And when I asked why he had turned down multiple opportunities to leave his dead-end job at his firm, his answer was always "I don't know."

I later found out that there was also no reason for Mark to stay in New York City, outside of this job. His family was in California, and he was divorced, had no kids, and wasn't seeing anyone. His social life had completely dried up as a result of years of being chained to his desk. He didn't even love the city itself or the small studio apartment in Brooklyn that he had been renting for nearly ten years.

Mark was beyond stuck; Mark was a *dead-inside* human. Every once in a while, he would awkwardly burst into laughter, and I'd get a glimpse of the lively person he'd once been. But that flickering of life was quickly snuffed out again by the inertia that had become part of his persona. I sometimes thought he was depressed, but he told me his primary doctor had put him on some low-dose medication. At other times, I thought Mark might be addicted to anti-anxiety meds and that he had been chomping down on too much Ativan or Xanax. But no, Mark didn't take any of those drugs because he was scared of their addictive nature.

After three months of working together, I concluded that Mark was psychologically paralyzed; he was petrified of change. It seemed to me that he was addicted to being stuck and complaining about it. We weren't making any progress, and I wasn't prepared to be his merry-go-round coach for much longer. It's not uncommon for coaches to transition clients who are absolutely unwilling to take risks, stick to plans, or even budge from their current perch. We weren't a good fit, I concluded. Mark deserved to work with someone who could help him, and I wasn't that person. It was time for some hard truths.

"Mark, I'm going to be straight here, and you may not like what I have to say. But, after a lot of thought, I don't think it makes sense for us to work together anymore," I said to him during a session one fall afternoon.

"Why do you say that?" he asked, expressionless.

"Truth is, either you're going to fire me, or I'm going to fire you," I explained, alluding to the fact that we'd been in this hamster wheel for nearly three months, and if he wasn't willing to budge in any direction, I would never be effective as his coach. I was also frustrated for him because he tolerated an ongoing abusive relationship with his firm and the senior partner. Mark knew all this, and yet he was unable and unwilling to take that first step toward changing his life. It was genuinely futile, and I didn't know what else I could do.

"I still don't understand," Mark repeated several times.

In a moment of exasperation, I looked at him and said, "Look, Mark. You need to make some changes. You know that. But for whatever reason, this process is not helping you get unstuck; it just may be that we are not the right fit."

Mark was still looking at me blankly.

Sometimes powerful coaching demands absolute, brutal honesty. Without varnish. And sometimes, not always, there is a nugget of truth in that honesty that can make all the difference. Mark needed the truth, and I was ready to take my chances with the fallout.

"Mark, do I have your permission to be completely honest with you?"

He nodded.

I took a deep breath. This was not going to be easy.

"First, if what I'm about to say upsets you or insults you, I am prepared to apologize and clean it up later, but I really believe that you need to hear this. So here goes. You are not stuck, Mark. You are way past stuck. Truth is, between your job, your social life, and your living conditions, it's as if you are paralyzed. It's . . . it's more like you've given up on your life. There is no air. No way out. It's as if you've allowed yourself to be completely buried alive by your circumstances."

Mark's eyes widened for a moment; then he looked down at the carpet and folded his arms in front of his chest defensively. He was silent. Then, almost imperceptibly, he began to sway back and forth in his chair.

I immediately recognized his automatic, self-soothing rocking behavior as a tell-tale sign of trauma. I had spent nearly two years working as a clinical social worker at New York-Presbyterian Hospital in Westchester, New York, in the Borderline Unit, treating patients who suffered from depression, chronic suicidality, schizophrenia, drug-induced psychosis, and bipolar disorders. Something had just triggered Mark, and it was causing him to dissociate mildly. I had seen this type of defensive and regressive reaction in others before. It appeared to me that he was experiencing a flashback of some sort.

Mark had a fixed expression, had turned ashen, and still had his arms folded defensively across his torso. He was still staring at the carpet, rocking himself gently for what felt like ten minutes but in reality, was only a couple of seconds.

Looking away from me into the distance, he started speaking slowly.

"Tell me," he said in a monotone whisper, "where were you on 9/11?"

He was now looking past me, and I could see that his eyes were filling with tears. Caught off guard by the question, I briefly shared that I had been safe in Westchester with my little ones, watching the news in horror as everything unfolded.

Mark's story was a little different.

He went back to looking down at the carpet. He'd stopped rocking, but he was still in silent contemplation.

I tried to break the silence.

"Where were—" but he cut me off mid-question.

"I was there," he started.

I got caught mid-breath, and I gasped quietly.

Dear God . . . oh no . . . what did you just say to him?

I could feel the floodgates of guilt start to drown out his voice. But I refocused in time to hear him resume.

"I was there," he said even more flatly. "My office was across the street from the second tower. I watched it all happen. All I remember is running down twelve flights of stairs and out of the building. I needed to get to the subway, to try to get away. The moment I stepped outside, I was instantly covered head to toe in soot," he continued. "Someone fell on top of me, and seconds later, everything went dark."

He stopped speaking, and his breathing was heavy. He took a sip of water and then finally looked directly at me. And for the first time in nearly three months, Mark looked flushed, present, emotional—and very much alive.

Mark had been *literally* buried that fateful day, and his life from that day on had slowly begun to take on all the qualities of a buried, subterranean existence.

Even though this conversation was taking place more than ten years after that tragic day, Mark talked about it as if it had happened last week. He was reliving it all over again, right there in my office.

I later learned that despite the trauma, Mark hadn't sought out consistent support in the form of therapy, and he hadn't addressed the direct residual effects of PTSD caused by his experience on 9/11. He had thought he could "tough it out" and that seeking treatment would just make him "weaker." He'd decided to try to forget it, push it down, and just go on with his life and pursuits. But it was clear now that his PTSD from that day had crept up silently behind him and was choking the life force out of his world.

Our "failed" work together turned out to be anything but a failure. Over time, Mark uncovered that his paralytic stucked-ness was directly related to the trauma he'd suffered on that day.

What we were able to piece together was that because Mark had been in transit and trying to escape his office on the morning when tragedy had sent him hurling into complete horror, he had developed a deep-seated fear of any transition. Mark associated leaving his job, or going through any other change, with death and horror. He felt that everything would be destroyed amid any sort of change. His mindset was fixed in a loop that associated all change with horror. It then made sense why he was unwilling and unable to leave his current job and New York City.

Once Mark and I were able to pinpoint what was causing him not to take any risks or leaps to free himself from his toxic work environment, he realized that he needed to seek professional help for his PTSD. With more than a little convincing, I suggested that he start working with a cognitive-behavioral therapist who could better address Mark's thought distortions associated with change. He agreed to try it out. That was a massive step for him. Once he was in good therapeutic hands treating PTSD from a cognitive modality, he was better able to make the changes he wanted in his life.

Mark is an extreme, vivid example of how untreated mental illness can impact our day-to-day mindset in dangerous and sabotaging ways. Mark needed more than career coaching; he needed therapy and proper medical intervention for his PTSD. **Coaching can never serve as a replacement for psychotherapy or psychopharmacological intervention for those of us suffering from mental illness.** Only after psychological treatment for his PTSD could Mark embark on the career changes he wanted in his life. Over time, he realized that he didn't need to bury himself to remain safe, and he ultimately left his law firm and New York City, accepting an in-house role in California, closer to his friends and family.

In the past several years, the reality of chronic mental illness in high-achieving professions, like law, banking, business, and medicine, has been brought to light by professional associations such as the American Bar Association and numerous journalists. Until recently, admitting that you struggled with mental illness made you a professional pariah and could cost you your job, your promotion, and your growth and success.

Achievement Addiction

➤ enabled Mark to minimize the trauma and pain associated with his experience on 9/11 for fear that seeking treatment might compromise his career and his promotion to partner;

➤ exacerbated Mark's pre-existing mental and emotional challenges and diminished his sense of autonomy over his life's direction; and

➤ induced in Mark a form of Achievement Trance that had him stuck in a "go-nowhere" career.

Achievement Addiction DETOX helped Mark

➤ process some of the difficult emotions prompted by his failed marriage and career setbacks so that he could strategize his next step;

➤ seek out therapeutic intervention to address his 9/11 PTSD; and

➤ start on the road to recovery which allowed him to create a new vision for his life and career.

STEP 3: EMOTIONS
The IMAGO Coaching Questions

Now it's time for you to work on the third step—EMOTIONS—using several IMAGO Coaching Questions. All the questions below are designed to help you work Step 3 and deepen your understanding of how Achievement Addiction has impacted and/or suppressed your expression of emotions and feelings.

In addition, after each question, I offer you a way to summarize your third-step insights in the form of a declaratory sentence. These summarized insights will be essential to refer to should you choose to download and complete the Achievement Addiction DETOX Worksheets accessible at www.achievementaddictiondetox.com.

To recap, the IMAGO Coaching Method invites you to INQUIRE, MAGNIFY, ACT, GROW, and OWN.

The questions below can help you work this third step.

Inquire

What emotions have you suppressed in the past to pursue specific achievements?

_____

_____

_____

On any typical day, how would you describe your typical emotional set point?

_____

_____

_____

In my addictive pursuit of achievement, I have ignored or suppressed my emotions about . . .

_____

_____

_____

In my addictive pursuit of achievement, my emotional set point is . . .

_____

_____

_____

Magnify

Of the emotions and feelings you have suppressed, what singular emotion have you chronically suppressed?

_____

Has your emotional set point caused you pain, discomfort, or challenges with others? If so, how?

_____

_____

_____

In my addictive pursuit of achievement, the one emotion I have suppressed the most is _____, and it has caused me to feel . . .

_____

_____

Because my emotional set point is _____, I suffer in the following way:

_____

_____

. . . and the people around me suffer in the following way:

_____

_____

Act

Think about the most difficult emotional challenge you are struggling with right now. What action would you be willing to take to improve that situation?

_____

_____

I want to take the following action steps toward reconnecting with my genuine emotions:

Reconnecting with my true feelings and emotions about _____ would mean that . . .

_____

_____

_____

Grow

What might a shift in that emotional set point mean to you? To your family and friends?

_____

_____

_____

I want to grow and improve my overall ability to connect with my genuine emotions once again because it would mean that . . .

_____

_____

_____

Own

Hopefully, answering these questions has helped you increase your awareness of how achievement has impacted your emotions, feelings, and emotional set point. So, let's turn to owning that newfound awareness around your EMOTIONS.

When it comes to my emotions and feelings concerning achievement, I own and acknowledge that my present emotional set point is _____ and that if I could take steps to improve my connection to my emotions and feelings, it would mean . . .

_____

_____

_____

_____

_____

FINAL THOUGHTS
Emotions, Feelings, and Achievement Addiction

✓ Allowing our feelings and emotions (Step 3) to surface and inform our thoughts, actions, and beliefs is a crucial step toward reconnecting with and valuing our true selves.

✓ As Achievement Addicts, many of us were taught to ignore, suppress, deny, or devalue our feelings, leaving us disconnected from our real emotions, beliefs, and sense of self-worth.

✓ When we start to identify and process our feelings and emotions and allow them to surface, we begin to disempower the false self that drives and perpetuates our Achievement Addiction.

STEP 4

SUPPORT
Ask For Help

A Culture of Isolation Creates the Perfect Storm

*"Look around the room; everyone here is your competition in achiev-
ing your goals. Look at the person on your right and the one on your left.
At the end of law school, one of you won't be here and won't make it."*

I remember this speech given by one of my law school professors in the first week of my first semester. From the day I started law school, I was taught, like many others, that law was a solo act. Support systems were lacking at best, and I was on my own to compete for grades, positions, recognition, law-firm spots, clerkships, and any other key achievement indicators. Study groups in law school were purely efficient, temporary political and intellectual *Lord of the Flies* alliances designed to leverage the group effort to devour as much information as possible for the singular good.

The toxic impact of the highly isolative culture in law—along with other high-achieving professions—has not gone unnoticed. In the past decade, there has been some progress in reducing isolation, as certain workplaces promote the fact that their culture fosters a collaborative environment. But

149

despite well-intentioned efforts on the part of some workplaces, most are—by design—a breeding ground for institutionalized isolation. Everything is designed to maximize production and create compartments and sub-silos for resource leverage. Ever-increasing client demands and expectations make it nearly impossible to maintain friendships, interpersonal relationships, or a sense of community. Sadly, real collaboration frequently falls by the wayside as ambitious Achievement Addicts in various professions are still conditioned to believe they are on their own to survive. It is each man/woman for themselves.

But the gravitational pull toward these toxic environments has its roots in our past histories. As Achievement Addicts, many of us were bred in financially or emotionally deprived environments where we learned early on that we had only ourselves to rely on and that achievement was the surest way to maximize limited resources and praise. And as we grew up, many of us gravitated toward social, relational, and work environments that reinforced those familiar beliefs and habits. So if you have any trace of Achievement Addiction, I guarantee that at least one or perhaps all of the following thoughts have crossed your mind somewhere between one and a thousand times:

- I can do this alone.
- I should be able to do this alone.
- I have to do this alone.
- To be self-reliant means being alone.
- I have to push through this alone.
- I have to prove I can get through this alone.
- I have always done this alone and always will.
- The price of success is being alone.
- The price of high achievement is being alone.
- People of high achievement are loners and go at it alone.
- The more alone I am, the more I can achieve.
- I can't trust anyone around me.
- I can't really rely on anyone to help me.
- I can't ask too many questions.
- I can't ask for too much help or guidance.

- If I can't do this alone, maybe I'm not cut out for this profession.
- If I need help, something must be wrong with me.
- If I need support, something must be wrong with me.

Do any of these sound familiar to you? I thought so. For me, I know at least a handful of these thoughts still succeed in polluting my thoughts, even though I know better.

And when you couple an Achievement Addict's natural propensity toward isolation with a stressful work environment that culturally and operationally reinforces that tendency, you have the makings of a perfect storm.

Isolation culture is only growing. As law firms, banks, corporations, etc. continue to expand globally, as many continue (or are forced) to work remotely, and as clients are no longer willing to pay for training younger professionals, isolation culture in the workplace has run rampant. People on the same floor no longer get up to talk to one another; they email or text. People on the same client team have never seen some of their teammates face-to-face, much less had a non-work conversation. And during the pandemic, when we have all been forced to work and communicate exclusively through virtual/video conferencing, many workers "opt-out" of the video option altogether, preferring the obscurity of a disembodied voice. This isolation can trigger or exacerbate existing mental health concerns, such as anxiety, depression, addictions, or something more severe.

Corral together an Achievement-Addicted population operating from a fear-dominated mindset and then apply endless work demands, chronic stress, and perfectionistic expectations onto them in an isolative culture that also stigmatizes any signs of weakness or mental illness . . . and, well, what you've just created is the perfect fission reactor for real psychological disaster.

The full eruption of this psychological volcano has hit the news and has become the focus of many workplace studies and reports.

And for decades, many of these professional, highly successful Achievement Addicts—who were literally dying under the weight of Achievement Addiction—have been finding their way into my office under the guise of "career coaching," "executive coaching," or "business development coaching." They were desperate for support, help, and guidance.

Sebastian was one of many refugees from that perfect storm.

Suicidal Sebastian

Sebastian called me out of the blue one day after being referred to me by an acquaintance. I could barely hear him when he spoke, but I assumed there was just something wrong with the phone. Sebastian was initially very cryptic in his reasoning for why he was coming to me. He sent me his résumé and scheduled a time to meet at my office.

Sebastian showed up for our first appointment in a three-piece suit and tightly knotted tie. He sat down, robotically awkward and pin-straight, and his foot was nervously tapping. He looked visibly uncomfortable, but he was silent.

"I took a look at your résumé. Very impressive! So, what brings you to coaching?" I asked to break the awkward silence. Sebastian looked right through me with his dulled brown eyes and didn't say a word.

I waited; his blank stare continued.

"What's on your mind, Sebastian?" I probed.

More silence. Then Sebastian looked at me casually and answered my question.

"Killing myself. Yes. That is what is on my mind. Yes. That's about right." He mouthed those words with the deliberate, eerie calmness frequently typical of an actively suicidal person.

I said nothing and remained equally calm.

But under the surface, I knew I had the therapist I referred clients to on speed dial, my phone was next to me, and I was ready to call 911 and jump into an ambulance with Sebastian if I needed to.

I have done this before; people in this situation are not my preferred coaching clients, but after fifteen years in this job, I've come to realize that suicidality and other harmful thoughts are alarmingly common in the legal world. Unfortunately, it was so common that it helped drive my decision to focus my therapeutic and academic training on chronic suicidality.

So, having treated the chronically suicidal for nearly two years as an intern, I knew the drill cold:

- Determine whether the client has a plan.
- Call 911 and get the client to an ER for evaluation.
- Contract with the client for safety (either verbally or by having the client sign a contract with you stating that until they reach the ER they will not harm themselves).
- Refer the person to a psychotherapist immediately.
- Once the client is stabilized, make a joint determination with the therapist as to whether the client can tolerate coaching in addition to traditional therapy.
- Contract for safety again, then cross your fingers and pray.

"I was fired yesterday," Sebastian supplied. "On my way to your office, I strongly considered jumping in front of the uptown 6 train but reconsidered." His voice was flat and serene, like the coastline before a tsunami.

"Sebastian, how are you feeling right now?" I asked, controlling the alarm in my voice.

"Calm. Okay . . . numb."

"Sebastian, I believe you. And I want to help you in any way I can, but I am under an obligation to call 911 and get you to an ER ASAP. You will need to be okay with that decision. Do I have your permission?" I knew there was no need for me to delay that move. Sebastian had all the signs of someone ready to harm himself.

Silence.

I wasn't really asking permission. Sebastian was heading to the ER. This was happening. It was my job to keep him safe until the ambulance got to my office.

More silence. Sebastian wanted and needed help, and he wasn't fighting me.

"Yes," he finally answered.

"Do you have a therapist I can call, Sebastian?"

"Yes," he replied. "Let me speak to him. I'm okay to speak to him. I will call him right now. Is that okay?" he asked. He finally blinked for what seemed to be the first time since entering my office. He called his therapist, and the three of us spoke about Sebastian's condition. We then agreed to call 911 and that the therapist would meet Sebastian at the hospital, where he had admitting privileges.

While waiting for the ambulance to arrive, Sebastian continued his wooden monologue: "I'm sorry to burden you with all this. My wife left me. She's been having an affair with the managing partner of her law firm. I've known about this for years. I looked the other way. Thought it would pass. Thought I could make her happy. But she left me for him and is threatening to take away my two boys. And now I got fired from my firm because— according to them—I can't bring in business. I'm a partner, and they fired me like it was nothing. Like I was nothing."

I said nothing.

"That's when I called you."

He shared the devastation of spending fifteen years at a firm that could just drop him like a bad habit. And he started to describe all the years of self-sacrifice he had dedicated to making partner and keeping his wife in a lavish lifestyle.

I still said next to nothing. I was there to listen, abide, watch, and create a safe space for him until the ambulance came.

Then, out of the blue, as if he were telling me the breed of dog he had at home, he blurted out, "Oh. I have a gun."

"Where?" I inquired calmly despite the alarm bells that set off in my mind. I quickly eyed the briefcase and backpack he had with him. For all I knew, his gun might have been packed somewhere inside one of those bags.

"In my car. In the glove compartment. It's legal, registered, of course," he added for my comfort.

Police officers began to arrive at that moment, and Sebastian was back on the phone with his therapist. Sebastian walked out of my office building as if he and I were about to take a stroll along the East River. Once outside, I offered to accompany him to the hospital, but he declined, and the police assured me that he was in good hands. Then, as if in a scene from a movie, the window of the police car suddenly rolled down, and out popped Sebastian's face, expressive with concern.

"Everything here is confidential, right? I mean, you won't tell my firm about this, will you?"

"Of course not," I replied.

"Okay. Good. Thanks," he said, and the car sped off to the nearest ER, leaving me on the corner of Park Avenue and East 36th Street. As I watched the ambulance follow Sebastian, I finally exhaled. It would take a little longer for my heart to stop pounding in my ears.

Even while he was in the grip of a full-on suicidal episode, Sebastian was more concerned about appearances at the firm—at which he was no longer employed!—than about himself.

About a month later, I received a call from Sebastian telling me that his therapist would be calling me and that we should discuss the possibility of resuming our coaching relationship. Together with the therapist, we devised a plan that would keep Sebastian in therapy, medically stabilized, and positively focused on his career in a way that would not add to his stress. While Sebastian and I worked on his résumé, we talked about his passions and interests before law-firm life. In addition, we worked on a way to get him reconnected with his love for horses and journalism by exploring alternative legal careers outside of corporate practice.

Sebastian had hit rock bottom and was in a genuine state of crisis. But even amid that psychological chaos, there was a part of him that was well enough to know to seek help. He couldn't go at it solo anymore. So together we built a support team that got him stable, treated, and focused on the future in a manageable way.

His therapist and I connected weekly at first and then monthly. Sebastian managed to find an opportunity that focused on legal journalism, writing for legal publications. It was the professional pivot that ultimately saved his life.

Achievement Addiction

➤ compromised Sebastian's ability to handle personal and career setbacks;

➤ had Sebastian believing that seeking support would compromise his success as a lawyer; and

➤ exacerbated Sebastian's pre-existing mental condition that led to his suicidal ideation.

Achievement Addiction DETOX helped Sebastian

➤ recognize the impact that Achievement Addiction was having on his health, family, and well-being;

➤ process some of the difficult emotions prompted by his failed marriage and career setbacks; and

➤ find the support he needed to regain his mental stability and move on to the next chapter in his life.

We are not supposed to go at this thing called life alone. No matter who you are. Or how smart you are. Support has made all the difference for me and others.

Sebastian's story reverberates with lessons about self-awareness, negative self-talk, mindset, mental illness stigmatization, thought distortion, and Achievement Addiction, among others. Precisely because Sebastian embodied so many of the issues and challenges we've discussed so far, I chose to tell his story through the lens of support.

As Achievement Addicts, the worst thing we tell ourselves is that we are alone in our suffering and that "being successful" means having to endure all this suffering and self-sacrifice by ourselves. Sebastian's story reminds me every day that the difference between life and death is frequently a function of the support you have or seek out in your life.

Stigma, Mental Illness, and Achievement Addiction

So, let's talk about the elephants in the Achievement Addiction board-room: **mental illness and stigma**.

In our society, the stigma around mental illness continues to be real and palpable. And the fallout from this kind of institutionalized stigma includes minimization, denial, self-medication, addictions, and, frequently, self-harm.

Let's take a quick look at the numbers.

How prevalent is mental illness, and how is mental illness defined?

Health-focused medical organizations worldwide have collected data on mental illness (a.k.a. mental disorders) for many decades. The data has not changed much in the past decade or so, and it indicates that *in the United States,*

- almost **half** of the adults (**46.4 percent**) will experience a mental illness during their lifetime, and
- **one in five** adults (**18 or older**) experience a mental illness in any one year; this is the equivalent of **51.5 million** Americans in 2019.[1]

Although it sounds scary and there is a real stigma attached to even bringing the subject into conversations, the profession defines mental illness broadly as any "mental, behavioral, or emotional disorder."

Read that again:

Mental illness is any "mental, behavioral, or emotional disorder."

Regardless of the degree of severity of the affliction (mild to full-blown), this definition includes *depression, anxiety, schizophrenia, addictions, substance abuse, bipolar disorder, Alzheimer's disease, suicide*, and other afflictions.

Again, mental illnesses formally include:

[1] Sources: NIH/NIMH data.

depression, anxiety,
addictions and substance abuse,
suicide and suicidal tendencies,
bipolar disorder, schizophrenia,
and Alzheimer's disease.

Anxiety disorders are the most common mental illness in the US, affecting **40 million** adults (**18.1 percent** of us) every year. Anxiety disorders are highly treatable, yet less than **37 percent** of those suffering from them seek or receive any treatment. Add to this the fact that **33 percent** of the world's population (well over **2 *billion*** people) will suffer an anxiety disorder at some time in their lifetime.[2]

Depression is likewise a common human affliction. Nearly **a quarter *billion*** people worldwide suffer from depression in any given year.

All told, ***450 million*** people in the world—nearly **half a *billion*** individuals—experience some form of mental illness (i.e., among *all* identified mental illnesses, including depression) in any given year.[3]

So, why am I throwing these scary numbers at you?

Because Achievement Addicts are loath to seek support for their suffering, many let their mental illnesses go undiagnosed and untreated for decades. Their excuses? "I'm too busy." "I can deal." "I don't want anyone to know." "Mental illness will stigmatize me as weak, incapable, a risk." Worse, though, is that many go on to self-medicate in private so that they can continue with their Achievement Addiction. This only compounds their suffering. They are experts at minimizing and denial. They believe achievement should and will magically solve all their problems. And many deny the suffering they endure because their distorted thinking has them believing it is "the price" of achievement and success.

Stigma breeds denial.

And denial is a killer. It almost killed me. It nearly killed Sebastian. And it nearly killed Nathan.

---

2   Source: NIH, WHO data.
3   Source: NIH, WHO data.

The American Psychiatric Association defines *mental illness* this way:

*"Mental illnesses are health conditions involving **changes** in emotion, thinking or behavior (or a combination of these).*

*"Mental illnesses are associated with **distress** and/or **problems** functioning in social, work, or family activities."*

The Worth Health Organization defines *mental health* as:
- "a state of *wellbeing* in which the individual realizes his or her abilities,
- can cope with the normal stresses of life,
- can work productively and fruitfully, and
- is able to make a contribution to his or her community."

Nathan the Painter

Nathan was fresh out of law school when we were introduced, and he came to me for help adjusting to his new Big Law firm. Nathan was a sharp guy—a graduate of Columbia Law School with an undergraduate degree from Harvard. He was well put together, very charismatic, and he had an innate magnetism that made him a standout in any room.

He reached out to me during his first year at his firm after recalling a skill-building presentation I had done for his class at Columbia. We started down a standard path for a first-year associate looking to lay a solid foundation in law-firm practice. We worked on basic benchmarks like how to get the "good assignments," how to become professionally visible at a law firm, how to create boundaries, how to manage caseloads, time management tactics, and how to gently say no to partner requests—necessary survival skills for most young lawyers.

About two months into our sessions together, Nathan brought his notebook in to show me.

He was visibly excited; his eyes were wide and glistening, and he was very animated.

Nathan was usually an impeccable dresser and very well-groomed. But something was off that day. His suit looked a little wrinkled, as did his shirt, and he looked like he hadn't shaved in about two days. It seemed unlike him, but I chalked it up to him perhaps having pulled an all-nighter on a case or deal.

Out of his backpack, he pulled a metal cup.

"You know what this is?" he said loudly and excitedly.

Before I could answer, he was off.

"This is how you make yerba maté! Oh my God, have you ever had maté?! It's *amazing.* . . . I mean, better than coffee, better than any of those caffeinated drinks. I mean, maté tastes like shit in the beginning, but you have to get used to it, you know? I mean, not everything that's good for you tastes good, right? Take okra, for example. Seriously, who really likes okra? I guess some people do, but I don't, but I hear it's sooooo healthy for you. Anyway, back to the maté . . ."

This monologue about the maté went on for a bit. I couldn't get a word in edgewise if I tried. But after I'd waited a respectable amount of time to see how this might connect to the work we wanted to focus on during that session, it was clear that Nathan was on a rambling tangent that was going nowhere fast. So I interrupted him.

"Nathan, truth is, I hate to disappoint you, but I hate maté. Glad you like it so much. But unless there is something specific you want to work on or update me on about this week, let's talk about your assignment."

Nathan jumped straight to attention.

"Sorry, sorry, sorry. Right. Oh my God! I totally forgot to tell you what I worked on this week!" He leaned into his dusty backpack that looked like it was about to explode with papers and started rummaging around again.

"Great. Let's start there," I said, thinking he was going to share his completed assignment for this coaching session.

He triumphantly pulled out a black-and-white composition notebook and held it high in the air as he exclaimed with equal dramatic flair, "I'm writing a brilliant dissertation on how to be a lawyer. I mean a super-successful lawyer.

"This is the book that *has* to be written," he continued at a pressured pace. "I mean, who better than me to write it, right? Imagine if I wrote a book for young lawyers giving them the intestinal workings of the bowels of this big behemoth thing that we are all terrified of, you know, the law firm. . . . I mean . . ." He kept going on, talking faster and faster and elaborating more on the "animal" nature of legal practice. He was no longer making sense.

Something was off. His associations and word choices were getting stranger and stranger. He handed me the notebook, and I saw that it resembled something a spirograph could have created—graphological words written with tiny letters formed circle patterns all over every page. It was intriguing to look at but instantly concerning.

For the rest of that session, alarm bells were going off in my head all over the place. But with a lot of effort and redirecting, we were able to steer the session back on track, and by the end of it, Nathan's enthusiasm about "nailing this coaching thing" seemed a little over the top to me. I again chalked it up to his energetic way in the world.

Over the next two sessions, things grew progressively odder. The discussions were becoming even more tangential, erratic, grandiose, and disconnected, but I managed to peel back the layers and get closer to the truth about Nathan.

I learned that he was from an upper-middle-class industrialist family in Argentina. Lately, Nathan had had dreams that he was from a family of healers. During my last session with him, he was determined to talk only about his most recent dream despite multiple attempts to redirect the focus onto coaching.

"So in the dream, I'm speaking only Spanish, but I see my ancestor . . . and I look, and I see Jesus in the dream, and he is talking to me, Elena. He is looking at me and talking to me, and I think . . . I mean, I know you think I might be weird, but I saw him appear in front of me yesterday, and I really think he was sending me a message that my real calling in life . . ."

Okay. That was it! If there was one thing I learned in the locked ward at New York–Presbyterian Hospital (as an intern), it was that you do not ever, ever, ever indulge or accept a person's delusion. You don't challenge it, but you also don't give it validity by asking probing questions about it.

"Nathan. I am going to stop you right there. Okay?" I was firm but kind.

"Okay, but you haven't heard the part where . . ." His undeterred compulsion to share his messianic delusion confirmed my growing suspicions about what was happening.

"Nathan, I'm very concerned about you. First things first, are you sleeping at night?" I asked.

"No. But I don't need a lot of sleep. I mean, this project . . ." he said, trying to redirect the conversation back to the delusion.

I was forced to cut him off a second time.

"Nathan, how are you feeling right now? Does anything feel different to you? What do you think is happening to you right now? I have a sense, but I want to hear what you think. Answer my questions. Please."

Nathan stopped talking, looked at me sheepishly, and then started slowly wringing his hands nervously. He looked away from me and down at his hands and then spoke.

"I've been up all night painting. I went out and bought about 100 small, framed canvases so I can finish painting this picture of this recurring dream . . . and, well, I have been calling in sick to the firm to finish the paintings, you understand . . . but I know that once I finish the paintings and the book, I may not need to go back to the firm. . . ." He was still gazing at his hands as he spoke.

"Nathan, please listen to what I am asking. Do you think everything feels okay? Or does something feel a little off or different with you?" I needed to test his connection to reality. If Nathan knew that something was off, it was a good sign. If not, then I needed to get my speed dial ready for 911.

I held my breath. It could go either way.

Nathan looked up at me, and I saw clarity in his eyes that I hadn't seen since the session began.

"I know what you're getting at, Elena." He paused. "I know . . . I know that something is a little off."

An awareness that we are not well, even when our brains might be messing with us, is a sign of wellness.

I exhaled.

"What do you think I need to know, Nathan? How can you help me understand what is happening to you right now? I really want to understand so I can help you," I explained.

Nathan paused a long time. I could tell he was battling something. Finally, he spoke again.

"I stopped taking them," he blurted out.

"Taking what?"

"My meds, Elena. I stopped taking them, okay? They numbed me out and stifled my creativity. This happens every time I stop, but this time, I had it all together, you know? I had made it, a lawyer, a big firm, great life. I was certain I had this thing beat." He was very defeated.

It turned out that Nathan had stopped taking his bipolar medication about three weeks earlier, just about the same time I'd begun encountering a very off-kilter version of him when he came in person to our sessions. His stability had declined rapidly. He gave me permission to connect with his therapist; the therapist and I collaborated on keeping Nathan safe. Eventually, with Nathan's permission, we decided to contact his family. They ended up bringing him back to Argentina, where he entered a full-time inpatient program. He was getting the support and treatment he needed.

Two months after Nathan had returned to Argentina, I received a call from his father, who wanted to let me know that Nathan was doing much better now that he was back home, with support from his family and friends.

"He was all alone in New York, no family, no support, no friends. We understood why he insisted on going to Columbia University but isolating himself in NYC wasn't good for him or his condition. And I don't know why Nathan ever pursued law. He's a painter!" his father exclaimed. He then recounted all the ways he had encouraged Nathan to follow his passion for art. It seemed that Nathan was one of the lucky ones who had parents who were open to his pursuing a career aligned with his passion.

The research shows that latent mental illness comes to full fruition for many of us between ages eighteen and twenty-eight. Unfortunately, this is precisely when many of us start our careers. Many of my clients come to realize that their youthful Achievement-Addicted ambitions led them to choose a high-pressure, stressful career path that they discover is no longer sustainable for them as adults with mental illness. Nathan came to that realization at a very high price.

Nathan believed his bipolar disorder and his need for medication were stigmatizing. The law-firm culture he was in confirmed his beliefs. Unknowingly, he thrust himself into a highly stressful and isolative environment that severely exacerbated his underlying mental illness and further compromised his health. For many of my clients, the comorbidity of a pre-existing mental illness and unchecked Achievement Addiction frequently escalates into a full-blown crisis.

Achievement Addiction

➢ had Nathan believing that seeking support in the form of medication and therapy for his diagnosed mental illness would compromise his success as a lawyer;

➢ led Nathan to make choices that escalated into a genuine mental and physical crisis that culminated in a psychotic episode; and

➢ induced in Nathan an Achievement Trance that had him believing that achievement was worth sacrificing his mental and physical health.

Achievement Addiction DETOX helped Nathan

➢ find the proper mental health support and resources he needed;

➢ understand the toxic impact that his work environment was having on his health; and

➢ redefine success on his own terms and in a way that was better aligned with his natural talents and abilities.

Oh, Sweet, Sweet Betsy

For many of us, isolation and stress don't necessarily result in pathology, addiction, or mental breakdown. In fact, for many, these twin evils just leave us irritable and volatile.

Many, like Betsy, just end up becoming insufferable.

Betsy was all sunshine, butterflies, and rainbows. Overly polite, cloyingly sweet, instantly accommodating, and enviably efficient, she ultimately invited a swell of dislike from most of the folks at her firm. She was one of those phony, suffer-in-silence martyrs who refuse to delegate anything or collaborate with others. She peppered her sentences with passive-aggressive, backhanded comments about having to do everything herself. Because Betsy was a huge moneymaker, the firm had turned a blind eye to her bad behavior for years, but now she was beginning to try the patience of her partners.

Ultimately, Betsy's law firm referred her to me because her prickly and alienating style of practice presented a possible liability to the firm. As a senior associate, she was withholding work from partners and colleagues, isolating her matters so that no one else knew what she was doing, and working endless hours around the clock. Partners believed that Betsy was now putting the firm at risk should she slip up. The firm was more than happy to milk endless hours from her, but not at the cost of a possible malpractice suit down the road. Now Betsy not only was disliked but also couldn't be trusted. The firm wanted her "fixed," but not so much that she reduced her billable hours. They wanted my help reining her in a bit so that she would delegate more and become more friendly and collaborative.

So we arranged to meet.

Betsy floated into my office exuding a fairy-like demeanor and other-worldly smile. She was the embodiment of beauty pageant perfect, a former dancer standing no higher than five-foot-two with meticulously coiffed blonde hair. I immediately understood how her confectionary façade could be so off-putting.

After she'd slathered me with an abundance of flattering niceties, I cut to the chase and asked Betsy why she thought the firm wanted her to get some coaching.

"Truthfully, I genuinely have no idea why I'm here or what they want me to work on," she said sweetly with an accompanying childlike shrug of her shoulders and tilt of her head for good measure.

Oh boy. This one's gonna be tough.

"Neither do I," I replied flatly.

At that moment, something inside me was reluctant to spend time volleying the verbal tennis ball over the net with this one. She knew damn well why she was sitting across from me because the firm's managing partner had told me that he'd been direct and firm with her about what needed to change. She just wanted to waste our time.

But she stared at me silently for quite a while, with her fixed, lipsticked smile, and widened her big blue eyes as if to say, "Good try, but I don't break so easily. Your move."

Plan A had failed. Gentle confrontation wasn't going to work with Betsy. Time for plan B.

I have found that sometimes the best way to coax out a highly defended person reluctant to engage with me is by immediately surrendering the face-off and engaging the persona they are presenting with respect and a little flattery. People work very hard to build and maintain a false persona that protects them; no point in trying to storm a century-old stone moat. Let them come out when they feel it's safe.

So I tried again.

"Betsy, it's clear to me that you are a hugely accomplished woman, you are at a top firm, and the partners are clearly impressed enough by you that they want to invest time and money in your development, which is a testament to your importance to the firm," I gushed. "So tell me, I'm always curious about women who manage to make balancing family and a successful career effortless. With two small kids at home, I can barely make sure I have the same pair of shoes on each foot in the morning. So what's a typical day like for you?"

I could see from a brief flicker in her baby blues that Betsy wasn't terribly impressed with my half-assed effort to flatter her. Still, it was clear that she respected my new strategy—one that seemed to mirror her own passive-aggressive approach to handling people in her firm. (Every once in a while I take a gamble, and it works out.)

She had a well-rehearsed response.

In its first iteration, I learned that Betsy started her day at 4:30 in the morning, she worked out, and then she would get to the office like clockwork by 8:30 before the others arrived, so she could hit the ground running while the office was quiet. She worked through lunch and left the office by 7 p.m. because she had a four-year-old son who was very precious to her and demanded a lot of her time. She then would log back onto her computer from home once her son was asleep and work from about 10 p.m. until 2 in the morning. She needed very little sleep, she assured me with a smile. She also told me that she was married to a wildly successful man who worked in finance.

Betsy started opening up a bit about her career ambitions; she was single-minded and talked incessantly about her career, her clients, her plans for business development, her future, the firm, the partners, the likelihood of making partner, etc. She presented me with an impenetrable picture of perfection at work.

She was hell-bent on making partner no matter what. She was oblivious to the way others saw her, experienced her, and related to her. When I gently confronted her repeatedly with some of the law partners' concerns, she genuinely didn't understand why anyone's opinion about her should impact her making partner.

"So long as I keep the clients pleased and bill a ton of hours, nothing should get in my way," she insisted.

Subtlety was not working with her. Betsy needed to hear some brutal truths about what was happening in her career before we could embark on any meaningful change.

"Betsy, okay, so here it goes. Do I have your permission to speak plainly and bluntly about this? Gloves off?"

She nodded calmly.

"Okay, you may not like what I'm about to say, but I can always clean it up later. Betsy, you know as well as I do, that's not the way making partner works anymore. Many subjective requirements need to be met that are sometimes only shared with you once the die has been cast. And one of them is not pissing off partner after partner with a sharp-elbowed, solo-act approach to practice that keeps them in the dark about what is going on with their own damn clients. You are making them nervous, and they don't trust you. No one is gonna tell you the real deal because they want you to keep billing like a maniac, but you need to understand how you are being perceived at the firm."

She was incensed.

"Pissing off partner after partner?! Making them nervous?! Are you fucking kidding me? I make those arrogant, lazy idiots millions and millions of dollars by slogging away doing all the mind-numbing shit work they don't want to do for clients—even at my own expense, my own physical, health expense, and that of my son and family!" Her voice was getting louder as her outrage continued.

"I need to make partner, and I know no one will help me get there except me. I'm not in this for friends or 'community,' Elena, and I don't want to end up another female lawyer statistic with a huge bump on my forehead when I hit the glass ceiling! If I need to hoard work and lots of it with razor-sharp elbows so that some good-ol'-boy jock doesn't end up taking credit behind my back for work that I did, then that protects me and my prospects. What is wrong with that?! Tell me! What is wrong with my being selfish and smart enough to figure out that I need to be front and center on all deals to the exclusion of everyone else—even if it kills me—to make partner?" She was now red in the face and breathing hard.

Betsy had a point. Everything she was saying made sense to me, and she was right about women making partner at law firms. The glass ceiling and old-boy network were both alive and well in the legal profession and other high-achieving professions. I saw firsthand how many workplaces mentored men for promotion while leaving many talented women with the "housekeeping" work that burns them out but never gets them any closer to being promoted.

I respected her and her determination not to be another smart woman to fall victim to the statistics.

But something worried me.

"I hear you, Betsy. I really do, more than you know. I want to put a pin in this discussion and come back to this pointy-elbow solo strategy that unfortunately seems to be backfiring on you without you knowing it. But I gotta stop you for a minute and back up. What do you mean, at your own 'physical, health expense' and that of your son and family?"

Betsy was sitting upright and still in her seat and was drinking a glass of water to calm her nerves. She put down the glass, and that was when Betsy calmly and methodically explained that (1) she was a chronic insomniac and might be overdoing it with Xanax to sleep, (2) her four-year-old had recently been diagnosed with autism, (3) she was married to a man who always traveled and whom she never saw, and (4) she was now filing for divorce.

It all came out like a laundry list of disasters without an emotional quiver in her voice. She was just telling me the facts as if they were happening to someone else.

She took a breath. Not a hair was out of place. Then she looked at me with a hardened look that I will never forget and said, matter-of-factly, "And I found out yesterday that I have breast cancer."

I said nothing.

"And the truth is, I don't have time for cancer. I've gotta make partner," she pronounced, as she crossed her arms in front of her and finally sat back in the chair.

Betsy eventually admitted that she was feeling overwhelmed by all the challenges that were being hurled at her. She had zero support. She didn't seem to have time for anything. She was going for gold, all solo—and now it was literally killing her. Betsy was, figuratively and literally, dying to make partner.

By the end of that rocky first session, we agreed that we would use our time together to work on two challenges simultaneously. We would find her support in dealing with her health and family issues and, at the same time, overhaul her approach to pursuing partnership and design a strategy for making partner that didn't alienate everyone and put her life in jeopardy.

But first, we got down to the business of finding her an oncologist.

Betsy and I worked together on and off for almost two years on both her life and her career. By focusing her coaching on the support she needed, both personally and professionally, Betsy was able to identify and commit to taking action steps in a situation that otherwise felt unmanageable and overwhelming. I lost touch with Betsy after we finished, but ultimately her cancer went into remission, and I understand she left that firm and went on to make partner at a smaller firm.

Achievement Addiction

- ➤ convinced Betsy that seeking support of any sort would compromise her success as a lawyer;
- ➤ led Betsy to make less-than-ideal choices that escalated into a genuine mental and physical crisis that almost compromised her cancer treatment; and
- ➤ induced in Betsy an Achievement Trance that had her believing that achievement was worth sacrificing her mental and physical health.

Achievement Addiction DETOX helped Betsy

- ➤ shake off her Achievement Trance and seek the proper health support and resources she needed;
- ➤ recognize the toxic impact that her work environment was having on her health and her family; and
- ➤ find a work environment that was better suited to her needs, talents, and abilities.

I realize that telling stories about life-or-death situations can tread a slippery slope to hyperbole. The unfortunate truth here is that these scenarios are alarmingly common among Achievement-Addicted professionals. I am sharing them in solidarity and hope to convey that there are solutions and various paths to reach the ever-coveted light at the end of the tunnel. But I also share these stories to drive home the fact that it is up to you to be brave and build your support system. It can literally mean the difference between life and death.

STEP 4: SUPPORT
The IMAGO Coaching Questions

Now it's time for you to work on the fourth step—SUPPORT—using several IMAGO Coaching Questions. All the questions below are designed to help you work this step and deepen your understanding of how Achievement Addiction has increased your sense of isolation and compromised the level of support and community in your life.

Following each question, I offer you a way to summarize your fourth-step insights in the form of a declaratory sentence. These summarized insights will be essential to refer to should you choose to download and complete the Achievement Addiction DETOX Worksheets accessible at www.achievementaddictiondetox.com.

To recap, the IMAGO Coaching Method invites you to INQUIRE, MAGNIFY, ACT, GROW, and OWN.

The questions below can help you work this fourth step.

INQUIRE

How has Achievement Addiction contributed to your sense of isolation and/or compromised the level of support, help, or community you have in your life?

_____

_____

_____

_____

_____

In my addictive pursuit of achievement, I have ignored or suppressed my need for help, support, and/or community in the following ways:

_____

_____

_____

Magnify

How has your level of isolation or lack of support in your life caused you pain, suffering, discomfort, or challenges? With your health? With your mental well-being?

_____

_____

_____

_____

In my addictive pursuit of achievement, my isolation level has caused me to feel _____ and has created several challenges, including . . .

_____

_____

_____

Because of my increased isolation or lack of support, I suffer in the following ways:

_____

_____

_____

. . . and the people around me suffer in the following ways:

_____

_____

_____

Aᴄᴛ

Think about the most difficult challenge you are struggling with right now. What kind of support might help?

_____

_____

What action step would you be willing to take right now to seek out that support?

_____

_____

I would be willing to improve the level of support and community in my life, and I am eager to take the following steps toward reducing my isolation and asking for help:

_____

_____

Gʀᴏw

Take a moment to imagine what it might look like to have more support in your life. What feelings arise?

_____

_____

What would having more support right now mean to you? To your health? To your mental wellness?

_____

_____

When I imagine having more support in my life, I feel _____,
and seeking out more support and reducing isolation in my life would mean
that . . .

_____

_____

O<small>WN</small>

Hopefully, answering these questions has helped you increase your awareness
of how Achievement Addiction has impacted the level of isolation, support,
and community in your life. So, let's turn to owning that newfound awareness
of the role of SUPPORT in overcoming Achievement Addiction.

I own and acknowledge that because of Achievement Addiction, my present
level of isolation leaves me feeling _____, and if I
could take steps to improve the level of support and community in my life,
it would mean . . .

_____

_____

_____

_____

_____

FINAL THOUGHTS
Support, Community, and Achievement Addiction

✓ Finding support (Step 4), community, help, and guidance is a powerful step toward getting unstuck and correcting course. It is a sign of wellness and a practical, achievable step toward reducing isolation and regaining health and sanity.

✓ Many Achievement Addicts were taught that success should be a solo act and that the price of success is paid through isolation, loneliness, and disconnection.

✓ When we ask for help, seek out like-minded people, and invest in community, we start to debunk the myth that we are alone in our suffering and struggles, and that misery is our destiny.

STEP 5

BODY

Move a Muscle

I Think, Therefore I Don't Take Care of My Body

Achievement Addicts are a chair-bound nation. Sit, sit, sit. As Achievement Addicts, many of us barely find time for sleep, much less exercise. We are sedentary from one end of the day to the other. We are proud of our intellect, our power of analysis, and the impact of our own highly refined thinking and discourse. As a result of this mental focus, many of us have lost or thoroughly ignored our bodies' well-being.

Whatever we may know about nutrition goes flying out the window come crunch time in favor of oversalted, oversweetened, and over fatty crap food as our mainstay. Unless your profession has you focused on athletics/sports, many Achievement Addicts are prone to being overweight, under-fit, and vulnerable to all the dangerous chronic illnesses that quietly kill people the most often. They include cardiovascular-pulmonary disease (clogged arteries combined with bad respiratory health that can lead to heart failure and death), diabetes, cancer . . . the list goes on.

In my career alone, I have known of at least three people who suffered fatal heart attacks at their desks at relatively young ages. They were enormously successful attorneys at some of the most prestigious firms in the world.

The insidious price of Achievement Addiction keeps rising higher and higher as we complacently offer up both our mental and physical well-being in the hope of finally achieving that ever-elusive "success." We shrug our shoulders, sigh deeply, and tell ourselves, "This is the price I have to pay for success."

After nearly twenty years, I still struggle to incorporate some form of exercise or body movement into my own life consistently. And even though I know better, I slip backward sometimes into believing that all my troubles can be solved through the power and adeptness of my mind and thoughts.

When I'm stressed or troubled, I have to force myself to put on my running shoes, sit on my yoga mat, go for a bike ride, or set out for a walk. But when I turn to my body and body movement of some sort, invariably—every single time—I feel *better*. My stress is relieved. I am better able to handle whatever crisis appears.

Margaret came to that realization on her own and went on to turn her whole life around.

Fabulous-50s Margaret

Margaret came to me at age forty-nine. She had had a career in photography before the law. She was the youngest child of Cambodian immigrants who fled the genocide. She felt that photography (her love and interest) was an indulgence, so she chose law as her career instead.

She was a pretty, bubbly, heavyset, petite woman who had a talent for making you feel immediately at ease.

She came to me to talk about turning fifty, not her career. She was having a full-blown midlife crisis that had her preoccupied with death. Her father had recently died, and her surviving parent was ill, as was her much-older husband. Margaret felt that her career was "fine" but empty. In the shadow of all the death and illness around her, she wanted to find more meaning in what remained of her life. *If I have thirty or forty more years to live, what will those years be about?* she asked herself.

Two months into our coaching engagement, she came into the office sporting a shiny neon-blue spandex leotard, white Reebok high-top sneakers, a bright pink headband around her hair, and a huge, faded baby-blue sweat-shirt that proclaimed, "No Pain, No Gain." I took it all in. Margaret was genuinely pumped up and bursting with energy. Someone had bought her a package of personal-trainer sessions for her fiftieth birthday—and this was her first experience with exercising. She had been a bookish, driven, and intellectual person her whole life. Exercise was for "the beautiful people," she'd explained to me one afternoon; now she was accessing a wholly different culture by going to the gym. She seemed excited but wary. This was not her world, and to her family and culture, this exercise focus was "frivolous." Her mother even told her it was a "passing phase" and not to invest too much in overpriced running shoes or workout clothes (which now explained her '80s Jane Fonda outfit).

But Margaret didn't let her doubts or her family's ridicule get in her way. She was committed to giving it a try, and I was there to encourage her.

But as the weeks rolled by, I noticed that Margaret had started spacing her coaching sessions far apart and was skipping some altogether. One afternoon, she finally said, "I don't think I need coaching anymore. I've been working out. I'm getting healthier. I really think exercise and learning about the body is fascinating. It's been improving my mood, and I think this is what I want to do." I was all for it and wished her well with a big hug.

We stayed in touch periodically during that time.

A year later, Margaret had lost eighty pounds and completed her gym trainer certification to work with other women over fifty. She had a business card and a website. From having zero body awareness, Margaret was now passionate about body movement and exercise. She had discovered her health along with her calling through a connection to her body.

Achievement Addiction

➢ caused Margaret to ignore her physical well-being for nearly fifty years;

➢ led Margaret to believe that physical exercise wasn't something seriously accomplished professionals could or should focus on; and

➢ induced in Margaret an Achievement Trance that had her believing that achievement was worth sacrificing her physical health.

Achievement Addiction DETOX helped Margaret

➢ realize that physical exercise was a positive outlet for her anxiety about aging;

➢ recognize the many false beliefs she had about physical exercise and self-care that were generated by her Achievement Avatar; and

➢ embrace her new-found passion to make body movement and wellness her top priority, which resulted in changing her overall health and professional focus.

Achievement Addicts, Body Awareness, and Maternity

My practice as a coach has attracted an equal number of men and women. But I had my first big break as a coach when a top international law firm hired me to design and implement a maternity coaching pilot program to be launched as part of its Women's Initiative Network. The idea was that a maternity coaching program would help women navigate their maternity process and stay in the profession. For many reasons, personal and ideological, I jumped at the chance to work on this project.

But I knew from my own experiences that there is nothing more effective than pregnancy at hurling you headlong into a confrontation with your body. Pregnancy wreaks havoc on our psyche, hormones, body image, metabolism, sleep cycle, and executive functioning. Pregnancy teaches us pretty quickly that we have a solid but vulnerable body that needs care, attention, and rest. For many female Achievement Addicts, pregnancy is their very first body-awareness wake-up call. And for many of us, pregnancy is the first time we are forced to deal with our health, bodies, and overall well-being. Pregnancy compels us to make physical health a priority. And because these are new waters to navigate, many of us, like Morgan, find ourselves rudderless.

Morgan the Reluctant Mom

Morgan was six months pregnant with twins when she came in to meet with me. Her name had been given to me the week before, and when I'd asked the HR director why the firm had only given me Morgan's name in her last trimester instead of earlier, the director said, "She just told us yesterday. We all knew it by looking at her, but until she said something official to us, our hands were tied. We couldn't broach the subject. You'll see what I mean when you meet her."

Morgan was a petite woman, and she carried a perfectly shaped basketball belly. She sat down in the chair without the typical maneuvering associated with pregnant women (back holding, easing one hip at a time into a chair, deep sighing, and exhaustion at the effort involved in just sitting down). Nope. Not Morgan. Morgan popped into the chair and sat fully upright, and looked straight out at me with a defiant look that said, "See? I'm not *really* pregnant, and even if I am, I'm not prepared to act or talk like I am."

"Sorry I'm late," she began while looking down at her cell phone. "I am around the clock with depositions and dep preparations, and I need to contact the doctor to make sure they can provide me with a heart monitor should I need to keep doing depositions into my last month. Such a pain in the ass; the doctor is insisting that if I choose not to go on bed rest for the last several months, I would need to have a heart monitor at my desk to make sure everything is okay. Can you imagine? How are my partners going to deal with this? Much less my clients, who expect me to be at their beck and call. I guess I may need to have the monitor in the dep room. . . . Anyway . . . ugh, another annoying email from my husband. I will deal with it later. I'm sorry. How are you? What can I do for you?"

All in one breath. Not looking up at me once from her phone.

Now, if that wasn't comorbid Achievement Addiction, coupled with good old-fashioned denial bordering on the delusional, I don't know what is.

I knew I had to navigate this engagement strategically. Slow, careful. No quick moves on my part. So, in the same way you might talk to someone who was standing on the edge of a sixty-five-story building threatening to throw themselves off, I mustered a deliberately gentle and empathic, "Hello, Morgan. Nice to meet you, too."

My next thought was *I can't bullshit with this one—she can smell it a mile away, and she's already heard everyone give her great advice that she's ignoring.*

"So . . . you really don't want to be here, do you?" I said.

She perked right up.

"What? Wait. No! Wow. I'm sorry. Of course, totally fine with me if the firm wants to pay for me to talk about . . . about whatever it is we are going to talk about. I'm fine with whatever. Whatever the firm wants."

Morgan was an über-people-pleaser, and she made it immediately clear to me that she would do anything to please me, the firm, and her clients. In those first few moments, she revealed that she was prepared to do anything for anyone else but herself.

So I continued.

"Okay. Great. What do you want to talk about? I don't have an agenda here. I'm here to help navigate the whole maternity leave process and then onboarding . . ." I began to explain before she quickly cut me off.

Morgan's agreeable perkiness instantly shifted to defensiveness.

"Well, I am damn straight coming back, no ifs, ands, or buts about that. I mean, we already have the plan to have two nannies in place, one from six to six, then one from six to midnight. Right. That should cover it, right? Two nannies? Don't you think?" She looked at me anxiously, awaiting my approval.

"Okay, so you're coming back. Good. But let's back up a bit. What's this about a baby monitor?" I asked. Her breezy reference to having to have her fetus' well-being monitored had me more than a little concerned.

"Oh, yeah. That. What a pain in the ass. . . . So, turns out I'm carrying twins; typical overachiever, right?" she chuckled.

I failed to see the humor in any of it.

Morgan continued talking about her pregnancy as if it were happening to her neighbor or an office mate. "Well, they say it's high risk, something about the hips being too narrow, something about bed rest and making sure the twins aren't in distress . . . but seriously, how can I be on bed rest?! Like the firm would even allow it, like Allan, my partner, would agree to it." She was now going on about Allan and how demanding he was.

I was still processing that Morgan's pregnancy was deemed high-risk enough to warrant all that intervention. So I cut her off.

"Morgan, you're high risk?" I asked.

"Yes, I guess. . . . Maybe they're exaggerating. I mean, I feel fine." She was looking a little pale, and she was breathing noticeably heavily. That will happen when there's a blue-ribbon-size watermelon pushing up against your diaphragm when you're sitting.

"Do you?" I asked rhetorically.

Morgan shifted in her seat, readjusted the pillow behind her back, and uncrossed her legs, most probably to relieve the pressure on her back. That's when she opened up a little more.

"Well, I'm exhausted all the time, can't sleep at night, can't really keep any food down, and my mind is racing nonstop, but I was sort of like that before my pregnancy." She was accustomed to minimizing her bodily discomfort, and she was still doing it now that she was pregnant.

I gently confronted her with "But now there are two fetuses involved, too."

"Yes. I know that. I don't need you to tell me that." She paused and was reflecting on what she had just said. "I do know that I guess . . ." she repeated more quietly.

" 'I guess'?" I repeated back to her.

Silence.

"Morgan?"

Morgan was now flushed in the face, she started to quiver, and single tears were slowly rolling down her face. I handed her a tissue box. She put it back on the table and didn't help herself to one.

"What am I going to *doooo*? I can't deal with this, and my career and my clients and my partners, and if I get any bigger, I won't be able to even fit in the conference-room chairs. Do you know those effin' chairs bob backward on a whim?! I almost toppled the damn thing over the other day in front of a client. They are soooo going to fire me." She was now crying, recalling the embarrassment that day.

I actually had done the same thing when I was pregnant with my son, and I remembered my male partners rolling their eyes at me. Some things hadn't changed.

Morgan was the quintessential Achievement Addict; she was steeped in denial, preoccupied with pleasing others at her own expense. She was now neglecting her body and her pregnancy and putting her unborn children at risk. She admitted that she had missed doctor appointments and missed and resched-uled ultrasound appointments and that her sanity was hanging on by a thread.

The idea of her refusing to listen to her doctor's advice about going on bed rest struck me as the epitome of self-deprivation, self-abuse, and unchecked Achievement Addiction. Not taking care of her health and well-being had become baseline behavior for Morgan, so her inability to wrap her head around the need to take care of herself during her pregnancy was just a func-tion of years and years of chronic self-neglect in the interest of achievement.

But now the stakes were higher, and she wasn't only playing with her well-being, she was compromising the well-being of her unborn children.

These were the thoughts swirling around in my head, and Morgan must have seen the expression of concern on my face because she added, "Don't get me wrong. I mean, I want these kids," she whispered. "I really do. I've always wanted to be a mom. But I am on a hamster wheel that is speeding out of control, and it was barely manageable when it was just my husband and me, so how am I going to balance this? I can't even get my head straight to tell my firm about the pregnancy, and now I also have to tell them that I need to go on bed rest? My career will be over. . . ."

Morgan's worst nightmare was coming true, and her distorted way of thinking contributed to her misery. Her all-or-nothing, catastrophizing way of thinking had her convinced that all her years of hard work and achieve-ment would be erased, and her career would be ruined, all because of her pregnancy. She was terrified that she would be left jobless, pregnant, and without prospects.

We agreed that our work together would focus on two things: (1) managing her communications and messaging with the firm about her pregnancy, maternity leave, and return after leave; and (2) focusing on her overall wellness, which included changing the way she felt about the pregnancy and her mindset about her career and future.

Morgan and I met and spoke on the phone almost every day after that first meeting. Trust and listening without judgment would be the key to getting her to start making decisions that put her well-being and that of her infants first.

It turned out that, like many other Achievement Addicts, Morgan defined her self-worth by her achievements; fundamentally, she didn't feel entitled to be pregnant, take leave, or take care of her health. She needed "permission" to be pregnant and "permission" to take care of herself and her pregnancy. As tough as she was, Morgan was terrified of disappointing her partners, being fired, and ending up like "another woman attorney statistic."

But she was also terrified of inadvertently causing harm to her babies. Morgan was forced to face her Achievement Addiction and to choose her wellness over "pleasing and achieving."

She was overwhelmed and paralyzed by her circumstances. By focusing on body awareness and her physical needs in her last trimester, we created a clear action plan that Morgan felt confident she could execute. Over time, we rehearsed and re-rehearsed what she would say to her partners, her clients, and her colleagues about her need to be on bed rest. We partnered with HR to make sure that they supported her in her ultimate decision to work from home, and they helped set her up so she could continue working comfortably without jeopardizing her health or her babies' health.

Morgan ended up going on full maternity leave, returning on a part-time basis for the first year and then working full-time after that. Within a year of her return to full-time practice, Morgan and I started working together again. She wanted a reduced-schedule arrangement while her kids were still young.

We worked together on and off for about two years to craft and navigate a way that would work for her and her young family. As a result, Morgan never left the firm or the practice of law; instead, she learned that she was well-respected and valued at the firm and that she could use that to shape a career that worked for her. She ended up having a successful career in law that also took her well-being and that of her family into account.

Achievement Addiction

➤ had Morgan in denial about her pregnancy, her physical needs, and the needs of her unborn children;

➤ caused Morgan to make less-than-ideal choices that could have escalated into a genuine crisis that could have compromised her pregnancy; and

➤ induced in Morgan an Achievement Trance that had her believing that achievement was worth sacrificing her mental and physical health along with the well-being of her unborn children.

Achievement Addiction DETOX helped Morgan

➤ emerge from her Achievement Trance and seek the proper health support and resources she needed;

➤ recognize the toxic impact her work environment was having on her health and family; and

➤ negotiate a flexible work schedule that allowed her more time with her children.

Stress and the Achievement-Addicted Brain

The number one sentence I hear from the clients I coach is "I'm burned out," tied with "I'm beyond stressed out." Often it comes in the form of "I am swamped," "I am slammed," or "I am fried."

You don't need me to tell you that burnout and chronic stress will kill you. It kills you emotionally, psychologically, and—ultimately—physically.

Learning how to reduce and manage stress involves developing a user-friendly tool kit for addressing stress in real-time. And body movement and body awareness are central to stress reduction, stress management, and overall brain health.

What I have learned through repeated trial and failure is that you simply can't *think* your way out of stress. You need other tools. Body movement, breath work, general exercise, meditation, yoga, and tai chi, among others, are all *body-centric* ways to short-circuit and reduce your body's stress state and thereby improve brain functioning.

A basic understanding of your brain and the effects that stress has on your biochemistry, physiology, psychology, and behavior is key to getting it to sink in that *you* need to develop and commit to body-centric tools to manage stress. If you learn nothing else from this book, I hope you at least learn that *your body has the ability to self-regulate stress, which puts a whole lot of your wellness back in your hands*.

If you are anything like me, you need to really understand how things work before accepting them as universal truths. So, even though you may kind of know that stress and burnout impact your brain badly and that somehow body movement can help, you still may not understand it enough to buy into it completely. And I want your buy-in.

So, here is a brief and highly simplified tutorial on how all that crazy "I can't take another minute, my head is about to explode, my heart is going to implode" stress is impacting your entirety: your brain, your mind, and your body.

More and more research confirms the relatively new and somewhat circular principle that *general wellness starts and ends with optimal brain functioning and that body movement is pivotal to brain health*. An active body leads to a reduction of the stress hormone cortisol, and less stress leads to a healthier brain, which then leads to a healthier body.

The sequence that is important to this discussion goes something like this: chronic stress floods the brain with a harmful imbalance of hormones (cortisol and adrenaline), which in turn impairs proper brain functioning in your cerebral cortex, which then impairs and compromises your most valuable cognitive abilities: your *executive functioning*.

There are some super-duper critical *cognitive abilities and skills* that depend on your brain's optimal executive functioning. Cognitive abilities like:

- Paying attention
- Maintaining focus
- Organizing
- Planning and strategizing
- Prioritizing
- Time management
- Starting tasks
- Staying focused on tasks to completion
- Understanding different points of view
- Regulating or managing emotional states
- Conflict management
- Self-monitoring (i.e., tracking what you're doing)
- Empathy

Differently stated, a *healthy* brain learns, remembers, assesses problems, follows instructions, devises a plan, manages projects, manages time, makes and executes decisions, and regulates your moods. A chronically *stress-fried* brain swimming in a sea of stress hormones means that all those abilities and skills—the lifeline skills for most Achievement-Addicted professionals—are being severely compromised and weakened.

Ironically, the baseline chronic stress that Achievement Addicts live with and consider acceptable is actively impairing the very skills they rely on to continue to achieve.

Jonathan was about to learn that lesson the hard way.

Jonathan Chased by a Tiger

While I've always preferred to meet with my coaching clients in person, much of my practice is now conducted by phone or videoconference. Jonathan was a third-year associate at a large, prominent DC law firm focused on federal appellate litigation. For those of you unfamiliar with the unspoken caste system built into legal practice, federal appellate litigators are typically the gold-medal-winning Olympians of the legal industry.

Jonathan had graduated from Harvard undergrad, taken a sabbatical to get his Ph.D. in biochemistry from Stanford, then returned to Harvard for law school. He then clerked for the late Supreme Court Justice Antonin Scalia and was cherry-picked by the most prominent Supreme Court practice in DC to work on its appellate team. He worked with one of the most celebrated intellectual powerhouses in legal history.

Jonathan was a superstar in a constellation of other supernovas. He called out of the blue one afternoon and indicated that he felt he needed help.

"Hi, Jonathan. Okay, sure. . . . What kind of help do you need?"

"Well . . ." And then he paused. For a very, very long time.

"Hello? ... Uh . . . hello, Jonathan?" I prompted.

"Yes," he said slowly, "I'm here. Was just thinking about how to answer your question."

More silence.

One of the greatest skills I learned while training as a psychotherapist was the art of staying silent with clients and patients. Learning how to let a client's silence fill a room and finding a way to get comfortable with that silence, not knowing what might happen next, can be magical. And nerve-racking.

Back to Jonathan . . .

The silence went on.

"I . . . I guess I'm calling because I read your article on stress and procrastination," he began to explain. Then he stopped.

Silence.

"And . . . I find myself . . ."

Long pause.

"I find myself . . . for the first time . . . struggling with this very thing. For the first time in my life," Jonathan then sighed audibly, "I am procrastinating.

Not getting things done. Not meeting deadlines. And I have no idea why this is happening to me now."

Jonathan and I started working together, and it turned out that he was handling his appellate caseload brilliantly. He was very comfortable with the slow-cooking, academic nature of appellate litigation. He luxuriated in fine wordsmithing and enjoyed indulging in every intellectual tangent that might make his appellate argument more sophisticated and nuanced. That was his expertise. Procrastination had never been a problem for him in the past; he was trained to tackle complex legal issues by taking all the time he needed. That all changed once he landed in the bottom-line, revenue-driven environment of Big Law.

Jonathan was not prepared for the avalanche of various commercial litigation matters that also filled his day and that required deft and efficient management of time and projects. When it came to his appellate matters, he was shining, but he was drowning on every other project. And the more he felt he was drowning, the more paralyzed he became. The more paralyzed he felt, the more he procrastinated. Jonathan was caught in an endless game of catch-up, missing new deadlines as he tried to tackle the growing pile of already-missed deadlines.

He first called me after a very mixed performance review at the law firm. He was in shock; he had never received a bad review of his work or his performance. But he'd been told in no uncertain terms that if he did not find a way to overcome his procrastination, manage his litigation and trial caseloads, and improve his time management, his future at the firm might be in jeopardy.

Matter overload—coupled with his lack of time-management skills—jacked up Jonathan's stress level until he was a deer caught in headlights. He didn't know how to say no to new projects. He took them on, barely started them, then allowed himself to get sucked into the reverie of his appellate projects, promising himself he would turn to the discovery request, letter to client, quick research memo, settlement letter . . . tomorrow.

Many tomorrows came and went for Jonathan. And the appellate practice couldn't save him from the painfully accurate criticism that his procrastination was costing the firm its reputation with key clients.

Crippling stress had piled onto Jonathan until he basically could no longer function. He could not get through a project or assignment. For the first time in his life, he started to doubt himself and his ability as an attorney.

Stress had disabled Jonathan's executive functioning, decision-making ability, and judgment. The chronic stress of Big Law practice had triggered in him a fight-or-flight biochemical reaction. His body was reacting as if a tiger was chasing him. With a fight-or-flight choice, he was fleeing into procrastination, and it was going to devastate his career.

Jonathan and I worked together for several months. One afternoon I was on another excruciatingly slow and drawn-out coaching call with him, and I was growing impatient with the sanctified and silent pauses between questions. But I was also growing curious. Maybe there was something worth exploring behind this odd conversation tempo that could be useful in getting him unstuck. So I took a gamble.

"Jonathan, okay . . . bear with me here. I need to say what is so, and if I mess it up, or screw it up or offend you, I will clean it up. But I have to say this: I don't know why, but almost every time we are on a call, I get the image that you are, like, in a dark, cramped cave, with almost no room to move around, and that you can't seem to find the exit to even try to leave. And I have to ask, and I might be nuts here, but . . . where are you calling me from, and when was the last time you went outside for air? I don't know about you, but at this very moment, I feel the walls are closing in on me, and I can barely breathe."

And it was true: for no apparent reason, I was starting to feel suffocated, stuffy, and cramped in my airy, bright office.

As a therapist, I was trained to tune in to my body and thoughts during the course of engagement for insight into what might be going on for the client—especially if what I, as a therapist, sensed or thought felt "foreign." My office was cheery and well-lit; there was no reason for me to be feeling suffocated, so I shared it with Jonathan to see if something was going on in his world that might resonate with that.

"I work in a pit," he said without pausing, "a veritable pit of a tiny office, an interior office, an effin' tiny interior office painted in dark gray with no window. It's like I work in a tomb. . . . And I have piles and piles and piles of documents and files and books and articles I intend to read but never get around to, along with newspapers, and periodicals. I can't move around in this office. I can barely squeeze myself in behind the desk."

Exhalation. Jonathan dramatically and audibly breathed out loud.

Silence. Deep inhalation . . .

"And outside?" he snorted sarcastically. "There is an underground tunnel that connects my office building to my apartment, and there are shops and so on. But I don't ever really get outside at all these days. I walk from my apartment to the office and back, sometimes without even seeing daylight."

The pain I felt for Jonathan was intense; the image that came to my mind at that moment was of this brilliant man now in a cold sweat, running at lightning speed away from a huge tiger, catching his breath while trapped in a modern-day cave.

Jonathan was a brilliant US Supreme Court clerk caught in the LED headlights of Big Law practice. He was frozen in his tracks, and if he didn't adapt or run, it was going to be his demise.

"Jonathan, you need a plan. And I hate this term, but you also need a stress 'toolbox' and time-management plan to kick you out of your panic-induced paralysis that is manifesting itself as day-to-day procrastination."

"Toolbox?" he asked.

"Yes. Tell me, what do you do to relax?"

"Elena, I read to relax," he laughed. "And as for stress, I never really suffered from it much. Unlike my colleagues, I found law school to be hard work, but I never found it stressful, and the clerkship was really demanding and intellectually taxing, but again, never really stressful. Certainly not to the point of paralysis. But this law-firm thing is foreign territory. There's just . . . I don't know . . . there's just no *space* or time to . . . think things through clearly, and even when I set aside quiet time to 'work,' I now find myself lost and having to read the same paragraph over and over. . . ."

Jonathan had talent, intellect, training, and discipline in spades. What was missing?

- What he didn't have was adaptability in crisis.
- What he didn't have was a set of coping skills to manage real-time stress.
- What he didn't have was a tool kit to help him self-regulate his paralysis under stress so that he could execute and demonstrate his brilliance.
- What he didn't have were practical tools to succeed and shine in a giant law firm where time was money and where meeting deadlines was key to survival.

Jonathan and I worked together for about a year. We focused on body awareness specifically, working on his stress-management skills. Then we worked on his time-management skills, and ultimately, we worked on a two-year plan to get him out of law-firm practice and into an academic law professorship at a top law school in a rural area. Body movement was a part of that plan: Jonathan's apartment was located near Capitol Hill, and over time, he committed to a daily walk around the Reflecting Pool. That walk eventually turned into jogging, which turned into a daily run. Jonathan and I lost touch over the years, but his story always reminds me of the importance of developing intangible skills like time management, stress management, and delegation.

Achievement Addiction

➤ kicked Jonathan into an Achievement Trance that had him chronically stressed about achievement to the point of paralysis;

➤ blinded Jonathan to the reality that his temperament was ill-suited to the high-achievement workplace that he'd worked so hard to join; and

➤ caused Jonathan to suffer from a form of Achievement Amnesia about his real talents, abilities, passion, and strengths.

Achievement Addiction DETOX helped Jonathan

➤ control his negative self-talk about his procrastination, break free of his Achievement Trance, and reconnect with his true talents and strengths;

➤ learn and apply stress-management tools including body movement to manage the chronic stress that was compromising his success; and

➤ change his work environment to one that was better suited to his talents, abilities, and temperament.

Our executive functioning depends on our ability to modulate stress biochemically. And the quickest way to correct the biochemical imbalance induced by stress is through body movement. Of the 7 Steps, I have come to experience and believe that body movement is the most accessible way back to regaining health, sanity, and wellness.

My clients have repeatedly proven that when we make even the slightest commitment to regular body movement, we can change our bodies, biochemistry, neurological pathways, thoughts, and emotions.

STEP 5: BODY
The IMAGO Coaching Questions

Now it's time for you to work on Step 5—BODY—using several IMAGO Coaching Questions. All the questions below are designed to help you work the fifth step and deepen your understanding of how Achievement Addiction has impacted your body's well-being and/or suppressed your connection to your body's needs.

Following each question, I offer you a way to summarize your fifth-step insights in the form of a declaratory sentence. These summarized insights will be essential to refer to should you choose to download and complete the Achievement Addiction DETOX Worksheets accessible at www.achievementaddictiondetox.com.

To recap, the IMAGO Coaching Method invites you to INQUIRE, MAGNIFY, ACT, GROW, and OWN.

The questions below can help you work this fifth step.

INQUIRE

How has Achievement Addiction contributed to your neglect of or disconnection from your body, its needs, and your well-being?

_____

_____

On any typical day, how does your body feel?

_____

_____

In my addictive pursuit of achievement, I have ignored my body and/or suppressed my need to take care of my body in the following ways:

_____

_____

_____

Magnify

How has your level of disconnection from or neglect of your body caused you pain, suffering, discomfort, or other challenges? With your health? With your mental well-being?

_____

_____

_____

In my addictive pursuit of achievement, my level of body neglect/disconnection has caused me to feel _____ and has created several challenges, including . . .

_____

_____

Because of my neglect of or disconnection from my body, I suffer in the following ways:

_____

_____

. . . and the people around me suffer in the following ways:

_____

_____

Act

Think about the most difficult bodily challenge you are struggling with right now. What action would you be willing to take to improve that situation?

_____

_____

_____

_____

I want to take the following action steps toward reducing my body neglect and reconnecting with my body:

_____

_____

Reconnecting with and taking better care of my body would mean that . . .

_____

_____

G~ROW~

Take a moment to imagine what it might look like to have a better relationship with your body. What might a shift in bodily health and well-being mean to you? To your family and friends?

_____

_____

_____

I want to grow and improve my relationship with my body because it would mean that . . .

_____

_____

_____

O~WN~

Hopefully, answering these questions has helped you increase your awareness of how Achievement Addiction has impacted your level of care for and connection to your body and its needs. So, let's turn to owning that newfound awareness of your BODY.

When it comes to my body, I own and acknowledge that my Achievement Addiction has caused the following harm to or neglect of my body:

_____

_____

. . . and that if I could take steps to improve my relationship to and care of my body, it would mean . . .

_____

_____

 FINAL THOUGHTS:
Body Awareness, Movement, and Achievement Addiction

✓ Developing body awareness (Step 5) and committing time every day to some form of body movement is a powerful and achievable step toward regaining health, sanity, and wellness.

✓ As Achievement Addicts, many of us believe that body movement or exercise is not essential, so we continue to ignore, neglect, and devalue our bodies' needs and self-care.

✓ When we start to introduce regular body awareness and movement into our lives, we begin to regulate our moods, improve our physical health, and optimize our brain and executive functioning.

STEP 6

FAITH

Widen Your Perspective

There's Just Gotta Be More
To Life Than Achievement, Right?

Writing this particular chapter was tough, for lots of reasons—some personal and some cultural. I am many things: a lawyer, a psychotherapist, a coach, an entrepreneur, a writer, a mom, and a wife. But let me tell you what I am not.

I am not a theologian, guru, priestess, rabbi, imam, or prophet. I am, however, a storyteller, a seeker, and an acute observer of human nature.

So, let's also start with what this chapter is *not*.

This chapter is not about God or religion. It is not a clever way for me to proselytize or enter into a debate about ideologies. It is not about promoting any given practice, tradition, belief, or ritual.

This chapter shares a simple concept based on my story and other human stories.

And the simple concept is this: cultivating a posture of faith in something greater than ourselves defuses the fear underlying Achievement Addiction and, as a result, widens our perspective and creates space for intentional choice.

This concept may be easier to relate to for those whose faith is anchored firmly in organized religion or a set of beliefs or practices. But for those who may not feel connected to an organized religion or who may identify with secular spirituality or experience faith without religion, I offer this understanding of faith.

Faith, as I use it here, refers to the mysterious, nonrational perspective and posture that surfaces when we intentionally invest our time, focus, and actions toward something greater than ourselves.

The most articulate definition of this kind of faith—that is, secular spirituality—is offered by Roger Housden in his book *Keeping the Faith without a Religion*. He explains:

> *Secular spirituality is founded on faith as distinct to belief. By faith, I don't mean something that's irrational, but rather it is non-rational. Faith in what? Faith in life. Faith in the moment as it is presenting itself to me. Faith that there's an inscrutable (or unsayable)* intelligence *that is present at every moment. The non-rational faith I'm speaking of is an* intuition *of that intelligence, whereas belief is more a mental concept . . . Belief is more connected to opinion. Faith is like a fragrance, if you like, of the heart's knowing. There's an intuition of the transcendent that is not confined to a church or a mosque, or a synagogue. It's secular in the sense that it can be part of our everyday ordinary existence if we are open to it.*

No matter how you define or access faith, it has been my experience that when we mindfully connect with faith, cultivate it, and incorporate it into our life, somehow we start seeing things, people, and circumstances differently. Faith is a tool, like any other, that, when accessed, offers us more peace in that it allows us to shift perspective and frees us up to feel more connected to our true selves, to our wisdom, and to what is meaningful.

Simply, I think of faith as a new camera lens on our life—a new lens that offers a fresh, wondrous, and different way of looking at ourselves, others, our world, our challenges, and our blessings. And by accessing faith—and using it to serve as a lens, posture, worldview, or practice—we start the process of dismantling the Achievement Addiction that has a stranglehold on our thoughts, actions, beliefs, and behaviors.

Okay, if you're still with me, let's go into what I have learned about faith and its power to undermine the fear that drives our Achievement Addiction.

Faith and Fear

At any given moment in time, there are only two operating principles at work in our lives: **fear** or **faith**. These binary opposites are at play every time we make a decision, every time we are stuck, every time we fall in love, every time we are confronted with either welcome or unwelcome change. At any given moment, each one of us gets to choose over and over again, multiple times a day, which principle we operationalize. We get to choose. Do we live (i.e., think, feel, act) from a place of fear or from a place of faith?

Let's use something relatively benign to demonstrate the principle.

When we go to the deli to order our lunch, we choose to operate from a place of faith. Faith that the deli is clean, that the cook is competent, that the place has its health certificate, that we are being sold fresh food, that the server isn't messing with our order, and on and on. We all know people who choose to operate from a place of fear, even on that level of decision.

So, when I use the word *faith*, I do not necessarily refer to any particular ritual or religion. I am not even referring to God, or the Higher Power, or the I Am, or the Universe, or Shiva, or Jesus, or Allah. Rather, when I speak of faith, I am referring to a person's consciously chosen

> *inner posture, perspective, and operating framework that directs them to intentionally choose to embody, feel, and enact the exact* opposite *of what fear and its operating framework, perspective, and posture indicate.*

Let's parse that out.

Faith is
- an inner posture and/or
- a perspective and/or

- an operating framework
- chosen consciously and intentionally
- to embody, feel, and enact the opposite of what fear might indicate.

Faith can be thought of as a posture we choose, again and again, over fear. When we reject a posture of fear and intentionally embody a posture of faith, we may find that we suddenly have more

Faith in ourselves
Faith in our decisions
Faith in our intuition
Faith in others
Faith in the universe
Faith that we are safe
Faith that we are protected
Faith that all things work out somehow, even if it gets messy
Faith in our accomplishments
Faith in our resilience
Faith in our God
Faith in goodness
Faith in nature
Faith in life

As we have come to understand, our Achievement Addiction is deeply rooted in fear. Achievement Addiction has us believing that our self-worth depends on our achievements and that we are worthless without them.

Ultimately, faith offers an alternative to our fear-driven Achievement Addiction. When we choose faith over fear, we begin to support a sense of self-worth independent of our achievements. Faith gives us a perspective beyond fear, and when we can embrace a worldview that is no longer fear-driven, we can begin to question our robotic, Achievement-Addicted choices. **If fear drives automatic Achievement Addiction, then faith offers freedom of choice.**

In the chapter on mindset, we talked about our power to monitor and control our thought life. Just as we can change our thoughts, we also, at any given moment, can choose the belief system, posture, and operating principles that underlie those thoughts. As I understand it, free will offers us the choice to look at every situation through the lens of either fear or faith, and then to choose the pattern and collection of thoughts that will inform our mindset, our feelings, and ultimately our actions. The great news is that we get to choose.

And from what I have learned, embedded within that freedom of choice lies the difference between living one's life in heaven or hell.

Achievement Addiction and the Culture of Fear

If we go back to the Achievement Addiction assessment, we can see how many of our Achievement-Addicted choices, thoughts, and behaviors are driven by fear.

Many high-achieving professions, like law, banking, medicine, accounting, consultancy, academia, and media, are firmly rooted in the language and culture of **fear**.

These workplace environments thrive on a fear-based hierarchy and ethos. Many of my clients have not stopped to think about the fact that their language, career, worldview, and mindset have all been governed by a belief system based on raw fear.

Remaining steadfast in a place of faith and not letting fear dominate has often been complicated for me and others—complicated by the fact that many of the world's religions, unfortunately, conflate fear and faith and inspire adherence to their particular orthodoxy with terror-inducing stories of a vengeful, punitive, easy-to-anger God-entity.

I'm not about to take on the canonical principles of the world's faiths. I am here to propose a simple concept that has helped me and others develop a saner thought life.

And the simple concept is this: **At any given moment, you can choose fear, or you can choose faith.**

Learning how to rejigger my own fear-based mindset is what swept me up into decades of learning, studying, and spiritual practice. It led to developing language and rituals that could replace my automatic, fear-based thoughts with an intentional, faith-based perspective.

What I have experienced is that when we choose fear, things can feel stuck, concretized, immovable, oppressive, stagnant, grim, and insurmountable, and we often feel victimized. When we learn to choose faith over fear, somehow things start to ease up, get some color, shift a little, loosen up, lighten up, and feel more possible, and we feel more wonder or curiosity about what comes next.

Tanya had religion but needed to learn how to choose faith.

Tanya, Faith, and Home Depot

Tanya came up to me after a presentation I gave at the Princeton Club on branding and business development for lawyers. She was an African American woman who was elegantly dressed in a bright blue Tahari dress, Hermès scarf, and high heels, and in her ears were two diamond studs the size of plump summer blueberries. Tanya was disarmingly soft-spoken, but it was clear she was a formidable force of nature. She asked for my business card, and she emailed me later that evening wanting to set up a meeting to work on her business development plan.

Tanya was at one of those super-mega-powerhouse law firms in New York City. She had stellar credentials: Brown undergrad, University of Chicago School of Law, federal clerk for the Third Circuit. She explained that she had recently been told by the law firm she was on track to make partner within the next eighteen months, but the firm needed to see that she had business development talent. That's where Tanya was stuck.

"I have a huge network from undergrad and law school," she told me. "I was president of my sorority in college and have maintained many of those relationships. I am also on the boards of two nonprofit organizations in New York that have led me to meet some of the more influential leaders in the banking, manufacturing, and venture capital worlds." Tanya seemed like she was doing everything right.

She had kept an ongoing list of her top contacts; she'd had her assistant create a calendar to remind her to stay in touch and set up drinks/lunches/pings with her top thirty prospects, and she was following through on all of it.

"Tanya, it sounds to me like you know what you are doing on the BD side of things. What seems to be the problem?" I asked.

She got to the point very quickly. "I can't make the ask. Actually, I am terrified to make the ask. These are my friends. I can't make the ask." She was adamant.

Tanya was slowly getting agitated. "I just can't imagine asking lifelong friends, colleagues, mom-group acquaintances, board members. . . . I can't just go from 'Hey, let's have a drink' to 'Can you give me some business?' I mean, who does that? It seems so . . . so . . . phony and false. Like I've been tricking them the whole time, waiting for the kill."

I said nothing. I had heard this complaint before. I've heard it from almost every partner and associate I have worked with on BD. The question has been "How do I go from friend to future client without embarrassing myself and losing the friendship, and how do I live with the icky, schmoozy, phony feeling of essentially asking my friend for money?"

Tanya went on. "My friendships and relationships are real. And I hate fake people. This just compromises . . . compromises my integrity . . . my way in the world. It's not how I was taught to be in the world. It's not our way."

It's not our way. That phrase stuck in my head for some reason. I hadn't heard that term used before, and I had a sense that Tanya had something specific in mind that she was referring to. So I started probing.

"Tanya, I hear you. Making the ask is very delicate and tricky stuff that we can work on, but something caught my attention. What did you mean by 'not our way'?" I asked as delicately as I could.

Tanya was no-nonsense. And she launched right in.

"So, I was raised Baptist," she said. "And I have a very strong belief in God. My father was a preacher, so God and living a God-fearing life was part of my upbringing. Granted, I don't always agree with how the Church does things, and my family wasn't thrilled that I became a corporate lawyer. But I feel strongly about the need for women of color to take their seat at the corporate table and being part of a corporate monolith like my firm enables me to help a lot of people from the inside. I do a lot of pro bono work, mentor other women of color, and devote a lot of time to my nonprofits. But I was raised not to lie, not to be two-faced, and to make sure my reputation and word were always well-regarded. I have worked hard to stick to those values. Selling out my friendships and relationships for the firm or my financial gain just doesn't feel right to me. It's just flat wrong." Tanya was calm as she explained this to me; it came from her core values, and I respected that. She felt that business development, at least as she understood it, would compromise her faith.

But still, something didn't sound right to me. So I pressed on.

"Tanya, explain this to me some more. You are okay working for a law firm that knowingly represents less-than-noble corporate interests, and we both know what that can mean, but you feel your faith is getting in the way of you asking for business? I'm a little confused." I knew that I was pushing her, but before she gave up on business development, I felt an obligation to have her clarify her logic and reasoning. Her career was on the line.

Tanya was quiet. She looked at me for a moment and then said with shaded lids, "Look, I know who and what my law firm represents. And when those morally troublesome cases hit my desk, and the partner asks me to work on files that I'm uncomfortable with, I bite the bullet and do it because the way I see it, I didn't choose those clients, and I have a job to do. I know that can seem like an arbitrary boundary for some, but it works for me. But . . . this is different. I mean, I am going to be peddling my wares like some two-bit salesperson? That doesn't feel right, and anyway, how am I going to feel when they all say no?! Then what? I've lost my self-respect, I've compromised my dignity, probably lost friendships in the process, and for what? To try to bring in a client that the firm probably won't be able to service anyway because our rates are too high? Nope. No way. Too high a risk for me." Tanya then exhaled, folded her fingers into a tight little ball, and placed them decidedly in her lap. Her facial expression and body language silently proclaimed, "Counsel rests its case."

But, without knowing it, she had given me the answer I was looking for. The real truth was that Tanya was scared. Scared of being rejected, embarrassed, and then abandoned by her friends.

Tanya may have been raised in a God-fearing home premised on a strong faith in God, but she was now operating exclusively from a posture of fear. And from what I was hearing, faith had taken a backseat.

It was time to gently confront her with the fact that her aversion to business development had less to do with fearing God and more to do with fearing disapproval from other people.

This was getting messy, and I knew that phrasing it the right way would make all the difference.

"So, let me get this straight. From what I'm hearing, it sounds like your decision isn't so much based on fearing God. What you are terrified of is rejection and embarrassment from other people. Does that sound right?" I blurted out.

Sometimes, in the moment, my best intentions fall away no matter how hard I try.

But Tanya didn't look offended by my summary. She was very animated when she said, "You bet I'm scared! I worked too hard to develop these connections to just blow them all with one misstep or stupid ask that comes out the wrong way at the wrong time for the wrong thing."

I continued.

"I can't blame you. But what if we were to find a way, a comfortable way, for you to do this slowly, using your language and only language that suits you and makes you comfortable. Would you be willing to entertain that?"

Tanya considered what I had just proposed and nodded her head, saying, "If you can find a way for me to make the ask without tripping all over myself and alienating my friends, I'd consider it."

Tanya and I started working together on crafting language that felt authentic to her. That allowed her to gradually broach the subject of possibly giving work to the firm in a slow and methodical way. That approach also involved bringing in some partners from the firm to help her pitch when the time was right. Tanya didn't feel comfortable promoting herself to her friends, but she felt comfortable pitching her partners and the firm, so we followed that route.

One afternoon, Tanya called me in a bit of a panic and asked if we could have an emergency session that afternoon to talk about a recent development that had her very nervous.

Tanya walked into the office, and she was visibly rattled. "Home Depot." She threw herself into the chair and looked at me sidelong.

"Home Depot?" I echoed, confused.

"Yup, Home Depot," she began. "I submitted my BD plan with my list of top prospective client contacts to my department chair as part of my partnership dossier, and we had a meeting today to walk through them, as you and I had discussed."

"And?"

"And of all the contacts she wants me to pursue, she said it would be a huge win and a home run for me if I could land Home Depot," she said, rolling her eyes with equal frustration and sarcasm.

I said nothing.

She stopped and looked up at me.

"I know what you're thinking. I know, and the answer is no. I can't do that one. . . I just can't. I have known this guy since when I was in high school. I mean, we have stayed in touch over the years, and lately, we have connected as business colleagues because we serve on the same nonprofit board. But it's too close. Too close for comfort. He's gonna say no, and then what if it gets back to my parents? I mean, our parents used to belong to the same church, and . . ."

I let her go on with her catastrophizing and even encouraged it. Sometimes, when clients are genuinely stuck in fear, I help walk them through the "worst-case scenario" aloud. It allows them to see how stuck in terrorized fear they are and lets them hear how extreme their fear is.

"So he tells his parents, who tell your parents. Then what happens?" I asked.

"Then I get a call first from my mom, warning me my dad's gonna call. Then my dad calls."

"And then what?"

"And then he asks me a million leading questions about how it was that I got it into my head to embarrass the family that way by asking for business like some two-bit salesperson from a family friend. And didn't I think about them? And him? And he didn't raise me that way . . ."

"What way?"

"To be a huckster. A salesperson."

"And then what happens?" I continued my line of questioning.

"Then he makes me feel like crap, lower than crap, and then he asks me why I didn't take that job in Atlanta, closer to the family, because maybe my values wouldn't be so mercenary then." She was on a roll.

"And then what?"

"Then I, then I . . . I don't know. I disappoint him, embarrass my family, and then don't make partner after all, because no way, no how is Home Depot going to give me business!" she shouted with exasperation.

"Are you finished?" I closed.

"Yes." Tanya was beat.

"Anything else?" I pushed.

She was exasperated but still very much in control.

"No. Nothing else. I think that's plenty," she said, deflated, crossing her arms defensively.

"Okay, Tanya. I'm going to say something here that may feel insulting, but hear me out, okay? Can you bear with me?"

"Yes, sure," she said flatly.

I took the plunge. "Okay. So here goes."

Serving up business development coaching with a side order of faith can be tricky.

I took a deep breath. "Tanya, where's your faith?"

She raised her eyebrows at me in disbelief. "Excuse me?" She was slightly offended.

"You heard me. Right now, at this moment, after telling me this story of calamity and destruction, I would like to know, where is your faith in all this?" I repeated.

She looked at me hard. She was quietly weighing whether she should pick up the gauntlet I'd just thrown down. I was quietly wondering if she was going to walk out.

"Okay. I'll play along," she finally said. "My faith, huh? My faith is . . ."

She was thinking. The silence went on a bit, but after a while, the expression on her face started to soften as she thought.

"My faith is . . . my faith is . . . Well, I guess my faith in this moment is nowhere. My faith isn't in this equation," she said quietly as if to herself.

"That's right. Your faith isn't in this equation at all. It's clear that fear is dominating every single scenario you just rattled off to me."

She sat back in her chair and exhaled.

"So, let's try to move you. Move you from calamity to wonder. What if faith walked in the room right now? What would faith have to say to you?" I was quiet now. She had a lot to think about.

This idea visibly moved Tanya. After some thought, she answered my question.

"Faith would say, 'Fear not, for I am with you.'" She was quoting from the Bible.

"What else?"

"Faith would say, 'I can do all things through Christ,'" she quoted again.

"What else?"

"Faith would say, 'All things work together for good for those who believe.'"

"What else?"

"Faith would say, 'No weapon formed against me shall prosper.'" She was on a roll. "And faith would say that God wouldn't have presented this to me if he thought I couldn't do it," she concluded.

I get goosebumps writing this story still to this day.

Tanya's face was streaming with one long tear stain down her face, and she needed a moment to compose herself.

"Tanya, you have the benefit of knowing what it is to truly rely on faith. You know, better than most people, the power of faith. It may be one of your strongest powers of all. Yet, you've let the law-firm fear-culture dominate your thinking. It might be time to let faith out of the closet and see what happens when you start operating and thinking strategically through a posture of faith. It might surprise you."

She solemnly nodded her head in quiet agreement.

Faith had just entered Tanya's business development strategy, and Home Depot would never be the same.

Tanya and I worked hard on a strategy for making the ask of her contact at Home Depot.

And when she panicked, we worked on her reframing her fear through a lens of faith. It kept her clear-headed, focused, and action-oriented.

I hadn't heard from Tanya for about two months, during which time she was planning on making the initial ask of her contact to see if he would be willing to take a meeting with the department chair who could speak regarding the firm's abilities. Tanya was going to be the connector, and the chair would try to close it.

One afternoon I got a call from Tanya while I was out. She left me a short voicemail that said, "Just thought you should know Home Depot has agreed to meet the chair. I did it. . . . Faith landed Home Depot. I'm heading to Atlanta for the week and actually meeting up with my contact while in Atlanta, too. We are both going to a wedding in our community. Will let you know how it goes. By the way, my dad would loooove you. Talk to you soon."

Achievement Addiction

➤ caused Tanya to adopt a fear-based mindset that ultimately compromised her ability to grow professionally;

➤ allowed Tanya's Achievement Avatar to dominate her mindset and what she was capable of in her career; and

➤ induced in Tanya a form of Achievement Amnesia that had her suppressing her true self, her talents and abilities, and the role of faith in her life.

Achievement Addiction DETOX helped Tanya

➤ recognize the impact her fear-dominated mindset was having on her career and well-being;

➤ learn how to master control over her negative self-talk that had her convinced that business development was not possible for her; and

➤ reconnect with her faith and incorporate a faith-based mindset that helped support her during challenging moments in her career.

Fear can grip even the most talented, pedigreed, capable people and reduce us to quivering and paralyzed shadows of ourselves. Fear will convince us to stay put, compromise, settle, give away our power, and tolerate the intolerable. "Better the devil I know . . . ," says fear.

But faith—faith in ourselves, in something bigger than ourselves, in the magic of possibilities—often has us believing once again that change is possible, that the impossible can be achieved, and that we are bigger, better, and more capable than fear would have us believe.

Facing Down Fear

At some point in all of our journeys toward sanity, balance, and transformation, we will come face-to-face with fear and all the terror and catastrophe it has to share with us. It is in that very moment that we get to choose. In that moment, maybe we can pause and remember that faith may offer an alternative to our fear-dominated life and mindset. And perhaps, just perhaps, there is something bigger than ourselves that we can tap into that may offer another perspective. By learning to choose faith over fear, we can access a wider outlook on our life, a broader perspective filled with more optimism, more hope, more vision, more creativity, and even more magic.

Blake needed to be reminded of the role that faith had once played in his life to widen his perspective and redesign a more meaningful life and career.

Blake the Choirboy

As I have stated before, not all clients who have confided in me as their coach have been sufferers of serious mental illness or addiction. The lion's share of them were just burned out, stressed, situationally depressed, and looking for tools or a way to recover their health and personal lives.

Blake was one of these clients. His law firm sent him to me to help him through a very stressful time in his life. Blake was a superstar at the firm and was on track to make partner within a year. However, he had just told his managing partner that he wanted to leave the law firm for an in-house position with a client because he was burned out with law-firm life.

The managing partner was smart enough to tell Blake to take some time off before he made a final decision and that the firm would pay for him to work with a coach to figure out a way to reduce his stress and make his life at the firm sustainable over the long term.

When I met Blake, I thought that perhaps the firm had sent me the wrong attorney.

He was sitting in the waiting room, comfortably slumped in his chair, reading the *New York Times* and drinking some coffee that my receptionist had offered him. When we met, he looked up from his paper with a wide, open smile.

This did not look like someone who was struggling with stress or burn-out. He looked like he'd just taken a stroll around the park with his dog. Calm, relaxed . . . nothing was wrong with Blake.

He sat in my office and started to tell me about his life.

He was from Alabama, the first generation in his family to go to college, much less law school. He'd moved to New York to attend Columbia Law School, where he'd met his fiancée. They were supposed to get married in about five months. She was a doctor, finishing her residency in Virginia. They had not seen each other in about three weeks because of his work demands.

Blake was working around the clock, flying all over the world for the firm; he couldn't recall the last time he'd had a vacation. And then he said with a chuckle, "Now that I think about it, I can't recall the last time I didn't work on a weekend or came home before 2 a.m. Ha . . . isn't that something?"

Blake was still Bermuda-breezy as he said this. "I guess I'm just one of those people who don't need sleep or vacations; I guess I function best when I'm working around the clock."

Admittedly, to this day, I envy those people who can pull all-nighters or manage to thrive on only four hours of sleep.

"So, why do you think the firm wanted us to connect?" I genuinely couldn't see what the challenge was. Blake had decided to take another position, and it seemed to make sense to me.

"Well, I had a minor incident—no big deal—about a month ago that kind of gave me pause. And my fiancée said that if I didn't make a change, she would call off the wedding. Can you believe that? Call off a wedding because I had a minor dizzy spell and I had to go to the ER? So I . . ."

"Wait. Sorry, but dizzy spell? ER? What happened exactly?" I asked.

Blake was masterful at burying unpleasant information behind his pleasant, gee-whiz demeanor. But an ER visit wasn't something that even he could conceal or disguise.

But boy, did he try!

"Well, I guess I was overtired or something, and suddenly I couldn't focus on the computer screen anymore. The numbers became all blurry, and when I went to stand up, the room started spinning fast. I guess that was when I fell to the floor. . . I guess I may have zonked out a bit because I opened my eyes and realized the room was still spinning and my heart was beating out of my chest like it was going to just damn near pop out of my body. I have diabetes, which, don't worry, I have it under control, so I thought it was a blood sugar drop. But I still couldn't get up. I got to the phone to call 911 and my fiancée, and the next thing I know, I'm in an ambulance with all these wires attached to me. I mean, I'm a young guy. . ."

"Sounds pretty scary and serious. What did they say it was?"

"Well, it was no big deal," he smiled with assurance. "Turns out I have a streak of drama queen in my gene pool, and I had a full-on panic attack, an anxiety attack, or something you shrinks diagnose when we get too stressed. I was sent home and told to take it easy." Then he took another sip of his coffee and barely blinked as he looked up at me, took me in, and smiled.

"So did you?" I asked.

"Did I what? Oh, take it easy? Of course not. I had to be on a plane to China the next day. But then something like this happened in China, and that freaked my fiancée out. And she gave me an ultimatum to quit my job or quit her."

Again, cool as a mint julep on a hot August day. Nothing disturbed this guy. And yet, two panic attacks in one month were a clue that his mind wasn't planning on sticking with his cool charade for much longer. I know firsthand that when we ignore our bodies, they can devise new and ever-louder ways to get our attention so that we make the changes we need.

"So, you had another panic attack in the course of a month, but this time in a foreign country. That must have been harrowing. Have you had similar symptoms since China?"

I knew the answer to that question, but I was building a case.

"Oh yeah. One or maybe two more times. Not a big deal. It's to be expected, I guess, now that the wedding is getting closer, and my mom, well, she was diagnosed recently with pancreatic cancer, and my fiancée keeps threatening to leave me, and then I almost got into a major car accident the other day because I almost fell asleep at the wheel. Well, you see my point? Things seem to be getting a bit out of hand. So, it was becoming clear that I needed a change. . . . That much was becoming very clear to me." Blake smiled at me once again, trying to sell me the notion that he had it all under control.

He continued, "I needed an escape route, and the firm wouldn't change my hours or level of responsibilities, so I took an offer with one of the firm's clients to go in-house." He seemed satisfied with this dizzying storyline.

But I wasn't buying it. Anxiety attacks can increase in frequency and severity if left untreated or if you don't make a serious change in the circumstances that are underlying the anxiety. Your body will up the ante until you pay attention. Blake wasn't paying attention. He'd just bought a really big Band-Aid.

"Wow. That's a big change to make without missing a beat. Just up and out and into the next thing, it sounds like. But explain to me, how exactly is going in-house going to change things for you?" It was clear to me that not only was Blake a prize-worthy Achievement Addict, but he was also in a full-on Achievement Trance that had him sleepwalking through his life as he made some major personal and career decisions.

"Well, they promise me fewer hours, a more regular schedule, less travel, and no billable hours to worry about," he explained genuinely.

"But if I understand you, isn't this the same client that had you flying on a plane to China twenty-four hours after a panic attack to close a deal?"

Achievement Addiction can have us swirling in a whirlpool of endless denial that is both fascinating and potentially deadly.

And Blake was trapped in the whirlpool.

"Yes. So what? It's not a law firm. What's your point?" He sounded a little defensive.

"My point is that this lateral move to a hard-pressing client sounds more like a cosmetic change at best, no?" I was trying to confront him gently with the reality of his decision.

"Funny, that's what the law firm's managing partner said to try to keep me. He—along with my fiancée—said that I needed life tools to deal with the stress so I can continue adding value. So here I am, Doc. What's the plan?"

Blake was the living embodiment of a Ken doll; nothing fazed him, nothing bothered him, and nothing could tousle up his well-manicured demeanor. And here he was asking for "tools" so that he could continue with his Achievement-Addicted life, as long as his health allowed. Suddenly, I felt a surge of anger well up inside me; it felt weird.

Why was I angry? This was Blake's life, not mine. Why was I taking this personally?

"I'm not a doctor, Blake, and I don't have a plan. It's your life, your health, your diabetes, your anxiety attacks, your career, your fiancée. But it sounds like your body is telling you in no uncertain terms that it's going to keep upping the ante until you make some changes. So, sounds to me like you need more than a job change. You need a plan. Do you have one?" I was doing a relatively good job of containing the anger, but I could detect the edge in my voice.

Sometimes, some of the most pleasant, most intelligent, most talented, most capable people simply aren't coachable. They don't want to make a change; they will resist all efforts to embark on self-awareness and simply aren't ready to entertain the concept that they are the ones who need to take action. As well-intentioned and likable as he was, Blake was starting to look like a classically "uncoachable" client.

"Isn't that your job? To give me one?" he asked naïvely.

Now my anger was palpable, and I could feel my heart racing. I still had no idea why Blake was triggering me this way. But I went on.

"Nope. Not my job to tell you what to do, Blake. Even if it were, it doesn't sound like you're too good at listening to what other people tell you to do anyway. So that model doesn't work. Not for me and not for you."

Wow. That had come out all wrong. What was going on?

"So . . . why am I even here wasting my time with you?" he asked with an annoyed tone.

By this time, I had regained my composure because I was beginning to understand why I was feeling this foreign, sudden flash of anger. Blake's suppressed anger was in the air, and I was experiencing it even if he couldn't articulate it at that moment. So I continued.

"I don't know. Why are you here? What do you want? Everything you've been telling me about yourself has at least you convinced that nothing really needs to change. I'm not going to force you to make changes you aren't ready for. So why are you here? What do you want, Blake? Really, what is it that you want to happen in your life?" I asked calmly and empathetically.

I saw a flicker of uneasiness ripple across Blake's face. Something was going on under the surface of that perfected demeanor, and it was bubbling to the top.

"I want to stop passing out. It is scaring me," he said somberly after a pause.

"Okay, and what else do you want?" I asked softly.

"I want to not be working 24/7 and traveling all the time." His voice was getting edgy.

"Okay. What else?" Even softer.

"I want my damn fiancée to get on a plane to New York so we can spend some time together. I'm getting married, and I haven't seen her in months. This is just crazy."

Blake's composure was starting to crack. He was visibly pissed, getting overheated, and he began loosening his tie. Then he unbuttoned and took off his jacket.

"What else?" I pushed.

He cleared his throat and poured himself a glass of water.

"I want my life back. I want my damn life back," he retorted as he turned and looked past me and out the window. "I don't know how I got here, and I don't know where to start unraveling what went wrong along the way. All I know is I just, I just want to live my damn life a little more peacefully. Is that so damn much to ask?" He looked up at me with a flushed face and with absolute rage and hurt in his eyes.

"No. I don't think so. And I can't blame you for being angry. Sounds like your life has been hijacked out from underneath you."

"Hijacked is damn right, right out from under my nose. I just can't keep going on like this. It's . . . it's inhuman."

Now we were getting somewhere.

"So, what do you want to do about this?"

"I don't know. I really don't know," he said, shaking his head. "All I know is work and stress and push, push, push. My dad died of a heart attack at sixty. I don't want that for me. It seriously scares me sometimes."

"Nobody wants that, Blake. It's not what any of us signed on to."

Silence.

"So, what do you do for sorry cases like me?" he smiled sheepishly.

"Me?" I said, smiling back. "I do nothing. *We* work together to figure out what needs to be eliminated from your life and what needs to be added. Then you take real responsibility for your life and start to take some action to save your own damn life."

Blake was nodding in agreement.

"So, let me ask you a question, Blake. How good are you at saying no to other people?"

He started to laugh. "Honestly, I don't think I have said no to another person in about five years."

"Oh yes, you have. You have been saying no pretty regularly and successfully to yourself for a damn long time, don't you think?"

"Oh, I am super good at saying no to the things that matter to me," he quipped sarcastically.

"Like what?"

Blake was thinking.

"Well, I say no to vacations, to weekend plans, to seeing my fiancée, to regular exercise, to eating well, to my hobbies . . ."

"What hobbies?"

"Well, I used to sing in the church choir growing up, and it gave me a lot of peace just being there. I loved going to practice, singing worship, finding time for me and God to just hang out. It's hard to explain, but I don't know . . . I just feel His presence when I sing and feel something more important than my own bullshit life. Wow. I haven't thought about that in years."

"So, you had a spiritual practice that fed you growing up, huh?"

"Yes, singing worship kept me focused on my goals, kept me out of trouble in high school, and was a real comfort when my dad died." Blake was now quiet and thinking to himself.

218

"So, what made you stop?"

He hadn't heard my question. Instead, he was caught up in the nostalgic memory of something that had once given him joy and solace.

He went on.

"You know, I even continued singing in law school; it was the one thing I knew would clear my head. I haven't done this since I was a first-year associate . . . wow, nearly seven years ago."

"What do you think it would mean to you if you started to go back to worship singing now?" Blake needed to take some action, and it didn't involve a lateral move to a corporation.

Blake got very quiet and stared at me for a long time. Finally, he looked down at his hands and said, "I think it would mean the difference between life and early death for me."

"How so?"

"Singing worship just connects me to God, to my spirit, to the other worshippers. It feels other-worldly when I sing, and it just feels like I'm alive and vibrant and filled with energy. It's the difference between feeling alive and feeling numb," he added gently.

"And what do you want to choose?"

"Life. I want a life again," Blake said firmly.

There it was.

Blake was articulating and owning what he wanted. And the look of deep relief on his face suddenly made him look ten years younger.

"You're going to have to learn to say no," I added. "But to other people who may not be used to hearing it from you. You do realize that, right?"

He nodded his head and added with a smile, "Yes, I get that, 'Lady No,' I get that."

"Lady No" was his nickname for me during our work together, and Blake would tell me that whenever he was tempted to say yes to others about things that weren't healthy for him, he would conjure up an image of me in his head and ask himself, *What would Lady No say?*

Blake and I worked together for about a year to figure out how to create healthy boundaries in his work and private life. He decided to take a leave of absence from his firm for about three months to focus on his health and recovery. During that time, he discovered that his spiritual practice was the bedrock of his wellness and stability. He realized that it was pivotal for him to have time for worship in his life. We worked on introducing his worship singing back into his life. Blake created the space he needed to start questioning some of his Achievement-Addicted patterns by grounding himself in his faith.

During those three months' leave, Blake took stock of his values, what was important in his life, and what he needed to do to keep his diabetes in check and manage his mental health. Ultimately, he ended his engagement with his fiancée and started to go to Bible classes at a church in NYC. After that, he returned to practice at his law firm for about another year but soon discovered that law-firm practice in New York was no longer aligned with his wellness or his moral and religious values.

I lost touch with Blake for a while. But about six months after he left Big Law, I received a text from him saying, "Hey there, Lady No, hope you're well. Wanted to let you know that I moved back to Alabama and joined a midsize firm. Life is easier down here. I am also enrolling part-time in chaplain school so I can serve as a chaplain for those who suffer. I can't afford not to practice law, but I'm lucky that the firm I'm with supports my worship efforts and my interest in volunteering as a chaplain. So I guess I didn't have to say no to law after all, but just no to practicing law in NYC."

Blake's story is a constant reminder to me of the power of faith to shift perspective, experience, and even direction.

Achievement Addiction

➤ launched Blake into an Achievement Trance that blinded him to his physical ailments and compromised his health and personal life;

➤ had Blake pursuing achievement after achievement despite the physical and mental strain that it was causing; and

➤ caused Blake to suppress his true self and the role that faith played in his life.

Achievement Addiction DETOX helped Blake

➤ recognize the impact Achievement Addiction was having on his health and well-being;

➤ learn how to control the Achievement Avatar that had him convinced he should continue to pursue achievement after achievement at the expense of his physical and mental health; and

➤ reconnect with his true self and incorporate a faith-based mind-set that helped support him during transitions in his career.

I like to think about this analogy when discussing the power of faith: When you want to cross an ocean, you need a strong vessel, some training, a crew, specific maps, radar, GPS, etc. These are very concrete and specific objects and actions that need to be put into place. But other less obvious and unseen forces of nature are also required to make the trip successful. Elements like wind speed, wind direction, the tide, currents, sunshine, and other factors invisible to the naked eye and well outside of our control are also needed. When you sail, there's an implicit understanding that both the tangible and the intangible elements must work in tandem for the boat to reach its destination.

And so it is with faith. We are all very good at mastering the tangible skills we need. But imagine how far we might go if we were to acknowledge, nurture, and engage those less tangible forces invisible to the naked eye but perhaps equally vital for us to reach our destinations.

Omar was someone who rediscovered the power of his faith and its ability to heal the damage caused by Achievement Addiction.

Omar the Somnambulist

Fatima reached out to me one snowy afternoon, leaving me a very abrupt voicemail message. It said I had been highly recommended to her by some friends and that I should call her back as soon as I possibly could. No details. Just a curt imperative followed by an international number and the time difference between Dubai and New York.

I called her the next day to discover that Fatima was not calling for herself but on behalf of her husband, Omar—the very Omar who was at that moment on a plane flying to New York City.

After some basic niceties, Fatima came straight to the point: "He will be in NYC tomorrow, he will be staying at the Four Seasons, and I would like you to meet with him. He knows that I am calling you, and he has agreed to meet you." Fatima was all business.

She concluded our brief discussion with a steely final directive: "If he doesn't show up at your office, you will call me immediately to let me know. He knows that, too. That was our agreement. Do we have an understanding?" Fatima was calling all the shots.

I agreed to her terms but told her that whatever Omar and I discussed would be confidential, and I wouldn't be able to share our meeting's details unless he gave me permission.

Unfazed, Fatima responded, "He will agree to it. Call me tomorrow after your meeting, please. Thank you. Goodbye." *Click.*

Omar arrived promptly at my office fifteen minutes before our scheduled meeting. He was average looking, with a slight frame. He was bespectacled and well-dressed but overall nondescript. In other words, he wasn't memorable or noticeable in any way. But I will remember his story for the rest of my life.

Before I could understand why he was sitting with me, Omar blurted out, "By the way, you have my permission to talk to my wife. Whatever she wants. Not a problem with me." Omar then sat across from me with a blank but somehow nervous look on his face.

"I guess you are wondering why I am here and why Fatima called you," he began.

"Yes, I am," I answered. Omar looked like he needed to unload whatever it was he had to share quickly. I didn't want to get in his way.

"So, here's the deal. Fatima has threatened to take the boys and leave me if I don't change. And that is not possible in our culture. So our families have come together to discuss the problem, and we have all agreed that I need to change. So here I am." *Aha, so Fatima isn't the only one calling the shots,* I thought.

"What needs to change?" I asked.

"Everything. My work hours, the drinking, the client dinners, my mistress and the hookers, my world travel, club memberships, and golf. It all has to stop. I have tried on my own, but I cannot do it alone. I cannot say no. Fatima says I am weak. I have always been weak. It's like I have been living these last five years in a bad dream, and I cannot seem to wake up from it. I don't know how it ever got this bad. But it is bad. It needs to change, or I will lose everything. My parents won't even talk to me right now. I have brought a lot of shame to them and our community. I have lost my way."

It turns out our nondescript Omar was a multimillion-dollar hedge fund genius. He was the youngest son of one of the most prominent Pakistani families that controlled much of that country's mining. Eton- and Oxford-educated with an MBA from Stanford Business School, he'd gone straight into founding one of the most successful hedge funds in existence.

Omar had been on a course of nonstop über-achievement from the cradle. His marriage to Fatima had been arranged by their families very early on, as was the cultural custom. They and their two sons lived in New York and Dubai.

But Omar had a lot to prove to himself, his older brother (a parliament member), his wife, and her family. His relentless drive to prove himself worthy had him working around the clock, flying around the world most months, and chasing achievement after achievement at the expense of his family, health, marriage, and mental stability.

Omar had recently been accepted as the first Muslim member of one of the world's most elite and exclusive golf clubs. But that wasn't enough. He was now networking his ass off, traveling the globe to become the president of one of the world's most exclusive business clubs.

However, it had all come to a head. All his success was on the verge of crashing down around him. Fatima had found out about his mistress, his nonstop womanizing, and his drinking (which was against their religion). And she and their families had given him an ultimatum: change your life—*now*—or suffer ex-communication from the families.

Omar's whole life had to change overnight, and all he had known since childhood was endless achievement.

That afternoon, he described his experience like this:

"It's like I'm waking up from a twenty-five-year nightmare. I honestly can't tell you how it all started or when it got so out of control. I genuinely thought I was doing everything right, pleasing everyone, doing what was expected of me, achieving everything everyone wanted me to achieve. Only to discover that I was sleepwalking through my life and quietly destroying myself—and the very life I had spent decades building up.

"I feel like I've just come out of a weird coma to discover that everything has been taken away from me," he went on. "Right now, I am just lost. I was the golden boy—the youngest son. I was adored. Envied. And I live for that, you know? That's what I was chasing. I live for that . . . for that look, that look of envy and admiration from others. You know what I mean, right?"

Omar was almost glowing as he reexperienced the sheer euphoria other people's approval, applause, envy, and admiration gave him. I decided this was my chance to push Omar a little further.

Omar had lots of people telling him what to do, where to be, and what to think. Even our coaching arrangement had been arranged by his family. During our sessions, I was starting to feel that Omar was just going through the motions. I was growing more certain that Omar was living a good portion of his life in an Achievement Trance—moving through his life in a semi-dream state without ownership of his decisions or their consequences. To transform his life in a lasting way, Omar needed to wake up from his Achievement Trance and regain some autonomy. And it needed to start with ownership. And ownership demanded a dose of unvarnished honesty.

I paused before I continued because I was about to drop a grenade into the conversation.

"I do know what you mean, Omar. Other people's approval can be very addictive. It can end up controlling our lives without our even knowing it. In fact, Omar, you may not like what I am about to say to you, but it seems to me that all the chaos in your life right now can be directly traced back to your worship of idols." I took a quick breath and continued before he could interrupt. "Omar, you worship other people's approval at the expense of everything including your autonomy and dignity. From where I sit, you have made other people your higher power...your God, and it has nearly cost you everything that is important and real to you, wouldn't you agree?"

Omar winced. Then he went pale. His eyes then narrowed in on me with steely anger. He scrutinized me for a good long while. Neither of us broke eye contact. I took a deep breath and said a quiet prayer for guidance. I realized that my observation could be interpreted as an insulting provocation. It could backfire and cause us both harm. But I followed my intuition. And my intuition told me to start talking to Omar about faith. At that moment, all I could do was hope that my good intentions hadn't been buried by my clumsy delivery.

But the message had its intended impact. Slowly Omar's face softened and he looked down at his thick gold wedding band with damp, sparkling eyes. I could tell that I did more than just hit a nerve. Something touched Omar deeply. He looked up at me and cleared his throat before he spoke.

"You know, Elena, I was taught that worshipping idols referred to other religions, you know, Jesus, Buddha... I never thought it might mean worshipping things or people. It's a different way of thinking about idolatry. What you said has hit me hard. And I'll need to think more about it. It's a different perspective, an interesting one."

He fell silent again before adding, "You know, there was once a time in my life when my faith was a central part of my life. I loved going to the mosque with my father, uncles, and brothers. I felt so alive. Part of something larger that was truly important. I felt connected to something...everlasting." Omar was looking out the window and into the far distance as he spoke.

"Whenever I prayed I felt 'seen' by God and it didn't scare me, it actually made me feel loved and protected." Omar went on to tell me more about his faith and personal relationship with God and how it had supported him through difficult times in his childhood. In our work together, Omar rekindled his faith practices, which offered him the guidance and solace he needed as he went about repairing his life and career. I have lost touch with Omar over the years, but his story still serves as a vivid example of the power of faith and how it can help in mitigating the impact of Achievement Addiction.

Achievement Addiction

➤ almost cost Omar his marriage, his kids, and his connection to the power and influence of his larger family network;

➤ induced in Omar an Achievement Trance that blinded him to the damage his Achievement Addiction was inflicting on his health, reputation, family, and career; and

➤ compromised Omar's personal autonomy which left him feeling numb, lost and confused about his ability to make good choices aligned with his values, faith, and sense of purpose.

Achievement Addiction DETOX helped Omar

➤ develop some awareness around the self-destructive nature of his Achievement Addiction;

➤ disentangle and simplify his life by reducing his non-family commitments; and

➤ reconnect with his strong faith and core values that offered him the solace, courage, and resilience he needed to make some serious changes in his life and lifestyle.

The Science Behind Faith

No matter what you believe in, science-backed evidence suggests that making time in your life to connect with faith can play a crucial role in mitigating some of the internal chaos that often fuels mental health issues, addiction, and feelings of isolation and victimhood. The research in this area confirms that

> *religious involvement* and *spirituality* are associated with *better health outcomes, including greater longevity,* **coping skills,** *and health-related quality of life (even during terminal illness) and* **less anxiety, depression, and suicide.** Several studies have shown that addressing the spiritual needs of the patient may enhance recovery from illness. *Faith has been proven to give structure and meaning to an individual's behaviors, his values, and life experiences.*[4]
>
> *(Emphases mine.)*

For many of us, it would never occur to us to make time to cultivate our faith during the workday. But for many who have, doing so can invite more sanity, serenity, and well-being into our daily life and activities.

If you have managed to keep an open mind until now about the impact of faith on our day-to-day lives, I offer these practical suggestions on how to access faith:

- Those of us whose faith is intertwined with meditation can commit to participating in an active breathing exercise at least once per day.
- Those of us whose faith resides in nature, the environment, and the outdoors, in general, can commit to spending time outside and to connecting with nature and the wonder and energy that it inspires.
- And for those of us whose faith is intertwined with religion, we can take measures to weave some faith-based practice into our every day, perhaps through prayer, reading, and connecting with others who share our belief system, rituals, or specific faith-based practices.

[4] Paul S. Mueller, MD; David J. Plevak, MD; and Teresa A. Rummans, MD, "Religious Involvement, Spirituality, and Medicine: Implications for Clinical Practice," *Mayo Clinic Proceedings* 76 (12): 1225–35. doi: 10.4065/76.12.1225.

Achievement Addiction has us in a trance-like haze, living our present lives entirely focused on the future to the point that we lose all sense of connection to our day-to-day existence. By introducing a spiritual or secular faith practice in our lives, we are better able to short-circuit our Achievement-Addicted fixation on the future so we can connect to the present moment. And by finding a way to focus solely on the present moment, we are better able to pause, reflect, and examine many of our Achievement-Addicted compulsions and automatic responses. Only then can we start to see a broader range of possibilities beyond Achievement Addiction.

STEP 6: FAITH
The IMAGO Coaching Questions

Now it's time for you to work on Step 6—FAITH—using several IMAGO Coaching Questions. All the questions below are designed to help you work this sixth step and deepen your understanding of how Achievement Addiction has impacted and/or suppressed the role of faith in your life.

In addition, following each question, I offer you a way to summarize your sixth-step insights in the form of a declaratory sentence. These summarized insights will be essential to refer to should you choose to download and complete the Achievement Addiction DETOX Worksheets accessible at www.achievementaddictiondetox.com.

To recap, the IMAGO Coaching Method invites you to INQUIRE, MAGNIFY, ACT, GROW, and OWN.

The questions below can help you work this sixth step.

INQUIRE

How has Achievement Addiction contributed to increasing your overall level of fear?

_____

_____

How has your Achievement Addiction compromised your level of faith?

_____

_____

_____

In my addictive pursuit of achievement, I have ignored or replaced faith with fear in the following ways:

_____

_____

Magnify

How has increased day-to-day fear caused pain, suffering, discomfort, or challenges? With your health? With your mental well-being? With others?

_____

_____

_____

In my addictive pursuit of achievement, the increased level of fear in my life has caused me _____ and has created several challenges, including . . .

_____

_____

_____

Because of fear, I suffer in the following ways:

_____

_____

. . . and the people around me suffer in the following ways:

_____

_____

Act

Think about the most difficult challenge you are struggling with right now. What does fear tell you?

_____

_____

What would faith tell you?

_____

_____

What action steps can you take to access the voice and wisdom of faith more frequently?

_____

_____

I want to take the following action steps toward reducing my fear and accessing the voice and wisdom of faith:

_____

_____

_____

Reconnecting with my faith would mean that . . .

_____

_____

Grow

Take a moment to imagine what it might look like if you increased your level of connection with the voice and wisdom of faith. What might a shift away from fear and toward faith mean to you?

_____

_____

_____

To your health? To your family and friends?

_____

_____

_____

I want to reduce my level of fear and grow my faith because it would mean that . . .

_____

_____

_____

Own

Hopefully, answering these questions has helped you increase your awareness of how Achievement Addiction has impacted the roles of fear and faith in your day-to-day life. So, let's turn to owning that newfound awareness around fear and FAITH.

When it comes to faith, I own and acknowledge that my Achievement Addiction has increased my day-to-day level of fear in the following ways:

_____

_____

_____

. . . and that if I could take steps to increase my connection with the voice and wisdom that faith has to offer, it would mean . . .

_____

_____

_____

FINAL THOUGHTS:
Faith and Achievement Addiction

✓ Choosing faith over fear (Step 6) is both a cognitive and a spiritual practice that invites us to expand our perspective and alter our experience of any given circumstance in real-time.

✓ Many Achievement Addicts operate from a fear-driven worldview that leaves them feeling anxiety-ridden, paralyzed, and reactive. It is a worldview that narrows their perspective and leaves them believing their options for change are limited.

✓ When we embrace a posture of faith instead of fear, we invite wonder, curiosity, play, mystery, and hope back into our lives, which automatically expands our perspective and range of possibilities.

ALIGNMENT
Trust Yourself

Thriving Beyond Achievement Addiction

As I have said before, many of my clients who come to coaching do not come for reasons related to chronic mental disorders. Instead, they come seeking what can best be described as "life-career coaching." Many come to me suffering from situational depression, a low-grade malaise primarily caused, in these instances, by an overall misalignment between their values and careers. This misalignment leaves them feeling miserable and disconnected from their lives.

The truth is, many of us have never spent time getting clear on our values, much less on our passions or what gives us meaning and purpose. For many, it is only when we enter therapy or a coaching relationship that we are invited for the first time to identify our core values and talk about our passions and our vision for ourselves.

When we first set our destinies toward achievement, many of us were too young to reflect on and articulate our core values. Some of us might have been swept up by the dominant Western values of achievement, prestige, power, and monetary success that were perhaps driving our decisions at the time. For many, like Blake or others, we got to know in the previous stories, core values only become clear in a moment of crisis, illness, or tragedy. For others, core values slowly start to take form in the context and contrast of our relationships with colleagues, our firm, our clients, our spouse, and our friends. And the truth is that our core values can change with our life experiences. Regardless of where we are in our lives, understanding our core values allows us to test their veracity; only then can we assess whether our lives and work align with those values. Alignment is key to feeling whole, integrated, authentic, and grounded. When our values and behaviors are aligned, there is harmony, and we are more likely to find meaning and purpose in our lives.

However, when we are out of touch with our values, don't even know what they are anymore, or find that our values and life circumstances are out of sync, we can encounter dissonance and a sense of disconnection from just about everything and everyone.

Julia was someone who discovered the power and impact of alignment.

Julia the Singing Lawyer

When you're an executive law coach, there are law firms that you just want the privilege of working with. They are the top handful of law firms that evoke admiration, respect, awe, and, admittedly, envy. They are the superstar firms that get all the Supreme Court clerks, do all the deals on the front page of the *Wall Street Journal*, and have offices in the glitziest Class A buildings with partners who make an average of $5 million to $7 million annually. One afternoon, I got a call from the head of professional development at one of the country's top three firms.

She was calling about a senior associate named Julia who was on track to make partner in the firm's highly competitive mergers and acquisitions practice. Julia was one of those people who could pull several all-nighters in a row and still manage to pull it together the next day. She was also a painfully shy social introvert who—I later found out—struggled with social anxiety.

Clients loved Julia and were continually inviting her to dinners, happy hours, and $2,500-a-plate gala dinners.

But Julia was turning them all down—methodically, intentionally, and consistently. It was now causing partners to reconsider whether she "had what it took" to make partner. Julia was not being asked to generate clients because this firm didn't need associates—or even partners, quite frankly—to do that. She was asked to take a leadership role at the firm and engage socially.

And for the first time in her life, Julia was failing and felt terrified.

My job was to work with Julia to improve her social skills. The firm didn't know about her social anxiety, for which she'd been prescribed medication. The firm was also unaware that she was a recovering alcoholic who struggled with social environments that involved alcohol. She felt trapped, sabotaged by her own body and addictions, and like an overall failure, so she agreed to see an executive coach.

Julia and I worked together weekly for about a year. During that time, we experimented with all kinds of ways to mitigate her social anxiety, but none worked. Fear had her by the throat and was slowly squeezing her career prospects to death.

It was the dead of winter, and I was sitting in my office waiting for Julia to knock on my door. I suddenly became aware of a beautiful voice singing—in an almost operatic voice—a breathtaking version of "Ave Maria." I checked my radio to see if I had left it on, and then it occurred to me that the voice was coming from the private waiting area outside my office door.

It suddenly stopped, and seconds later, there was a knock on the door. I opened my door to find Julia bundled from head to toe in her coat, hat, scarf, and mittens. She padded into the office, took off her winter gear, and plopped into the chair.

I waited for her to get comfortable and began wracking my brain for some genius way to ask her about the singing.

"Was that you?!" was the best I could come up with. I was met with silence. "I heard the most angelic voice singing 'Ave Maria' several seconds ago, and thought—"

"Yes," Julia cut me off quietly.

"Tell me," I said.

"Tell you what?"

"About your singing. Tell me about it." I was met with more deafening silence.

"Please?" I tried one last time.

She looked up with tears in her eyes, and she could barely speak. After several seconds she said, "That was a previous life. The Julia who loved to sing is no longer here. I was accepted to Harvard Law at the same time I was offered a spot in the Westminster Vocal Choir. I went to Harvard. That's that."

Julia's face fell; I was stunned. This wallflower who had spent the past six months too terrified to interact socially with her clients was capable of standing before an audience to sing choral music!

Every now and then, as a coach, you are given synchronistic clues about the direction to take to help a person. A book called *When God Winks* talks about how the Universe sends us signs—a "God wink"—to let us know that we are heading down the right path. Julia unconsciously singing to herself in the quiet of a snowy winter evening was a God wink.

Julia was undoubtedly living in fear. Her whole worldview was fear-driven and fear-based. Nevertheless, here was a sign that there was a fearless part to Julia. My hope was that if we focused her coaching on what was meaningful to her and reconnected her with her vocal performance skills, she would develop faith in herself once again, which might spill over and give her the confidence she needed to interact socially with her clients.

Over the coming months, Julia and I worked closely to understand how, when, and why she could become fearless when she sang before audiences. She explained that when she sang in the choir, she knew that everyone there wanted to hear her and shared the same passion for music. That shared passion and shared value system created safety for her—safety enough to belt out complicated classical songs in Latin. When she felt safe, and with like-minded people, Julia had faith that she could be herself with ease.

That became the key to our work on her ability to slow down her racing mind, find common ground with clients based on their passions and interests, and view her social interactions with clients as musical performances. This enabled her to engage clients on topics regarding music, opera, classical arts, choral arts, etc. As a result, she was able to reconnect with her core values, which helped her shift her mindset away from fear.

In our work together, Julia was able to reconnect and realign her life with that passion that gave meaning and purpose to her life. In the process, she was able to leverage the self-confidence and mastery that she felt in the musical arena as a template for socializing with clients. She made music a priority in her life again; she dusted off old lyric sheets, listened to choral music again, and joined a local choir. Julia made attending her choir practice a priority; it was hard at first for her to commit, but over time, she managed to create flexible boundaries around this passion that she honored and, eventually, those at the firm honored, too. By committing time to something that she was passionate about, Julia explained that she felt more herself, more like that eighteen-year-old person who thought she could conquer anything. Connecting with her passion allowed her to reconnect with something that had real meaning to her alone. That reunion with something of passion and significance fueled her ability to take on interpersonal and social challenges that she'd thought she couldn't handle.

My understanding is that Julia is now a partner at that firm. I recently received a note from her telling me that her networking and business development were finally becoming second nature. She also shared that she had joined the board of a local choral music association and integrated her passion with her law work. Julia embraced her passion, rediscovered what gave meaning and color to her world, and used it all to get her fear under control and step into the leadership role that was waiting for her at the firm.

Achievement Addiction

➤ induced in Julia an Achievement Trance that distanced her from her true self and her values, talents, and passions;

➤ allowed Julia's Achievement Avatar to dominate her mindset, pushing her to pursue achievement after achievement at the expense of all her interests, talents, and values; and

➤ induced in Julia a form of Achievement Amnesia that caused her to forget her prior achievements in music and how confident, capable, and talented she truly was.

Achievement Addiction DETOX helped Julia

➤ recognize the impact Achievement Addiction was having on her self-confidence and sense of self-worth;

➤ control over her negative self-talk and the Achievement Avatar that had her convinced that she should continue to pursue achievement after achievement at the expense of all her other passions and interests; and

➤ reconnect with her true self and focus on incorporating music back into her life as a way to create a greater alignment of her true passions, talents, and values.

Alignment, Meaning, and Purpose

Many of my clients ended up pursuing their high-achieving careers by default. Many of us started out as wannabe doctors, writers, playwrights, performers, academics, astronauts, or scientists. Many more of us encountered obstacles, failure, or disapproval on the road to those destinations and felt a need to reassess our dreams. So we looked into going to law school, medical school, or business school, and before we knew it, what started as "I'll just take the LSAT and see what happens" somehow catapulted us into our first constitutional law class only a few months later.

For many of us, these high-achieving career paths offered a "safe, well-respected" career. Perhaps choosing these paths allowed us to rise socioeconomically and exceed our families' expectations. And maybe these high-achieving, über-professional career paths allowed us to feel seen, influential, and accomplished.

Whatever the reason, anything done by default has its pitfalls and risks. And for many default professionals, the risk has been that our core values became sidelined, our actions became misaligned with our core values, and along with that, our sense of meaning and purpose in our work slowly dissipated.

We know that people who believe that their lives are aligned with their values and that their lives have meaning and purpose are generally happier and healthier.

But rediscovering our personal passions, values, talents, and interests later on in our careers can feel overwhelming and difficult to imagine. Yet, sometimes, putting in the hard work to reacquaint yourself with your core values and past passions can make all the difference between misery and joy.

Charlotte discovered the transformative power of reconnecting with her values and past passions.

Southern Belle Charlotte

Charlotte heralded from the South with a capital *S*. She'd been a finalist in the US Junior Miss competition and had been a cheerleader for the Dallas Cowboys before heading to law school to do IP/copyright law. She was petite and lovely and had a model's face with airbrush-perfect makeup, and never a strand of hair out of place. She always looked like she was ready for a photo shoot. Along the way, Charlotte had married a prominent, wealthy financier who was significantly older than she was and who truly worshipped her. She was introduced to me by her husband, who had called me to find out about coaching on her behalf.

You might be surprised to know that that happens more times than you might imagine. A loving or frustrated spouse, partner, sibling, or parent will sometimes initiate a call or meeting with me on behalf of their loved one. Their loved one simply won't take any action, won't budge to make a change, or feels too stuck or confused even to take the first step to talk to a coach or advisor.

It was immediately clear to me from the way he described Charlotte that Allan truly adored his wife and worshipped the ground she walked on; but recently, he explained, he'd noticed that Charlotte had lost her sparkle and that he knew she was "stuck, maybe even a little depressed and lost." She needed a gentle nudge toward figuring out the next step in her life, and Allan hoped I might be able to help. Before ending our call, I asked Allan why she didn't reach out to me directly. Allan stated matter-of-factly, "Embarrassment, or pride, I guess. Charlotte isn't the kind of woman . . . how should I put this? Charlotte isn't the kind of woman who wears her heart on her sleeve. You'll see what I mean when you meet her. She'll be at your office next Monday at noon, even if I have to show up with her." And then he hung up.

Meeting Charlotte was like meeting a Hollywood starlet from the '40s. Charlotte was a five-foot-nothing, girl-next-door, all-American beauty with a pure, milky-white complexion that gave off a gauzy, luminous aura around her. She moved consciously with the precise posture of a ballerina. Everything about her was purposefully put together; nothing was left to chance or nature.

It was clear within seconds that Charlotte worked hard to cultivate this image. It was damn impressive. But, as Allan had warned, the impenetrability of her well-crafted façade was as thick as her perfectly applied makeup. It took a lot of time to figure out what she was doing in my office. "Everything is truly lovely in my life. I am blessed. Truly. Life is truly wonderful." Three uses of the word *truly* in one brief utterance make someone like me pause with measured skepticism.

And with good reason.

It took several sessions for Charlotte to feel comfortable enough to share with me her less-than-perfect inner struggles.

"I just don't know about my career anymore. Should I or should I not go back into law?" She was a "pro/con" list maker. She read me her list of pros for returning to practice. She then read me her equally long list of cons. She then would return to listing the pros again . . . and then the cons. This cycle happened several times. Charlotte was spinning and stuck. In almost every session, she would plead, "What do you think? Can't you just tell me what I should do? I mean, should I go back, or shouldn't I?"

And time and time again, I would explain that what I thought or believed didn't matter; she was more than capable of realizing what was right for her. What I wanted for her was to reach the point where she could get in touch with her own values and make a decision that was grounded in her own process.

After three weeks of not moving from her list of pros and cons, I started the next session calmly, saying, "Charlotte, I'm going to tell you what is true for me and see what comes up for you when you hear this. Truth is, Charlotte, I'm dizzy. Really about to throw up, room-spinning, nauseated, and dizzy from going around and around and around in circles with you on this one question. . . . And something tells me you are even dizzier than I am. 'Saying what is so' can be helpful to clear the air. So, 'what is so' is that we are now *both* stuck and unable to answer this question. So, here's my thought: We need to move away from the pros and cons. We need to move away from the question you're posing altogether. We need a fresh approach—a new angle. So I am going to stop there. I really want to hear your thoughts on this. What do you make of what I'm saying?"

I was taking a risk by saying what was so, but sometimes you need to dive into the heart of a whirlpool to get out from under its grip. It was now time for me to be quiet and see what she said.

Charlotte's expression was calm.

She said nothing. She then smiled at me and nodded as if to say, "I heard you. I'm thinking."

So I let the silence fill the space between our seats.

On my little table between us was a copy of that month's *Vogue* magazine that I had carried in but forgotten to put away before the session.

Charlotte picked it up and thumbed through it; the ruffling sound of its glossy, thick pages was the only sound in the room.

"You know," she slowly started without looking up from the magazine, "growing up on a small farm in Texas, I used to take my allowance from doing chores around the farm and use every single cent to subscribe to *Vogue*."

She kept flipping the pages ever more slowly, savoring each image. "I saved every single copy of my *Vogue*s from the age of thirteen until I came to New York in my mid-thirties. I was this itty-bitty southern girl living in the middle of nowhere, but . . . when I read *Vogue* . . . somehow . . . the world became bigger, and so did my dreams. I dreamed with these magazines. I kept them all in Ziplock bags in boxes in my closet."

I said nothing but kept watching her turn the magazine pages as if in a dream. Something was slowly coming alive for Charlotte, and it needed a whole lot of time and space. The air was no longer stale but a little bubblier.

She went on in an animated but softer voice, still not looking up from the pages.

"I still have those magazines, you know. I held on to them; I don't know why. I was always really passionate about glamour, fashion, and design. It was magic to me. How something like a pair of shoes or a perfectly designed chair in just the right painted room could transform . . . transform a person or a whole room or house from something . . . from . . . I don't know, the mundane and boring to . . . magic. To something truly unique."

She was now on a roll.

"In addition to the magazines, I'd beg my mom to take me to the fabric stores in town so I could pick out pieces of shiny, elegant fabric scraps or remnants. I'd take them home and put them in a bin under my bed. Somehow, having the fabric made the images I saw more real."

Charlotte was still lovingly flipping through the *Vogue* when I asked, "So, what comes up when you think about that Charlotte who was crazy about *Vogue*, fashion, and fabric? Why do you think that's coming up now?"

She was silent as a single tear cut through the layers of makeup to her real skin.

She wiped it away and looked at me with composure regained.

"My biggest dream was always to be in fashion and to design fashion and clothing or accessories. I taught myself how to sew when I was fifteen, and I used to make all my own clothes." She sighed deeply, fixing her eyes back on the magazine as she continued to pore over its pages. "But being a designer wasn't going to pay my bills or get me out of Texas. I was pretty enough to get recruited as a cheerleader and tried out for Junior Miss, which gave me a college scholarship. . . I mean, what college in Texas could have taught me fashion? So I ended up studying French. I was good with languages, and I wanted to be able to read French *Vogue!*" She laughed to herself.

The reverie went on.

"It was the closest I thought I would get to Paris or the fashion industry. But then one thing led to another, and one of my advisors thought I would make a good lawyer. So I ended up going to law school on a scholarship. Didn't really think too much about it at the time. It was a way up and out of Texas and got me to New York. The closest my practice could bring me to fashion or design was to focus on trademark law."

Charlotte then took a big sigh, closed the *Vogue*, and placed it neatly back on my desk.

"Sounds to me like you need to get off the merry-go-round," I offered.

"What merry-go-round?" She was perplexed.

"The law merry-go-round. The one that you got on—for lots of good reasons—back when you were in your twenties, and the one you got off once you were more financially stable. It served you well, no?"

"Well, yes. . . . I mean, it got me to New York, where I worked hard for many years and paid my bills, loans, helped my family back in Texas. . . . And it allowed me to meet my husband." She smiled whenever she mentioned him; she adored him as much as he adored her.

"And now?" I asked.

"And now . . . and now, maybe I don't only have to think about law?" she asked hesitantly.

"Let's stay with that. Let's play. What if you didn't have to go back to law?" Suddenly she beamed.

"Well, I would do something, anything having to do with design or fashion. . . ."

Charlotte was now animated and talking fast about her list of design ideas that she had had over the years. When she finished, she looked radiant and excited.

"So, tell me, if you knew you couldn't fail, what's your moonshot? What's your vision for yourself?"

It turned out that Charlotte wanted to design very high-end swim-wear and accessories. High-price-tag, beautiful, high-quality bathing suits, matching clothing, and accessories. But she admitted she didn't know the first thing about the fashion industry.

I told her the only way to do this was to jump fully, experientially into the place she wanted to be. See how that played out, how it felt, who the people in the field were, and how they seemed. I said, "Next time I see you, bring the Fashion Institute of Technology course catalog to our session."

She did. She was excited about the various courses she could take. She was nonstop engaged, over-the-top ecstatic, and completely aligned with her lifelong passion for fashion. Charlotte signed up for her first class several weeks later. We worked together for a year. She began an apprenticeship with a fashion design professional. Her glossy, perfected lawyer persona was no longer burying the creative, inspired, and visionary fashion maven she really was and wanted to be.

Charlotte was able to reconnect with her passion and values. Through that reconnection, she could think beyond the immediately apparent and limited options life presented to her. She was able to envision work that held more creative meaning for her and reflected those passions, interests, and talents that had once had to be sidelined in the interest of more practical choices.

Achievement Addiction

➤ induced in Charlotte an Achievement Trance that distanced her from her true self and her values, talents, and passions;

➤ allowed Charlotte's Achievement Avatar to dominate her mind-set, spurring her to pursue achievement after achievement at the expense of all her interests, talents, and values; and

➤ induced in Charlotte a form of Achievement Amnesia that caused her to lose touch with her prior passion for fashion.

Achievement Addiction DETOX helped Charlotte

➤ recognize the impact Achievement Addiction was having on her self-confidence and sense of self-worth;

➤ gain control over her negative self-talk and the Achievement Avatar that had her convinced she should continue to pursue achievement after achievement at the expense of all her other passions and interests; and

➤ create more alignment in her life as she redesigned her career to incorporate her life-long passion for fashion.

Connecting with our core values and rediscovering what once excited us is a powerful step toward introducing meaning and purpose back into our lives and toward mitigating some of the malaise caused by years of misalignment.

This final story about Melody, a non-lawyer, will forever be a reminder to me of what can happen to us when we dare to reconnect with those hidden passions that once gave meaning to our lives.

Melody and Her Sweet Potato Pie

When I started as a career coach, I ran my practice out of my home office. Our home had a small, cottage-like shed in the backyard, and I turned that space into my office. My first clients were Scarsdale moms—brilliant, accomplished, pedigreed women, many of whom had left successful careers on Wall Street as bankers, brokers, lawyers, marketing directors, computer programmers, fundraisers, analysts, consultants, journalists, editors, or entrepreneurs to become stay-at-home moms. Many, if not all, were married to equally successful and wealthy men who enabled, if not preferred, that domestic arrangement. And those moms came to me in droves, looking for something meaningful to do with themselves once their second or third child was in elementary school.

Some wanted to re-enter their previous professions and found themselves lacking confidence, skills, or recent experience. Others didn't know what they wanted to do, only that they wanted and needed to do something, *anything* beyond their daily responsibilities of carpooling, extracurricular activities, tennis leagues, and school fundraising. These women felt that they had lost their sense of selfhood in the decade they had been raising their children. They spent their days taking care of everyone else in their lives, and they were desperately trying to find a way back to themselves.

Melody, who had been a very successful hedge fund banker ten years earlier, came to me in early September. She had four children, and the youngest one had just started first grade. As a result, Melody wanted to find a second career for herself. She didn't want to go back into banking; she had a natural artistic talent that she had never pursued, and she and I were exploring what visual arts career options might be available to her.

She was also a baker, and for the first month, to my great delight, she made a point of bringing that day's baked goods to each and every coaching session. Brownies, blondies, oatmeal cookies, tartlets, red velvet cupcakes, fudge . . . the list went on. I was incredibly grateful because, as my children could attest, I was a great cook, but I wasn't a baker. So much so that I was the proud owner of a black T-shirt with pink bedazzled lettering that read "I DON'T DO CUPCAKES." So, Melody's baking was a welcome treat every week.

But by the second month, I started to notice an increase in the volume she would bring. First, it was a paper plate with a couple of items for us to share. Then she would give me small plastic containers that were about half full. After that, she started bringing larger tins, enough for me and the kids.

And then one afternoon, a week before Thanksgiving, Melody came into my office carrying a 24-inch-high, Rubbermaid, two-tiered cake carrier. She carefully placed the plastic container on my desk, took off the bright red cover, and revealed about ten hefty slices of sweet potato pie. She then proceeded to take ten small paper plates out of her designer satchel, place each slice onto a plate, and put five different slices of sweet potato pie in front of me. Then she reached back into her bag, pulled out a chilled whipped cream can, and with all the solemnity of a holy benediction, proceeded to anoint each piece with a frothy swirl of God's own sweet, white goodness.

All the while, Melody explained, "God! I hate Thanksgiving. So much damn work. I am hosting again this year, and we expect about twenty people. But last year, I left the desserts to my sister-in-law, and they were store-bought, and they were terrible. So this year, I decided to make homemade sweet potato pie!" She was visibly excited as she arranged the plates of pie in front of me in perfect alignment.

That's when she turned around and handed me a white plastic fork.

"Go ahead!" she exclaimed. "Oh, and sorry about the canned whipped cream. Normally, I'd make that myself, but I didn't have time before our session. Dig in. I want your opinion." Melody stood over me and waited.

"My opinion?" I asked. I tried my best to keep up with her, but the whipped cream can at the ready in her left hand was throwing me off. I was so confused.

"Yes, your unbiased opinion. I was up until three this morning making five different versions of sweet potato pie so that I know which one is perfect and which one to make next week." She looked tired but also somewhat elated.

"You made five different pies in one night?!" I asked in shock.

"Yes. Yes, I did. I didn't know which one to make or which one would be the best or which one would make the best impression, so . . . I started researching recipes that morning, and there was no way I could know which one was the best just by reading the recipe. I was hell-bent on making each one until I knew which one was the best."

I was quiet as I gazed at the ten slices of sweet potato pie lying between us on a small table.

This was impressive, but it was also a little alarming.

"My husband thinks I'm nuts." She sounded slightly deflated.

"Actually, he thinks I need to get a life. Those were his exact words to me this morning. My kids even say it to my face. And maybe they're all right. But I wanted this Thanksgiving to be perfect! You know? I mean, I really wanted everyone to see . . . I don't know, I wanted everyone to admire me, I guess. You know, gush a little about me, about the pies I made, about the beautiful table . . ." She was starting to get a little hoarse and choked up.

Melody suddenly stopped talking and stared at all the sweet potato pies. She started to shake her head to herself. Then she began to cry silently.

"I must be out of my mind," she said flatly, shaking her head, and staring at the pie slices.

"I don't know what's wrong with me or who I am anymore. . . . I mean, five pies?! What the hell is that?" She was beating down on herself, and it was my job to stop it. But coaching is an alliance, and first, I needed her permission before I could speak freely.

After she nodded in assent, I said, "You're not nuts, and you're not a loser, and you're not crazy. You happen to be brilliantly talented as a baker. And at many other creative things. But you attacked this pie project as if you were designing a hostile takeover of an undervalued company. And you were on autopilot because you have been driven to achieve and win and be the best your whole life.

"You're a trained racehorse without a racetrack. And you've spent ten years without a place to express yourself or your abilities or your passion. Your drive is a fantastic asset. It will be amazing jet fuel in your next career. But making five pies in one night has more to do with your need to be seen as the *best* than it does with anything else. It has to do with being . . . number one," I added.

Melody stopped crying and was still gazing at her pies as she spoke.

"You know . . . I worked like crazy when I was in Greenwich at the hedge fund. I was the best. Everyone envied me, my ability to work long hours, my crazy dedication to the deal, to the client. I was a machine of excellence . . . unstoppable," she said wistfully.

"That's me. I only have one speed—and that speed drove me to make five pies so that the one I end up making for Thanksgiving . . . levitates." She was smiling again.

She leaned over and took a large forkful of the first slice, swallowed, puffed herself up, and said, "I knew this one would be the best . . . but of course, it's the last one I made."

I leaned over and took a forkful of a different delicious slice and glanced up to find Melody looking at me with all the wide-eyed, hopeful earnestness of a Labrador puppy. "So, what do you think? Maybe I'm wrong? Is that the best one? Maybe I need to go back to the first recipe and make it better. I can't have my sister-in-law gloating that her fucking $30 Balducci's bought pie last year was better than mine. . . ."

I said nothing, swallowed the morsel still in my mouth, pushed aside the table overflowing with pie slices, leaned over, and said without much finesse, "Melody, how about we forget the damn pies and focus on you? Just you. And all of you. And how about we figure out how to get you feeling connected to your life, passion, and purpose again? Because maybe, just maybe, you really are a baker, and maybe we need to start talking about what it means for you to 'only' be a baker when everyone around you is a lawyer, doctor, banker, etc."

Melody was nodding her head. Something resonated for her.

"I've always wanted to be a baker . . . and just own a small shop. . . . But that just wasn't ambitious enough in my family. My mother laughed at me and would say things like, 'Really? A baker? Susan B. Anthony fought for women's rights so you could end up in the kitchen making pies?' It made me feel stupid and worthless, to tell you the truth."

I was beginning to understand that Melody's mom was her Achievement Avatar, and at that moment, her mom had figuratively just pulled up a chair next to her and was shaking her head in disgust at all the pies Melody had made. I wanted to punch Melody's mommy-Avatar in her perfect figurative nose.

But Melody was still staring at her pies. She sat quietly for a while and then spoke.

"You know, I obsess about every detail when I work, to the point that I drive myself and everyone around me crazy. But this pie thing is a little extreme even for me. I guess you can't bury your true passion, even if you want to. And it looks to me like baking is my passion. What do you think?"

I had mindlessly shoved another piece of pie into my mouth while Melody was speaking, so my mouth was packed cheek to cheek; all I could manage in response without choking was a feverishly animated nod back at her in embarrassment. And we both cracked up laughing.

"I bet this nutty story is one for the books, huh?" Melody said, wiping away her laughter tears.

"You bet it is, sister, you can be damn sure of that."

I wrote this story ten days before Thanksgiving because, even fifteen years later, a Thanksgiving has not passed when I don't think of Melody and her five sweet potato pies. Melody battled her formidable Achievement Avatar and ended up finding meaning and purpose in her life once again by honoring her lifelong passion and talent for baking. She had been looking for her self-worth in other people's approval, and it had her depressed and stuck in a decade-long cycle of people-pleasing, perfectionism, and negative self-talk. Melody and I worked together for about a year, and she opened an online baking business that caters to her banking hedge fund network that she revived after ten years. By realigning her talents, passion, and values, Melody found meaning and purpose in her life and created a successful business that allowed her to manifest her most authentic love and talent.

Achievement Addiction

➢ induced in Melody an Achievement Trance that had her equating her self-worth with her achievements;

➢ allowed Melody's Achievement Avatar to dominate her mindset and urge her to pursue achievement after achievement at the expense of all her unique interests, talents, and abilities; and

➢ induced in Melody a form of Achievement Amnesia that caused her to forget her prior confidence and competence.

Achievement Addiction DETOX helped Melody

➢ recognize the impact misalignment with her true passion was having on her self-confidence and sense of self-worth;

➢ gain control over her negative self-talk and the Achievement Avatar that had her convinced she should continue to pursue achievement after achievement at the expense of all her other passions and interests; and

➢ create more alignment in her life by allowing her talent and passion for baking to direct her next career choice.

The truth is, almost all the stories told in this book, including my own, could have been included in this last chapter, as *each one of us suffered terribly because of a misalignment of values, meaning, and purpose*. Like Charlotte and Nathan, some of us took the plunge, left our jobs, and made drastic changes to our careers and lives. Others, like Blake, Julia, and Gustav, stayed in their original careers and made modifications to their time, schedule, location, or way of being in the world. But what has become clear to me over and over again is that reconnecting with our values and with those passions that color our lives with meaning can make the difference between a joy-filled life and a dejected, empty one.

Invariably, I believe we are all seeking the wholeness and happiness that alignment with our true selves can offer. For decades, many of us thought that the way to reach wholeness and happiness was through achievement. And perhaps, for a while, achievement and all its toys gave us that feeling.

But when achievement turned into Achievement Addiction, and when that feeling of authentic wholeness became more and more elusive, it was a sign that something was misaligned. Alignment and *not* achievement is the goal now. Aligning ourselves with our passions, values, purpose, and those things that give us meaning is the path that will help strengthen our innate and unconditional self-worth. And I believe that by accessing our innate self-worth we bring about the wholeness, balance, and happiness we once sought through Achievement Addiction.

STEP 7: ALIGNMENT
The IMAGO Coaching Questions

Now it's time for you to work on Step 7—ALIGNMENT—using several IMAGO Coaching Questions. The following questions are designed to help you work this step and deepen your understanding of how Achievement Addiction has compromised your sense of alignment with your values and sense of purpose.

Following each question, I offer you a way to summarize your insights working this seventh step in the form of a declaratory sentence. These summarized insights will be essential to refer to should you choose to download and complete the Achievement Addiction DETOX Worksheets accessible at www.achievementaddictiondetox.com.

To recap, the IMAGO Coaching Method invites you to INQUIRE, MAGNIFY, ACT, GROW, and OWN.

The questions below can help you work this seventh step.

Inquire

How has your Achievement Addiction compromised your values and your sense of purpose?

_____

_____

In my addictive pursuit of achievement, I have ignored or compromised my values or sense of purpose in the following ways:

_____

_____

Magnify

How has compromising your values and sense of purpose caused you pain, suffering, discomfort, or challenges?

_____

_____

Compromising my values and sense of purpose has caused me to feel _____ and has created several challenges, including . . .

_____

_____

Because I have compromised my values and lost my sense of purpose, I suffer in the following ways:

_____

_____

. . . and the people around me suffer in the following ways:

_____

_____

A<small>CT</small>

Think about the most difficult challenge you are struggling with right now. How does it relate to your compromised value system or sense of purpose?

_____

_____

What immediate action step can you take to realign your behavior and/or choices with your values and sense of purpose?

_____

_____

I want to take the following action steps toward realigning my life with my values and my sense of purpose:

_____

_____

Realigning my behavior and choices with my values and sense of purpose would mean that . . .

_____

_____

G<small>ROW</small>

Take a moment to envision what it might look like to have your choices and behavior more aligned with your values and your sense of purpose. What might a shift toward your values mean to you? To your health? To your sense of purpose and meaning?

_____

_____

_____

_____

I want to align my behavior and choices with my values because it would mean that . . .

_____

_____

O<small>WN</small>

Hopefully, answering these questions has helped you increase your awareness of how Achievement Addiction has impacted your alignment with your values and sense of purpose. So, let's turn to owning that newfound awareness around ALIGNMENT.

I own and acknowledge that my Achievement Addiction has caused me to be misaligned with my values and sense of purpose in the following ways:

_____

_____

_____

. . . and that if I could realign my behavior and choices with my values and sense of purpose, it would mean . . .

_____

_____

_____

FINAL THOUGHTS:
Alignment and Achievement Addiction

✓ By integrating our core values and what is meaningful to us (Step 7) into our lives, we start to align with our true selves, and we begin to create more authentic foundations for living lives that allow us to thrive beyond Achievement Addiction.

✓ As Achievement Addicts, many of us have never taken the time to identify and assess our core values and beliefs and integrate them into our adult life choices, leaving us feeling disconnected from those things that infuse meaning and purpose into our lives.

✓ When we incorporate our core values into our work and our lives in general, we start to thrive as we introduce activities and pursuits that hold meaning and purpose back into our day-to-day lives.

CONCLUSION

So, here we are. You've read a boatload of stories about Achievement Addiction and now understand the 7 Steps that can help you find your way back to health, sanity, and meaningful transformation.

Jay, Luisa, Blake, Charlotte, Trevor, Margaret, and all the others . . . *They are us.* Each one was misaligned, misguided, and caught up in the trance of Achievement Addiction. Each of their stories reflects back to us an Achievement-Addicted aspect of ourselves that compromises our own health, joy, and sanity.

All of my client stories can be boiled down to one essential truth. And that truth is this:

As Achievement Addicts, we live with the tyranny of perfectionism, negative self-talk, people-pleasing, low self-worth, self-neglect, multiple addictions, bottomless denial, self-destructive behaviors, and, worst of all, the self-delusion that more achievement is still the answer.

But now we know that these compulsions no longer serve us. And we are aware that deep down in our spirit lives a wiser inner knowing that there must be something more for us beyond Achievement Addiction. And it is that quiet inner knowing that belies the existence of a vibrant, authentic true self that still longs to be seen, heard, and manifested. A true self that wants you to thrive and that recognizes your innate self-worth that is not contingent on achievement.

By working these 7 Steps—as often as you need to work them—we gain clarity, reconnect with our true self, rediscover our innate self-worth and thrive beyond Achievement Addiction.

1. AWARENESS   Wake up!
2. MINDSET   Make a shift.
3. EMOTIONS   Honor your feelings.
4. SUPPORT   Ask for help.
5. BODY   Move a muscle.
6. FAITH   Widen your perspective.
7. ALIGNMENT   Trust Yourself.

The 7 Steps act as a portal--reconnecting you to your **innate and unconditional self-worth** not contingent on any achievement-past or future.

All the clients you just read about worked the 7 Steps, rediscovered their innate self-worth, and went on to transform their lives and careers. In the process, they regained sanity, health, joy, and a reconnection with their true selves.

Hopefully, in recounting these twenty-plus real-life transformative coaching sessions, I've been able to show my coaching method in action.

But still, I don't think that is enough.

What I want for you now is not only to understand the self-destructive nature of Achievement Addiction and put the 7 Steps into action; I want to inspire you. I want to leave you feeling optimistic and eager to make these changes in your own life. My wish for you is that you'll start working the 7 Steps so that you, too, can experience Achievement Addiction DETOX, reclaim your sanity, and start creating the life you deserve without killing yourself.

My goal with this book is to make Achievement Addiction DETOX doable. And I hope that one or more of these stories resonated with you; that your reflections on these stories surprised you, excited you, or reminded you of a former true self that you thought no longer existed. My wish is that you finish this book feeling so inspired to detox that you go on to download and complete the Achievement Addiction DETOX Worksheets available to you at www.achievementaddictiondetox.com.

Wriggling out from under decades of Achievement Addiction is not easy stuff. I know how hard it can be, and I genuinely applaud you.

But remember: We are addicted to achievement, and we have to expect that our addiction is none too pleased with any changes that might deprive us of our habit. Our Achievement Addiction will try to get in the way of our best efforts to try something new. Be vigilant and aware that when embarking on any change, you are guaranteed two things:

1. that it will be initially uncomfortable, and
2. that your body and mind will give you all kinds of reasons not to take actions leading to change.

But perhaps now you know you are not alone. You have taken the first step. And with guidance and support, maybe you'll take the next step. And the next one.

One Last Curtain Call For Leona

As for me, my Achievement Avatar, Leona, reared her siren-like head on more than one occasion while I was writing this book. On her nastier days, she told me I was wasting my time. "No one cares what you have to say, and no one is going to read your stupid book," she'd repeat. "Go back to working for a law firm," she'd say.

And on her more grandiose days, she told me, "The book *must* be a number one best seller, or else why bother?" On other days, she would taunt me with shame: "What will your college classmates think? Or those fancy clients?" She told me that I shouldn't publish it until one of the best publishing houses picks it up. She told me I shouldn't publish it myself because "only losers self-publish."

The list of nasty and grandiose self-talk that filled the space between my ears as I lumbered through this writing was driven by my Achievement Addiction.

And the truth is, these defeatist thoughts sometimes still live in me. And sometimes, they still trip me up. But if I listened to and abided by everything my Achievement Avatar, Leona, would have me believe, my Achievement Addiction would have me giving up just about everything that is good, healthy, balanced, and meaningful to me in the name of achievement.

Today, I no longer let myself be seduced by what Achievement Addiction promises me.

With awareness, most times, I can catch myself when the voice of my Achievement Avatar rises up to fill me with dread or tries to get me to go "back to the good old days" when all that mattered to me was higher achievement, prominence, recognition, material objects, respect, etc.

For help, I turn to the 7 Steps I wrote about in this book to keep me connected to my innate self-worth and aligned with what is healthful, sane, meaningful, and purposeful to me. And that's usually when I take another step outside, sit on my meditation cushion, talk to my therapist, coach, or support group, go for a walk, get on my mat, write, cook, connect with family, or get some sleep. That's my cue to take care of myself.

As for this book, I wrote it because I just wanted to. And if it succeeds in helping one person, then it will have been worth it.

I know this book is not perfect. So be it. But it was meaningful to me, and hopefully, some of the stories resonated with you, inspired you, and offered you some more hope.

As a precocious, curly-headed little girl growing up in Bensonhurst, Brooklyn, I wanted to be a doctor and a poet. I wanted to live on a mountaintop farm overlooking the sea. Life got in the way. And Achievement Addiction kept me running in the wrong direction for years. But I knew there was something meaningful I was supposed to do with my time here on this earth. And it kept gnawing at me until I pursued it. These days, I can honestly say that I am living my healthiest and most authentic life mostly because achievements no longer define my self-worth. My life and work are finally aligned with my values and purpose, and my self-worth is permanently tethered to my everlasting true self, and my idealized image of myself as a kid—I help people, I write books, and I live in a small farmhouse in the mountains.

I wish you courage, faith, self-compassion, patience, and an extra dose of good humor as you start on your path of recovering the health, sanity, and joy that is your birthright.

May you be happy.
May you be healthy.
May you be safe.
May you live with ease.
May you be free.

REFERENCES AND RESOURCES

Books

Aguilar, E. *The Onward Workbook*. San Francisco: Jossey-Bass, 2018.

Beattie, M. *The Grief Club*. Hazelden, 2006.

Carroll, D. *A Lawyer's Guide to Healing*. Hazelden, 2006.

Cho, J. *The Anxious Lawyer: An 8-Week Guide to a Joyful and Satisfying Law Practice through Mindfulness and Meditation*. American Bar Association, 2016.

Chodron, P. *The Places That Scare You*. Boston: Shambala, 2002.

———. *Start Where You Are*. Boston: Shambala, 1994.

———. *Welcoming the Unwelcome*. Boulder: Shambala, 2019.

———. *When Things Fall Apart*. Boston: Shambala, 2000.

Ciaramicoli, A. P. *Performance Addiction*. Hoboken, NJ: John Wiley & Sons, 2004.

Daicoff, S. *Lawyer, Know Thyself: A Psychoanalysis of Personality Strengths and Weaknesses*. American Psychological Association, 2004.

Dispenza, J. D. *Becoming Supernatural*. Hay House Publishing, 2017.

———. *Breaking the Habit of Being Yourself*. Hay House Publishing, 2012.

Duckworth, A. *GRIT: The Power of Passion and Perseverance*. New York: Scribner Book Company, 2016.

Dweck, C. S. *Mindset: The New Psychology of Success*. Ballantine Paperback, 2008.

Fassel, D. *Working Ourselves to Death*. Lincoln, NE: iUniverse, 2000.

Helmstetter, S. *Negative Self-Talk and How to Change It*. Gulf Breeze, FL: Park Avenue Press, 2019.

Hendrix, H. *Getting the Love You Want*. New York: Simon & Schuster, 2003.

Housden, R. *Keeping the Faith without a Religion*. Boulder, CO: Sounds True, 2014.

Kasser, T. *The High Price of Materialism*. Cambridge, MA: MIT Press, 2002.

Killinger, B. *Workaholics—The Respectable Addicts*. Toronto: Key Porter Books, 1991.

Levine, S. *The Best Lawyer You Can Be*. American Bar Association, 2018.

Nerison, R. *Lawyers, Anger, and Anxiety: Dealing With the Stresses of the Legal Profession*. American Bar Association, 2010.

Oates, W. E. *Confessions of a Workaholic*. New York: Abingdon Press, 1971.

Peterson, T. J. *The Mindfulness Workbook for Anxiety*. Althea Press, 2018.

Rath, T. *Eat, Move, Sleep*. Missionday, 2013.

Schiraldi, G. *The Resilience Workbook*. New Harbinger Publications, 2017.

Simpson, M. *Unlocking Potential*. Grand Harbor, MI: Grand Harbor Press, 2014.

Twerski, A. *Waking Up Just in Time*. New York: St. Martin's Press, 1990.

Other Publications and Articles

Alim, T., Lawson, W., Feder, A., et al. "Resilience to Meet the Challenge of Addiction: Psychobiology and Clinical Considerations." *Alcohol Research: Current Reviews* 34, no. 4 (2012): 506–15.

Austin, D. S. "Killing Them Softly: Neuroscience Reveals How Brain Cells Die from Law School Stress and How Neural Self-Hacking Can Optimize Cognitive Performance." *Loyola Law Review* 59 (2013): 791-837.

Bibelhausen, J., Bender, K. M., and Barrett, R. "Reducing the Stigma: The Deadly Effect of Untreated Mental Illness and New Strategies for Changing Outcomes in Law Students." *William Mitchell Law Review* 41, no. 3 (2015): 918–47.

Blatt, W. S. "What's Special about Meditation? Contemplative Practice for American Lawyers." *Harvard Negotiation Law Review* 7 (Spring 2002): 125–41.

Britt, W., Greene-Shortridge, T. M., Brink, S., Nguyen, Q. B., Rath, J., Cox, A. L., Hoge, C. W., and Castro, C. A. "Perceived Stigma and Barriers to Care for Psychological Treatment: Implications for Reactions to Stressors in Different Contexts." *Journal of Social & Clinical Psychology* 27, no. 4 (2008): 317–35.

Buckley, A. "The Mental Health Boundary in Relationship to Coaching and Other Activities." *International Journal of Evidence Based Coaching and Mentoring* 45 (Summer 2007): 17–23.

Chu, H., Buckworth, J., Kirby, T. E., and Emery, C. F. "Effect of Exercise Intensity on Depressive Symptoms in Women." *Mental Health and Physical Activity* 2, no. 1 (2009): 37–43.

Cooper, C., Flint-Taylor, J., and Pearn, M. *Building Resilience for Success: A Resource for Managers and Organizations*. Springer, 2013.

Crawshaw, L. "Coaching Abrasive Leaders: Using Action Research to Reduce Suffering and Increase Productivity in Organizations." *International Coaching Psychology Review* (2010).

Crum, J., Salovey, P., and Achor, S. "Rethinking Stress: The Role of Mindsets in Determining the Stress Response." *Journal of Personality and Social Psychology* 104, no. 4 (2013): 716–33.

Dingemans, E., and Henkens, K. "How Do Retirement Dynamics Influence Mental Well-Being in Later Life? A 10-Year Panel Study." *Scandinavian Journal of Work, Environment & Health* 41, no. 1 (2015): 16–23.

Filsinger, C. "How Can Maternity Coaching Influence Women's Re-engagement with their Career Development: A Case Study of a Maternity Coaching Programme in UK-Based Private Law Firms." *International Journal of Evidence Based Coaching and Mentoring* S6 (2012).

Frone, M. R. "Work Stress and Alcohol Use." *Alcohol Research & Health* 23, no. 4 (1999): 284–91.

Hammen, C. "Stress and Depression." *Annual Review of Clinical Psychology* 1 (2005): 293–319.

Herring, M. P., Jacob, M. L., Suveg, C., and O'Connor, P. J. "Effects of Short-Term Exercise Training on Signs and Symptoms of Generalized Anxiety Disorder." *Mental Health and Physical Activity* 4, no. 2 (2011): 71–77.

Hoffman, S. G., Sawyer, A. T., Witt, A. A., and Oh, D. "The Effect of Mindfulness-Based Therapy on Anxiety and Depression: A Meta-Analytic Review." *Journal of Consulting and Clinical Psychology* 78, no. 2 (2010): 169–83.

Hopkins, V., and Gardner, D. "The Mediating Role of Work Engagement and Burnout in the Relationships between Job Characteristics and Psychological Distress among Lawyers." *New Zealand Journal of Psychology* 41, no. 1 (2012): 59–68.

Houlfort, N., Fernet, C., Vallerand, R. J., Laframboise, A., Guay, F., and Koestner, R. "The Role of Passion for Work and Need for Satisfaction in Psychological Adjustment to Retirement." *Journal of Vocational Behavior* 88 (June 2015): 84–94.

Jennings, K. S., Cheung, J. H., Britt, T. W., Goguen, K. N., Jeffirs, S. M., Peasley, A. L., and Lee, A. C. "How Are Perceived Stigma, Self-Stigma, and Self-Reliance Related to Treatment-Seeking? A Three-Path Model." *Psychiatric Rehabilitation Journal* 38, no. 2 (2015): 109–16.

Kalisch, R., Muler, M. B., and Tuscher, O. "A Conceptual Framework for the Neurobiological Study of Resilience." *Behavioral and Brain Sciences* 38 (2014).

Krieger, L. S. "Institutional Denial about the Dark Side of Law School, and Fresh Empirical Guidance for Constructively Breaking the Silence." *Journal of Legal Education* 52, no. 1–2 (2002): 112–15.

Krieger, L. S., and Sheldon, K. M. "What Makes Lawyers Happy? Transcending the Anecdotes with Data from 6200 Lawyers." *George Washington Law Review* 83 (2015): 554–627.

Krill, P. R., Johnson, R., and Albert, L. "The Prevalence of Substance Use and Other Mental Health Concerns among American Attorneys." *Journal of Addiction Medicine* 10, no. 1 (2016): 46–52.

Muratore, A. M., and Earl, J. K. "Improving Retirement Outcomes: The Role of Resources, Pre-Retirement Planning and Transition Characteristics." *Ageing & Society* 35, no. 10 (2015): 2100–2140.

Organ, J. M. "What Do We Know about the Satisfaction/Dissatisfaction of Lawyers? A Meta-Analysis of Research on Lawyer Satisfaction and Well-Being." *University of St. Thomas Law Journal* 8, no. 2 (2011): 225–74.

Organ, J. M., Jaffe, D., and Bender, K. "Suffering in Silence: The Survey of Law Student Well-Being and the Reluctance of Law Students to Seek Help for Substance Use and Mental Health Concerns." *Journal of Legal Education* 66, no. 1 (2016): 116–56.

Patthoff, A. "This Is Your Brain on Law School: The Impact of Fear-Based Narratives on Law Students." *Utah Law Review* 2015, no. 2 (2015): 391–424.

Rikleen, L. S. "The Cost to Law Firms of Ignoring Harmful Workplace Behavior." *American Lawyer*, July 9, 2018.

Rikleen, L. S. "Fear-Fueled Silence, Power Imbalance Perpetuate Bad Behavior at Law Firms." *ABA Journal*, August 21, 2018.

Rikleen, L. S. "Solving the Law Firm Gender Gap Problem." *Harvard Business Review*, August 20, 2013.

Rikleen, L. S. "Survey of Workplace Conduct and Behavior in Law Firms." Women's Bar Association, June 2018.

Robertson, I. T., Cooper, C. L., Sarkar, M., and Curran, T. "Resilience Training in the Workplace from 2003 to 2014: A Systematic Review." *Journal of Occupational and Organizational Psychology* 88, no. 3 (2015): 533–62.

Rock, L., Roiser, J. P., Riedel, W. J., and Blackwell, A. D. "A Cognitive Impairment in Depression: A Systematic Review and Meta-Analysis." *Psychological Medicine* 44, no. 10 (2014): 2029–40.

Sheldon, K. M., and Krieger, L. S. "Does Legal Education Have Undermining Effects on Law Students? Evaluating Changes in Motivation, Values, and Well-Being." *Behavioral Sciences & the Law* 22, no. 2 (2004): 261–86.

Sheldon, K. M., and Krieger, L. S. "Understanding the Negative Effects of Legal Education on Law Students: A Longitudinal Test of

Self-Determination Theory." *Personality and Social Psychology Bulletin* 33, no. 6 (2007): 883–97.

Snyder, H. R. "Major Depressive Disorder Is Associated with Broad Impairments on Neuropsychological Measures of Executive Function: A Meta-Analysis and Review." *Psychological Bulletin* 139, no. 1 (2013): 81–132.

Southwick, S. M., Bonanno, G. A., Masten, A. S., Panter-Brick, C., and Yehuda, R. "Resilience Definitions, Theory, and Challenges: Interdisciplinary Perspectives." *European Journal of Psychotraumatology* 5 (2014).

Teper, R., Segal, Z. V., and Inzlicht, M. "Inside the Mindful Mind: How Mindfulness Enhances Emotion Regulation through Improvements in Executive Control." *Current Directions in Psychological Science* 22, no. 6 (2013): 449–54.

Violante, C. "Law360's 2016 Lawyer Satisfaction Survey: By the Numbers." Law360, Sept. 2, 2016. https://www.law360.com/articles/833246/law360-s-2016-lawyer-satisfactionsurvey-by-the-numbers.

Woo, J. M., and Postolache, T. T. "The Impact of Work Environment on Mood Disorders and Suicide: Evidence and Implications." *International Journal on Disability and Human Development* 7, no. 2 (2008): 185–200.

Additional Helpful Resources

If you or someone you know is experiencing suicidal thinking, please seek help immediately. The National Suicide Prevention Lifeline can be reached at 1-800-273-8255 or https://suicidepreventionlifeline.org.

24/7 Crisis Hotline: National Suicide Prevention Lifeline Network
www.suicidepreventionlifeline.org
1-800-273-TALK (1-800-273-8255) (Veterans, press 1)

Crisis Text Line
Text TALK to 741-741 to text with a trained crisis counselor from the Crisis Text Line for free, 24/7.

Veterans Crisis Line
Send a text to 838255.

Substance Abuse and Mental Health Services Administration
(SAMHSA) Treatment Referral Hotline (Substance Abuse)
1-800-662-HELP (1-800-662-4357)

ABOUT THE AUTHOR

Elena Rand, JD, LMSW, has spent over 20 years working as executive coach and leadership guru for Fortune 500 companies and Am Law 100 law firms throughout the world. Trained as a former NYC litigator, licensed psychotherapist, and certified executive coach Elena founded LawScope, LLC one of the first executive coaching companies to introduce executive coaching to the legal profession. She then went on to serve as the Chief Marketing Officer for Wiggin and Dana and Director of Business Development for Paul Weiss.

Elena is a highly sought after leadership trainer, panel moderator, motivational speaker and executive coach. She has worked for such institutions as *EY-Canada, Google, Guggenheim Partners, SONY, British Airways, Applied Insurance, The U.S. Department of Commerce Columbia Law School, Fordham Law School, University of Toronto School of Law, The Princeton Club of NY, The Legal Marketing Association, The Chicago Bar Association, The City Bar of New York, PLI* and *The NY State Bar Association* among others.

Elena graduated from Princeton University, The Georgetown University Law Center, The NYU School of Social Work and completed a fellowship at the NYU Institute of Psychoanalytic Psychotherapy. Elena also received certification in *Mindfulness Based Stress Reduction Meditation* from the Yale University Stress Center and is also a licensed Level II Reiki Master.

Elena was inducted into the 200th Legione D'Oro of the Accademia Tiberina di Roma, and serves as an International U.S. Delegate for the Fodazione Accademia di Tiberina Pontificale, dedicated to the promotion of Latin and Italian science and letters and to the preservation of Roman art and culture.

Elena is fluent in Italian, Sicilian, Hebrew and Spanish.

Elena is the mother of two children, step-mother to two children and now lives in the New York Hudson Valley with her husband doing what she loves the most-writing books and coaching others.

Elena can be reached at www.elenarand.com and her online Achievement Addiction: DETOX workbook, resources and virtual courses can be found at www.achievementaddictiondetox.com.

ACKNOWLEDGMENTS

This book would never have been written without the support and encouragement of my husband, Rob. You are the one who called me "writer" before I found the courage to call myself a writer. You listened patiently to my obsessive vision for this book when it was still a messy amalgam of voices, places, and ideas. It is rare to find a person, who can step away from his own creative processes and generously inspire others in their own art. You, Rob, are that man and that artist. You are among my many unexpected blessings in this lifetime.

As are my children, Maxim and Gabriella, two incredible young adults who each inspire me in different ways with their fearless departures from society's expectations and norms. Each of you has followed your passions, values, and intuition. And each of you, in your own way, has given me the courage and permission to step into my true self. I am crazy proud of both of you. And doubly blessed to be your Mama. I love and adore you both.

And then there is my dad, Archie. Mommy always said you took us both on as a package deal, which ended up saving all three of us in the process. As always, she was right. You taught me how to look. How to see. How to listen. How to hear my own voice. How to be very silly—and deadly serious. And you taught me how to be alone. Survival skills needed for any creative endeavor. I hope this work makes you equally proud of me.

Mommy, words were never your way. Fierce loyalty. Unbounded love. That was your way. This book is my eternal love letter to you.

Grazie a mia Nonna Rosa. Ti ringrazio per tutto. Ti amo, come una mamma. Tu m'hai insegnatto tre cose molto importanti. Che: "*Dio è grande*"

(*"God is great"*), *"Passa u pede disupra"* ("Let it go"), e *"Tutto è possibile"* (*"Everything is possible"*). This book is my quiet homage to my wise and loving, one hundred-year-old Nonna Rosa, whose long life is a daily reminder of the power of faith and forgiveness.

Finally, this book would never have been published without the patience, professionalism, and honest input from people who have been at this writing gig longer than I have. Thank you to my editors Tina Koenig, Tamma Ford, and Beth Bazar for organizing my thoughts, filling in the gaps, humoring my endless "final-final edits," and navigating this rickety rowboat through personal and professional storms. Thank you to Danielle Anderson for your brilliant and meticulous editing, attention to detail, and help in tightening up my writing. Many thanks to Ellen Fleury for her brilliant cover design. Thank you to all my coaching clients who taught me everything I write about here. And lastly, I want to thank the God of my own understanding.

INDEX

Printed in the USA
CPSIA information can be obtained
at www.ICGtesting.com
LVHW050149020224
770731LV00022B/72/J